With You Every Day

A 365-Day Devotional
for a Faithful, Steady Walk with God

LaToya Banks

This book is intended for inspirational and devotional purposes only. The author is not providing medical, legal, or professional advice. Readers are encouraged to seek appropriate counsel when needed.

ISBN (Paperback): 979-8-9948651-0-1
ISBN (eBook): 979-8-9948651-1-8

Printed in the United States of America

First edition

Dedication

This book is lovingly dedicated
to my grandmother, **Jessie Mae Adams**.

She walked with God every day of her life,
not loudly, but faithfully.
Her presence carried peace, her love reflected grace,
and her spirit revealed a life rooted in the Lord.

You did not have to ask who she belonged to.
You could see it in how she lived,
how she loved,
and how she trusted God through every season.

Releasing this book on her birthday feels fitting.
Her life was a daily walk of faith, hope, and quiet strength.
This devotional carries forward the legacy she lived so well.

I love you, Grandmama.

Author's Note

This book was written as an invitation, not an assignment.

It is an invitation to walk with God daily, honestly, and consistently. Not perfectly. Not performatively. Simply faithfully. Over the years, I have learned that spiritual growth does not happen in grand moments alone. It happens in the quiet decisions to show up, to trust God again, and to keep walking even when clarity feels distant.

I grew up watching what a daily walk with God looks like. My grandmother, Jessie Mae Adams, lived her faith in a way that was steady and sincere. She did not rush God or try to impress people. She trusted Him. She prayed. She listened. She walked with Him through every season of her life. Her faith was not loud, but it was rooted. Her life showed me that walking with God is not about intensity, but about presence.

This devotional was shaped by that understanding.

Each day is designed to meet you where you are and invite you to take one step closer to God. Some days will feel full and hopeful. Others may feel quiet, uncertain, or heavy. Wherever you find yourself, this book is meant to remind you that God is present, faithful, and attentive. You are not behind. You are not overlooked. You are walking.

My prayer is that these pages help you build a rhythm of faith, deepen your trust in God's presence, and strengthen your hope through every season. May this devotional become a companion on your journey, reminding you daily that growth happens as you walk with Him.

Thank you for allowing me to walk with you through these pages.

How to Use This Devotional

This devotional is designed to be walked through, not rushed.

Each day offers a scripture and a short reflection meant to anchor your heart in God's presence and invite you into steady spiritual growth. You can use this book in the morning, during a quiet moment in the day, or in the evening as you reflect. What matters most is not the time of day, but the intention to meet with God consistently.

Begin each day by reading the scripture slowly. Let the words settle before moving on. You may find it helpful to read the verse more than once, asking God what He wants you to notice or receive. The devotional that follows is meant to guide your reflection, not replace your own conversation with God.

Some days will resonate deeply. Other days may feel quiet or simple. Both are part of the journey. Growth does not always feel dramatic. Often, it happens beneath the surface as you remain faithful to show up.

This book is dated to help establish rhythm, but it is not meant to create pressure. If you miss a day, do not rush to catch up. Simply return to where you left off. Walking with God is not about keeping pace. It is about staying connected.

You may choose to journal alongside this devotional, write prayers in the margins, or sit quietly after reading. Use it in a way that supports your relationship with God and your current season of life.

Most importantly, approach this devotional with grace. You are not here to perform or prove anything. You are here to walk. One day at a time. One step at a time. With a God who is faithful to meet you along the way.

Table of Contents

JANUARY

Fresh Starts and New Mercies

January is more than the beginning of a new calendar year. It is an invitation into renewal. This month calls you to pause, reflect, and acknowledge that God is always doing something new, even when life feels familiar or unfinished. Each day offers an opportunity to release what no longer aligns with where God is leading you and to step forward with renewed trust in His faithfulness.

God's mercies are not recycled or diminished by time. They are fresh, intentional, and sufficient for every moment you will face. As you journey through January, you are invited to let go of past disappointments, lingering guilt, and old narratives that no longer define you. This is a season to receive grace daily and to believe that God is faithful to meet you exactly where you are.

Fresh starts do not require perfection or clarity. They require willingness. As you open your heart to God's new mercies each morning, you will find strength to walk forward one step at a time. January reminds you that beginnings are sacred and that God delights in doing new work within you.

January 1

A New Thing Begins

Isaiah 43:19 (NIV)
"See, I am doing a new thing! Now it springs up; do you not perceive it? I am making a way in the wilderness and streams in the wasteland."

Devotional

God is a God of beginnings. He does not wait for perfect conditions or complete readiness before He moves. When Scripture says He is doing a new thing, it is not a suggestion. It is a declaration. God is actively at work, even when you feel unsure, unprepared, or still carrying remnants of what came before.

A new beginning does not require you to have everything figured out. It requires trust. Trust that God sees what you cannot yet perceive and that He is already making a way where things once felt barren or stuck. The wilderness and wasteland mentioned in this verse are not obstacles to God. They are often the very places where He reveals His power most clearly.

What prevents many from recognizing the new thing God is doing is not lack of faith, but lingering attachment to the past. Yesterday's pain, disappointment, or unmet expectations can cloud your ability to see what God is unfolding now. But God's invitation is always forward.

Today is not about resolution or performance. It is about posture. As you step into this new year, allow God to interrupt old patterns, renew your perspective, and reestablish your trust in His timing. You are not late. You are not behind. You are stepping into exactly what God is doing now.

Reflection

What might God be asking you to release so you can perceive the new thing He is doing?

Life Application

Spend ten quiet minutes asking God to show you where He is inviting you to begin again. Write down what comes to mind.

Prayer

Lord, I open my heart to the new thing You are doing. Help me release the past and trust You with what lies ahead. Amen.

January 2

New Mercies This Morning

Lamentations 3:22–23 (NIV)
"Because of the Lord's great love we are not consumed, for his compassions never fail. They are new every morning; great is your faithfulness."

Devotional
God's mercy is not carried over from yesterday. It meets you fresh each morning. This truth anchors your day before circumstances, emotions, or responsibilities begin to compete for your attention. No matter what you are carrying from the day before, mercy greets you before anything else does.

God's compassion does not diminish because of your mistakes or fatigue. You are not consumed by what went wrong. You are sustained by who God is. His faithfulness is steady, not reactive, and His mercy is not dependent on your performance.

Many begin the day already weighed down by regret or self-criticism. But God does not lead with disappointment. He leads with compassion. When you receive His mercy at the start of the day, you shift from striving to trusting. You begin grounded in grace rather than pressure.

Today is an invitation to start from love. Let mercy reset your thoughts, steady your heart, and remind you that God's faithfulness is sufficient for whatever this day holds.

Reflection
How would your day change if you truly embraced God's mercy this morning?

Life Application
Before beginning your day, thank God out loud for His mercy and faithfulness.

Prayer
Lord, thank You for mercy that meets me every morning. Help me release yesterday and walk into today grounded in Your faithfulness. Amen.

January 3

Releasing the Former Things

Isaiah 43:18 (NKJV)
"Do not remember the former things, nor consider the things of old."

Devotional

Some of the heaviest things you carry cannot be seen. They live in memories, regrets, and unresolved moments from the past. God's instruction to release former things is not dismissive. It is freeing. He is inviting you to loosen your grip on what no longer serves where He is leading you.

Holding tightly to the past often feels safer than trusting the unknown. Yet when your hands are full of what has already happened, you have little room to receive what God desires to give you now. Letting go is not denial. It is discernment. It is choosing not to allow yesterday to dictate today's obedience.

God does not ask you to forget your experiences. He asks you to trust Him with them. Healing begins when you stop rehearsing what was and start surrendering it. Faith looks forward, even when understanding lags behind.

Releasing the former things is an act of worship. It is a declaration that God's future is greater than your past and that hope is stronger than regret.

Reflection

What former thing is God inviting you to release today?

Life Application

Write a short prayer releasing the past to God. Be honest and specific.

Prayer

Father, help me release what I was never meant to carry. Heal my heart and guide my steps forward as I trust You with what lies ahead. Amen.

January 4

Created With Purpose

Ephesians 2:10 (NLT)

"For we are God's masterpiece. He has created us anew in Christ Jesus, so we can do the good things he planned for us long ago."

Devotional

Long before you took your first breath, God had intention in mind when He created you. You were not formed by accident or shaped by chance. Scripture calls you God's masterpiece, which means you were crafted with care, detail, and divine purpose. Even on days when you feel ordinary or overlooked, heaven sees you as intentional and valuable.

Many people spend their lives trying to earn worth through achievement, approval, or productivity. But God settles the question of worth before you ever do a single thing. Your value is not rooted in what you accomplish. It is rooted in who created you. You were designed by God, for God, and that truth stands firm even when your confidence wavers.

Ephesians reminds us that God not only created us with purpose, but He also prepared good works for us in advance. That means your life has direction, even when the path feels unclear. Purpose is not something you have to chase down or manufacture. It is something you discover as you walk closely with God and remain open to His leading.

When you begin to see yourself the way God sees you, comparison loses its power and insecurity begins to loosen its grip. You stop striving to become someone else and start embracing who you already are in Christ. Today is an invitation to stand confidently in the truth that you were created on purpose, with purpose, and for a purpose that God is still unfolding.

Reflection

In what ways have you been measuring your worth by performance instead of God's design?

Life Application

Write down one area of your life where you have been striving for approval. Ask God to help you rest in the truth that you are already His masterpiece.

Prayer

Lord, thank You for creating me with intention and purpose. Help me release the need to prove myself and rest in who You say I am. Open my eyes to the purpose You are unfolding in my life. Amen.

January 5

Strength That Is Renewed

Isaiah 40:31 (NKJV)

"But those who wait on the Lord shall renew their strength; they shall mount up with wings like eagles, they shall run and not be weary, they shall walk and not faint."

Devotional

Strength is not something you generate on your own. According to this verse, strength is renewed through hope placed in the Lord. That means endurance is not about pushing harder, but about trusting deeper.

God does not promise that you will never grow tired. He promises that when you place your hope in Him, He will meet you in your weakness and renew what has been depleted. Renewal is not instant energy. It is sustained capacity. It allows you to keep walking, running, and rising without losing heart.

This scripture also reminds you that growth happens in stages. Sometimes you soar. Sometimes you run. Sometimes you simply walk. Each pace matters. Faith is not measured by speed, but by persistence. God honors every step taken in trust.

When you stop relying on your own strength and begin leaning fully on God, renewal becomes possible. Hope shifts your focus from what you lack to who sustains you.

Reflection

Where do you feel most weary right now?

Life Application

Identify one area where you have been relying on your own strength and intentionally place it in God's hands today.

Prayer

Lord, I place my hope in You. Renew my strength where I feel tired and help me trust You through every stage of this journey. Amen.

January 6

Guarding What Matters Most

Proverbs 4:23 (NIV)

"Above all else, guard your heart, for everything you do flows from it."

Devotional

Your heart is the center of your inner life. It holds your beliefs, your desires, your wounds, and your hopes. That is why Scripture places such strong emphasis on guarding it. God understands that whatever shapes your heart will eventually shape your life. Your words, decisions, relationships, and reactions all flow from what is happening within.

Guarding your heart does not mean shutting people out or becoming emotionally unavailable. It means being discerning about what you allow to influence you. Every conversation, habit, and thought pattern leaves an impression. Over time, those impressions either draw you closer to God or quietly pull you away from Him.

Many people feel spiritually drained not because they lack faith, but because they have been pouring emotional energy into places God never asked them to. Constant exposure to negativity, comparison, unresolved offense, or fear can slowly harden the heart. God's instruction to guard your heart is an act of love. He desires to protect your peace and preserve your joy.

When your heart is aligned with God's truth, your life begins to flow with clarity and stability. You respond instead of react. You move with wisdom instead of impulse. Guarding your heart is not about fear. It is about stewardship. Today, God invites you to tend carefully to what matters most within you.

Reflection

What has been influencing your heart the most lately, and is it drawing you closer to God or further from Him?

Life Application

Take inventory of one influence in your life that may be affecting your heart negatively. Ask God for wisdom on how to adjust or set a healthy boundary.

Prayer

Lord, help me guard my heart with wisdom and grace. Show me what needs to be released or realigned so that my life can flow from a place of truth and peace. Amen.

January 7

Honoring Small Beginnings

Zechariah 4:10 (NLT)

"Do not despise these small beginnings, for the Lord rejoices to see the work begin."

Devotional

We live in a world that celebrates big results and visible success, often overlooking the quiet faithfulness of small beginnings. But God operates differently. He rejoices when the work begins, not just when it is finished. He values obedience more than outcome and movement more than magnitude.

Small beginnings often feel insignificant because they do not look impressive to others. A single decision to pray again. One boundary set. One step of obedience taken in fear. Yet these moments matter deeply to God. They are evidence of trust, and trust always moves His heart.

Many people delay starting because they feel behind, unprepared, or unsure. But God never asks you to begin from a place of confidence. He asks you to begin from a place of faith. What you bring may feel small, but when placed in God's hands, it becomes more than enough.

Today is a reminder not to discount where you are or what you are carrying. God is present in the beginning. He is breathing on the seed. And what starts small today can grow into something strong and lasting when nurtured with faith and obedience.

Reflection

What small step of obedience have you been tempted to dismiss or delay?

Life Application

Identify one small action God has been prompting you to take and do it today without waiting for perfect conditions.

Prayer

God, help me honor the small beginnings You place before me. Give me courage to start where I am and trust You with the growth. Amen.

January 8

Ordered Steps

Psalm 37:23 (NKJV)

"The steps of a good man are ordered by the Lord, and He delights in his way."

Devotional

There is comfort in knowing that your life is not unfolding randomly. Even when circumstances feel disjointed or unclear, God is actively involved in directing your steps. Scripture tells us that God orders the steps of those who seek Him, which means nothing in your journey is wasted or accidental.

God's ordering does not always look like straight lines or predictable progress. Sometimes His guidance comes through pauses, redirections, or seasons that stretch your faith. What feels like a detour to you may be a necessary preparation for what lies ahead. God sees the full picture, even when you can only see the next step.

Trusting God with your steps requires surrender. It means releasing the need to control outcomes and timelines. It means believing that even when you feel unsure, God is still delighting in your obedience and attentiveness to His voice.

Today, you do not need clarity for the entire journey. You only need trust for the step in front of you. God delights in walking with you, guiding you one step at a time.

Reflection

Where in your life do you need to trust God to order your steps instead of trying to control the direction?

Life Application

Bring one decision you are currently wrestling with before God. Ask Him to guide your next step and commit to following His lead.

Prayer

Lord, thank You for ordering my steps. Help me trust You even when the path feels uncertain. Teach me to walk closely with You, one step at a time. Amen.

January 9

Renewing the Mind

Romans 12:2 (NIV)
"Do not conform to the pattern of this world, but be transformed by the renewing of your mind."

Devotional

Transformation does not begin with changing your circumstances. It begins with changing how you think. Scripture reminds us that lasting change starts in the mind, where beliefs are formed and decisions are made. If your thoughts are shaped more by fear, comparison, or culture than by God's truth, your life will reflect that tension.

The world constantly pressures you to conform to its patterns. Those patterns tell you to strive harder, worry more, and measure your worth by external success. God offers a different way. He invites you into transformation through renewal, where your mind is continually reshaped by His Word and presence.

Renewing your mind is not a one-time event. It is a daily practice of replacing lies with truth and choosing faith over fear. As your thinking aligns with God's perspective, your decisions begin to change. Your peace deepens. Your confidence grows. You start to recognize God's will with greater clarity.

Today is an invitation to examine what has been influencing your thoughts. God desires to bring freedom, not pressure. As you allow Him to renew your mind, transformation will naturally follow.

Reflection
What thought pattern has been influencing your emotions or decisions lately?

Life Application

Identify one negative or unhelpful thought you have been entertaining. Replace it today with a truth from God's Word.

Prayer

God, renew my mind with Your truth. Help me release thoughts that do not align with You and transform my thinking so that my life reflects Your will. Amen.

January 10

Choosing Courage

Joshua 1:9 (NIV)

"Have I not commanded you? Be strong and courageous. Do not be afraid; do not be discouraged, for the Lord your God will be with you wherever you go."

Devotional

Courage is not a suggestion in this verse. It is a command. God speaks these words to Joshua at a moment of transition, when uncertainty and responsibility weigh heavily on his shoulders. God does not pretend the assignment will be easy, but He assures Joshua of something far greater than ease: His presence.

Fear and discouragement often surface when you are standing on the edge of something new. God knows this. That is why He does not tell Joshua to rely on confidence or skill. He tells him to rely on the truth that God will be with him wherever he goes. Courage grows when you remember you are not walking alone.

Choosing courage does not mean the absence of fear. It means deciding that fear will not have the final say. It means moving forward even when your voice shakes or your steps feel unsure. God's presence is what steadies you when your emotions try to overwhelm you.

Today, courage may look like obedience in a small but uncomfortable place. It may look like trusting God again after disappointment. Whatever form it takes, remember this: God does not command courage without also providing the strength to walk it out.

Reflection

What situation in your life is requiring you to choose courage right now?

Life Application

Identify one step you have been avoiding because of fear. Take that step today, trusting that God is with you.

Prayer

Lord, help me choose courage over fear. Remind me that You are with me wherever I go. Strengthen my heart to move forward in obedience and trust. Amen.

January 11

God Finishes What He Starts

Philippians 1:6 (NIV)
"Being confident of this, that he who began a good work in you will carry it on to completion until the day of Christ Jesus."

Devotional

Confidence grows when you remember who started the work. This verse does not place the burden of completion on you. It places it on God. What He began in you was intentional, and what He begins, He sustains.

Growth can feel slow or uneven, especially when you focus on what still needs to change. But God's work is not measured by your awareness of progress. It is measured by His faithfulness. Even when you feel unfinished, God is still actively shaping, refining, and strengthening you.

This scripture invites you to rest in the process. Completion does not depend on perfection or constant momentum. It depends on God's commitment to you. Your responsibility is not to rush the outcome, but to remain willing and faithful along the way.

When doubt tries to tell you that you are falling behind, return to this truth. God is not done. What He started, He will finish. Hope is sustained when you trust His hand at work, even when the results are not yet visible.

Reflection

Where do you feel tempted to question your progress?

Life Application

When discouragement arises today, remind yourself that God is still at work and committed to completing what He began in you.

Prayer

God, thank You for being faithful to complete the work You started in me. Help me trust Your process and remain confident in Your timing. Amen.

January 12

Stillness That Reorients

Psalm 46:10 (KJV)

"Be still and know that I am God."

Devotional

Stillness is not simply the absence of noise. It is the intentional decision to stop striving and remember who God is. In a world that constantly demands your attention and urgency, stillness feels countercultural. Yet God invites you into it because He knows what it restores within you.

To be still does not mean your circumstances suddenly calm down. It means your soul does. Stillness shifts your focus away from what feels overwhelming and redirects it toward the One who remains unshaken. When you pause long enough to acknowledge God's sovereignty, fear begins to loosen its grip.

Many people struggle with stillness because silence exposes what busyness helps them avoid. But God meets you in the quiet, not to overwhelm you, but to reassure you. He is not anxious about your future. He is not confused by your questions. He is God, and He is present with you.

Stillness is where trust deepens. It is where perspective is restored. Today, God is not asking you to figure everything out. He is asking you to pause long enough to remember that He already has.

Reflection

What has been making it difficult for you to slow down and be still before God?

Life Application

Create five uninterrupted minutes today to sit quietly before God. No agenda. No requests. Simply acknowledge His presence.

Prayer

God, help me be still and remember who You are. Quiet my heart and calm my thoughts so I can rest in Your sovereignty and peace. Amen.

January 13

Living as the New Creation

2 Corinthians 5:17 (NIV)

"Therefore, if anyone is in Christ, the new creation has come: The old has gone, the new is here!"

Devotional

Becoming a new creation in Christ is not a gradual improvement of your old self. It is a spiritual transformation that takes place the moment you surrender your life to Him. Scripture is clear and bold here: the old has gone, and the new is already here. This truth is not dependent on how you feel or how well you perform. It is anchored in what Christ has already done.

Many believers struggle to walk in this truth because they continue to identify with past versions of themselves. Old habits, old mistakes, and old labels try to resurface and speak louder than God's Word. But your past no longer has authority over your identity. Who you were is not who you are becoming in Christ.

Living as a new creation requires intentional alignment with truth. It means choosing to believe God's declaration over your life rather than rehearsing old narratives of shame or inadequacy. When those thoughts arise, you have permission to remind yourself that they no longer belong to you.

Today is an invitation to step fully into your new identity. You do not have to earn it. You simply have to walk in it. The new is not coming someday. It is here now, and God invites you to live like it.

Reflection

What old label or belief have you been carrying that no longer aligns with who you are in Christ?

Life Application

Write down one truth about who you are in Christ and speak it aloud today whenever old thoughts try to resurface.

Prayer

God, thank You for making me new. Help me release the past and walk confidently in the identity You have given me through Christ. Amen.

January 14

Faithfulness Without Fainting

Galatians 6:9 (NIV)

"Let us not become weary in doing good, for at the proper time we will reap a harvest if we do not give up."

Devotional

Weariness often sets in when effort goes unnoticed and results seem delayed. You keep showing up, keep doing what is right, and yet nothing appears to change. God understands this tension, which is why Scripture speaks directly to the temptation to grow weary. Faithfulness can feel exhausting when the harvest feels far away.

God does not measure faithfulness the way the world measures success. He sees the quiet obedience, the unseen sacrifices, and the consistent choices to do good even when motivation runs low. Every act of faithfulness is a seed, and seeds take time to grow.

The promise in this verse is not just about reward. It is about timing. God assures you that there is a proper time for the harvest. Your responsibility is not to force the outcome but to remain faithful in the process. Giving up would mean walking away just before growth breaks through the soil.

If you are tired today, let this verse steady you. Your labor is not wasted. God sees it all. Stay the course. The harvest will come, and it will be worth the wait.

Reflection

Where have you been feeling weary or tempted to give up?

Life Application

Encourage yourself today by writing down one way you have remained faithful, even when it felt difficult.

Prayer

Lord, strengthen me when I feel weary. Help me stay faithful and trust Your timing, knowing that You will bring the harvest in the right season. Amen.

January 15

Holding Your Confidence

Hebrews 10:35 (NIV)
"So do not throw away your confidence; it will be richly rewarded."

Devotional

Confidence rooted in God is different from self-confidence built on circumstances. It is not loud or arrogant. It is quiet assurance anchored in who God is and what He has promised. This verse is written to believers who were growing tired and discouraged, tempted to let go of the very confidence that once carried them forward.

Confidence can erode slowly. Delays stretch your patience. Disappointments test your trust. Unanswered prayers make you question whether what you believed so firmly still applies. God's instruction here is both gentle and firm: do not throw it away. What He placed in you still matters.

Your confidence is not naïve. It is faith informed. It remembers what God has already done and trusts Him with what is still unfolding. Holding your confidence means choosing to stand on truth even when emotions fluctuate or outcomes remain uncertain.

Today, God invites you to gather up your confidence again. Not in yourself, but in Him. What He promised has not expired. The reward is not just what you receive one day, but the strength and steadiness you gain by trusting Him now.

Reflection

Where have you felt your confidence weakening because of delay or disappointment?

Life Application

Write down one promise from God that you are holding onto.
Reaffirm your trust in it today, even if you have not seen fulfillment yet.

Prayer

God, help me hold onto the confidence You placed in me. Strengthen my faith when I feel weary and remind me that Your promises are still sure. Amen.

January 16

Wisdom Without Shame

James 1:5 (NIV)

"If any of you lacks wisdom, you should ask God, who gives generously to all without finding fault, and it will be given to you."

Devotional

There are moments in life when you simply do not know what to do. Decisions feel heavy. Options feel unclear. Questions linger without easy answers. God does not criticize you for lacking wisdom. Instead, He invites you to ask for it freely.

This verse reveals the heart of God toward His children. He gives generously and without finding fault. That means He is not keeping score of how many times you have asked before or judging you for needing guidance again. Wisdom is not withheld as a reward for maturity. It is offered as a gift of grace.

Wisdom goes beyond knowledge. It brings discernment, clarity, and peace in decision-making. It helps you see not only what is possible, but what is wise. When you ask God for wisdom, you are acknowledging your dependence on Him rather than relying solely on your own understanding.

Today is an invitation to bring your uncertainty to God without embarrassment or fear. He delights in guiding you. When you ask, trust that He will respond in the right way and at the right time.

Reflection

What situation in your life requires wisdom right now?

Life Application

Take a moment today to ask God specifically for wisdom regarding one decision you are facing. Write down any insight or peace that follows.

Prayer

Lord, thank You for giving wisdom generously and without judgment. I ask for Your guidance today and trust You to lead me with clarity and peace. Amen.

January 17

Casting What You Were Never Meant to Carry

1 Peter 5:7 (NIV)

"Cast all your anxiety on him because he cares for you."

Devotional

Anxiety often builds quietly. It gathers in your thoughts, settles in your body, and weighs on your spirit until it feels normal to carry it. But Scripture reminds us that anxiety was never meant to be your permanent companion. God does not ask you to manage it. He asks you to cast it.

Casting implies movement. It is an intentional act of releasing what you have been holding too tightly. God does not minimize your worries or dismiss your fears. He invites you to bring them to Him because He cares deeply about every detail of your life. Nothing that troubles you is insignificant to Him.

Many people hold onto anxiety because they believe releasing it means losing control. But true peace comes not from control, but from trust. When you cast your cares on God, you are acknowledging that He is capable of handling what overwhelms you.

Today, God is not asking you to carry more. He is asking you to lay it down. You were never meant to shoulder everything alone. Let the One who cares for you carry what you cannot.

Reflection

What anxiety or worry have you been holding onto instead of releasing to God?

Life Application

Name one specific concern today and consciously release it to God through prayer. When it resurfaces, remind yourself that you have already placed it in His hands.

Prayer

Lord, I cast my anxieties on You today. Thank You for caring for me so deeply. Help me trust You with what I cannot control and rest in Your peace. Amen.

January 18

Trust Beyond Understanding

Proverbs 3:5–6 (NIV)

"Trust in the Lord with all your heart and lean not on your own understanding; in all your ways submit to him, and he will make your paths straight."

Devotional

Trust begins where understanding ends. This verse does not ask you to ignore wisdom or insight. It asks you not to rely on them as your final authority. God calls you to place full confidence in Him, even when clarity feels incomplete or direction seems uncertain.

Leaning on your own understanding often feels safer because it gives the illusion of control. But control is not the same as trust. Submission, as described here, is not weakness. It is alignment. When you submit your plans, decisions, and expectations to God, you allow Him to direct your path in ways you could not orchestrate on your own.

This scripture reminds you that straight paths are the result of surrendered hearts. God's guidance becomes clearer when you stop trying to figure everything out and start placing your confidence in His wisdom. Trust does not remove questions. It anchors you while you walk forward with them.

Hope is sustained when you release the need to understand every step. God does not ask for blind faith. He asks for wholehearted trust, rooted in relationship and obedience.

Reflection

Where are you leaning on your own understanding instead of trusting God?

Life Application

Identify one decision or concern you have been trying to control and intentionally submit it to God today.

Prayer

Lord, help me trust You with all my heart. Teach me to release my need for full understanding and follow You with confidence and obedience. Guide my steps and make my path clear. Amen.

January 19

Setting Your Mind With Intention

Colossians 3:2 (NIV)

"Set your minds on things above, not on earthly things."

Devotional

Where your mind settles, your life eventually follows. Scripture does not suggest that your focus will drift naturally toward what is eternal. It instructs you to *set* your mind. That word implies intention, discipline, and repeated choice. Left unattended, your thoughts will often gravitate toward worry, comparison, or distraction.

Earthly concerns demand constant attention. Responsibilities, expectations, and pressures can easily crowd out eternal perspective. But God invites you to lift your gaze. When you set your mind on things above, you are reminded that your life is anchored in something greater than what you see or feel today.

Setting your mind on heavenly things does not mean ignoring real life. It means filtering life through truth. It re-centers your priorities, softens your reactions, and steadies your emotions. When your thoughts align with God's perspective, peace begins to replace anxiety.

Today, you are invited to be intentional with your focus. You may not be able to control every thought that enters your mind, but you can choose which thoughts you allow to stay. Fixing your mind on God brings clarity, hope, and renewed strength.

Reflection

What has been occupying your thoughts most frequently, and is it drawing you closer to God or pulling you away from His peace?

Life Application

When you notice your thoughts drifting toward worry or distraction today, pause and redirect them by recalling a truth about who God is.

Prayer

God, help me set my mind on things above. Redirect my thoughts when they wander and anchor my focus in Your truth. Amen.

January 20

God Is Near to the Brokenhearted

Psalm 34:18 (NIV)

"The Lord is close to the brokenhearted and saves those who are crushed in spirit."

Devotional

Pain has a way of making people feel isolated, as though no one truly understands what they are carrying. But Scripture offers reassurance that God is not distant when your heart is heavy. He draws near. He is especially close in moments of brokenness and sorrow.

God does not rush your healing or minimize your pain. He meets you in it. When your spirit feels crushed and words feel hard to find, God remains present. His closeness is not dependent on your strength or your ability to articulate what hurts. He simply comes near.

Many people try to hide their brokenness, believing they must be strong in order to be accepted. But God invites honesty. He is not intimidated by your grief or discomforted by your tears. He draws close to restore, comfort, and save.

If today finds you carrying emotional weight, know this: you are not alone. God is nearer than you realize. Healing may take time, but His presence is immediate. Let yourself rest in the nearness of the One who holds your heart.

Reflection

Where are you experiencing emotional pain or heaviness right now?

Life Application

Take a moment today to speak honestly with God about what hurts. Invite Him into that space without holding anything back.

Prayer

Lord, thank You for being near to me in my brokenness. Comfort my heart and remind me that I am never alone. Amen.

January 21

Called to Shine

Matthew 5:14 (NIV)

"You are the light of the world. A town built on a hill cannot be hidden."

Devotional

Jesus does not say you *should* be the light of the world. He says you *are* the light. This identity is not earned through effort or achievement. It is given because of who lives within you. God's light shines through ordinary people who choose to live aligned with truth, love, and obedience.

Many people dim their light out of fear of standing out or being misunderstood. But light was never meant to be hidden. When you live authentically in your faith, your life becomes a quiet testimony of God's presence and goodness.

Shining does not mean perfection. It means consistency. It means showing kindness, choosing integrity, and reflecting God's character in everyday moments. Your light reaches places you may never fully see or understand.

Today is a reminder that your life matters. The way you speak, serve, and love has impact. God placed His light in you intentionally. Let it shine freely and boldly.

Reflection

Where might God be inviting you to shine more openly in your life?

Life Application

Do one intentional act today that reflects God's light through kindness, encouragement, or truth.

Prayer

Jesus, thank You for calling me the light of the world. Help me shine with humility, love, and courage so that others may see You through me. Amen.

January 22

Strength for Today

2 Corinthians 12:9 (NIV)

"But he said to me, 'My grace is sufficient for you, for my power is made perfect in weakness.'"

Devotional

There are days when strength feels scarce. You wake up willing but tired, faithful but worn. On those days, God does not ask you to muster more power. He offers His grace. Grace is not a consolation prize for weakness. It is the very place where God's power is most clearly revealed.

We often hide our weaknesses because we believe strength means having it all together. But God sees weakness as an opening. An invitation. When you acknowledge your limits, you make room for His sufficiency. What you cannot carry, He can. What you cannot fix, He already holds.

Grace does not always remove the struggle. Sometimes it meets you right in the middle of it. It sustains you when answers are delayed and outcomes remain unclear. God's grace is enough for today. Not tomorrow. Not the whole year. Just today.

You do not need more strength than what this day requires. You need to lean into the grace already available to you.

Reflection

Where have you been trying to rely on your own strength instead of God's grace?

Life Application

Acknowledge one area of weakness today without shame. Offer it to God and thank Him for His sufficient grace.

Prayer

Lord, thank You that Your grace is enough for me today. I release the pressure to be strong on my own and choose to depend on You. Let Your power rest on me. Amen.

January 23

God Is Near

Psalm 145:18 (NIV)

"The Lord is near to all who call on him, to all who call on him in truth."

Devotional

There are moments in life when God can feel distant, especially when prayers seem unanswered or circumstances feel heavy. But Scripture reminds us of a steady truth: God's nearness is not dependent on your emotions or your circumstances. He is near to those who call on Him, not with perfection, but with honesty.

Calling on God "in truth" means coming to Him without pretense. It means bringing your real thoughts, real questions, and real emotions into His presence. God does not require polished prayers or spiritual performance. He desires authenticity. When you approach Him as you are, you create space for intimacy rather than distance.

Many people assume closeness to God is achieved through consistency or discipline alone. While those matter, nearness is ultimately relational. God draws close when you invite Him in sincerely, even in seasons of doubt or weariness. He is not offended by your honesty. He welcomes it.

Today, let yourself be reminded that you are not praying into emptiness. You are calling on a God who leans in, listens attentively, and responds with care. His nearness is not fleeting. It is faithful, and it is available to you right now.

Reflection

What truth do you need to bring honestly before God today?

Life Application

Set aside a few quiet moments today to speak openly with God about what you are really feeling, without filtering or rehearsing your words.

Prayer

God, thank You for being near when I call on You. Help me come to You with honesty and trust, knowing You welcome me just as I am. Amen.

January 24

A Guarded Peace

Isaiah 26:3 (NIV)

"You will keep in perfect peace those whose minds are steadfast, because they trust in you."

Devotional

Peace is not the absence of trouble. It is the presence of trust. This verse reveals that peace is something God actively keeps and sustains when your mind remains anchored in Him. A steadfast mind is not one that never wavers, but one that continually returns to trust, even when circumstances try to pull it elsewhere.

Many people seek peace by changing what is happening around them. God offers peace by transforming what is happening within them. When your thoughts are fixed on fear, uncertainty, or what could go wrong, peace feels fragile. But when your mind is anchored in God's character, peace becomes guarded and secure.

Trust is the pathway to peace. Trust does not require full understanding or perfect clarity. It simply chooses to believe that God is faithful, present, and in control. As you trust Him, God does the guarding. He keeps your heart and mind from being overtaken by anxiety and unrest.

Today, peace is not something you have to chase. It is something you receive as you fix your mind on God. When you choose trust again and again, even in small moments, God faithfully surrounds you with the peace only He can provide.

Reflection

What thoughts have been competing for your attention and disrupting your peace?

Life Application

When anxious thoughts arise today, pause and intentionally redirect your mind toward God by recalling one truth about His faithfulness.

Prayer

God, help me fix my mind on You. Teach me to trust You fully so that Your peace can guard my heart and mind. Thank You for being my steady anchor. Amen.

January 25

Rooted and Established

Colossians 2:7 (NIV)

"Rooted and built up in him, strengthened in the faith as you were taught, and overflowing with thankfulness."

Devotional

A life that remains steady through changing seasons is a life that is deeply rooted. Roots are formed quietly, beneath the surface, long before growth is visible. In the same way, spiritual maturity develops through consistent connection with Christ, even when progress feels slow or unnoticed.

Being rooted in Christ means your faith is anchored in truth rather than circumstance. When challenges arise, you are not easily shaken because your foundation is secure. God strengthens your faith over time as you continue to lean on Him, drawing nourishment from His Word and presence.

As you grow in Christ, your life is also being built up. God is shaping you intentionally, strengthening your faith layer by layer. This growth is not rushed. It is steady and purposeful, producing resilience and confidence in Him.

Gratitude becomes the natural overflow of a rooted life. When you recognize how God has sustained you, even in quiet ways, thankfulness rises from a place of trust rather than effort. Today is an invitation to remain planted in Christ and allow Him to continue the work He is doing within you.

Reflection

What helps you stay spiritually grounded when life feels uncertain?

Life Application

Spend time today strengthening your spiritual roots by reading Scripture or reflecting on how God has been faithful to you in past seasons.

Prayer

God, help me remain rooted in You. Strengthen my faith and build my life on Your truth. Let gratitude overflow as I continue to grow in You. Amen.

January 26

Upheld by His Hand

Isaiah 41:10 (NIV)

"So do not fear, for I am with you; do not be dismayed, for I am your God. I will strengthen you and help you; I will uphold you with my righteous right hand."

Devotional

Fear has a way of making the future feel heavier than it actually is. It pulls tomorrow's concerns into today and convinces you that you are facing them alone. But God speaks directly into that fear with reassurance that is both personal and powerful. He does not promise the absence of challenges, but He promises His presence through them.

God's strength is not reserved for moments when you feel brave or confident. It meets you when you feel weak, uncertain, or overwhelmed. This verse reminds you that God is actively involved in holding you steady. You are not sustaining yourself. You are being upheld by Him.

When God says He will help you, He means He will come alongside you. His help may arrive as peace in the middle of chaos, clarity in the midst of confusion, or endurance when you feel depleted. His strength often shows up quietly, carrying you further than you thought possible.

Today, you are not asked to be fearless. You are invited to trust. God is with you, strengthening you for what this day holds. You do not need to borrow worry from tomorrow. His grace is sufficient for today.

Reflection

What fear or concern has been weighing on you recently?

Life Application

When fear surfaces today, pause and remind yourself out loud that God is with you and strengthening you in this moment.

Prayer

God, thank You for being with me and strengthening me when I feel afraid. Help me trust You with today and rest in the support You provide. Amen.

January 27

Peace in His Presence

Psalm 16:11 (NIV)

"You make known to me the path of life; you will fill me with joy in your presence, with eternal pleasures at your right hand."

Devotional

There is a difference between momentary happiness and lasting joy. Happiness often depends on circumstances, but joy flows from God's presence. This verse reminds us that when we remain close to God, He fills our lives with a peace and joy that cannot be manufactured or taken away.

God's presence brings clarity. When you draw near to Him, He gently reveals the path you are meant to walk. Even when life feels uncertain, His presence anchors you, reminding you that you are not wandering aimlessly. You are being guided by a faithful God who knows the way forward.

Many people search for fulfillment in accomplishments, relationships, or external validation. While those things may bring temporary satisfaction, true joy is found in intimacy with God. His presence nourishes the soul in ways nothing else can.

Today is an invitation to intentionally seek God's presence. Not because you need to earn peace, but because peace is found when you rest with Him. When you choose closeness with God, joy naturally follows.

Reflection

When was the last time you intentionally paused to be in God's presence?

Life Application

Set aside intentional time today to sit quietly with God, even if only for a few minutes, and invite His presence to refresh your spirit.

Prayer

God, thank You for the joy and peace found in Your presence. Help me remain close to You and trust You as You guide my steps. Amen.

January 28

Anchored in Hope

Romans 15:13 (NIV)

"May the God of hope fill you with all joy and peace as you trust in him, so that you may overflow with hope by the power of the Holy Spirit."

Devotional

Hope is not wishful thinking or blind optimism. Biblical hope is anchored in the character of God. It is the quiet confidence that God is faithful, even when circumstances feel uncertain. This verse reminds us that hope flows from trust, not from everything going according to plan.

God is described here as the God of hope, meaning hope originates in Him. When you place your trust in God, He fills you with joy and peace that steady your heart. This filling is not dependent on outcomes. It is rooted in relationship. As you trust Him, hope begins to rise from within rather than being something you have to chase.

Overflowing hope is the result of the Holy Spirit at work in you. It sustains you in difficult seasons and gives you strength to keep moving forward. Hope does not deny hardship. It acknowledges it while still believing God is present and active.

Today, if you feel weary or discouraged, let this be a reminder that your hope is not fragile. It is anchored in God Himself. As you trust Him, He will continue to fill you with joy, peace, and hope that carries you through.

Reflection

What area of your life needs renewed hope right now?

Life Application

Choose one promise of God to focus on today and remind yourself that your hope is anchored in His faithfulness, not in circumstances.

Prayer

God of hope, fill me with joy and peace as I trust in You. Strengthen my heart and help me overflow with hope through the power of Your Spirit. Amen.

January 29

Walking in Obedience

Deuteronomy 5:33 (NIV)

"Walk in obedience to all that the Lord your God has commanded you, so that you may live and prosper and prolong your days in the land that you will possess."

Devotional

Obedience is often misunderstood as restriction, but Scripture reveals it as a pathway to life. God's commands are not given to limit you, but to lead you into fullness and protection. When God calls you to walk in obedience, He is inviting you into alignment with His wisdom and care.

Walking in obedience is a daily decision, not a one-time declaration. It shows up in small choices, quiet moments, and unseen acts of faithfulness. Obedience requires trust, especially when God's direction challenges your comfort or understanding. Yet God promises that obedience leads to life, stability, and blessing.

Many people hesitate to obey because they fear what obedience might cost them. But Scripture assures us that God's ways are designed for our good. What feels like surrender often becomes the very place where peace and purpose meet.

Today, obedience may look simple or ordinary, but it carries eternal significance. As you choose to walk in God's ways, you position yourself to experience the life He desires for you, both now and in the days ahead.

Reflection

Where is God inviting you to walk more fully in obedience?

Life Application

Identify one area where God has been prompting you to obey. Take a practical step today to align your actions with His direction.

Prayer

God, help me walk in obedience to You. Give me the courage to trust Your ways and the wisdom to follow Your guidance each day. Amen.

January 30

Renewed Focus

Hebrews 12:1–2 (NIV)

"Therefore, since we are surrounded by such a great cloud of witnesses, let us throw off everything that hinders and the sin that so easily entangles. And let us run with perseverance the race marked out for us, fixing our eyes on Jesus, the pioneer and perfecter of faith."

Devotional

Focus is essential when the journey feels long. This passage reminds us that the life of faith is a race, not a sprint, and perseverance requires intention. Distractions, weights, and discouragement can quietly slow your pace if you are not attentive to what you are carrying.

God invites you to release what hinders you, not out of condemnation, but out of care. Some things are not sinful, yet they still weigh you down. Lingering guilt, misplaced priorities, unresolved wounds, or constant comparison can entangle your heart and blur your focus. God's desire is to free you so you can run with endurance.

Renewed focus comes when you intentionally fix your eyes on Jesus. He is not only your example, but your source of strength. When you look to Him, you remember why you started and who is walking with you. Jesus remains steady even when your energy wavers.

As this month comes to a close, today is an opportunity to reset your focus. Lay down what no longer serves your faith and recommit to the race God has marked out for you. With your eyes fixed on Jesus, you can move forward with renewed clarity and perseverance.

Reflection

What has been distracting or hindering your focus lately?

Life Application

Take a moment today to identify one thing God may be asking you to release so you can move forward with greater focus.

Prayer

Jesus, help me fix my eyes on You. Show me what I need to lay down and strengthen me to run the race with perseverance and faith. Amen.

January 31

Faithful Finisher

Psalm 90:12 (NIV)

"Teach us to number our days, that we may gain a heart of wisdom."

Devotional

Finishing well requires awareness. This verse is a prayer that asks God to help us live with intention, recognizing that our days matter. Numbering our days is not about fear or urgency. It is about wisdom. It is choosing to live thoughtfully rather than drifting through life on autopilot.

As this month comes to a close, God invites you to pause and reflect. Wisdom grows when you take time to consider how you are spending your energy, your attention, and your time. Every day is a gift, and how you steward it shapes the direction of your life and faith.

Being a faithful finisher does not mean perfection. It means staying present and attentive to what God is doing in each season. It means learning from what has passed and carrying that wisdom forward rather than rushing ahead unchanged.

Today marks the end of January, but it also marks a moment of clarity. God is teaching you how to live with purpose, depth, and intention. As you move forward, may wisdom guide your steps and help you continue this journey with faithfulness and trust.

Reflection

What has God been teaching you about how you use your time and attention?

Life Application

Take a few moments today to reflect on January. Write down one lesson you want to carry with you into the next month.

Prayer

God, teach me to number my days with wisdom. Help me live intentionally and finish each season faithfully, trusting You with what lies ahead. Amen.

FEBRUARY

Rooted in God's Love

February centers on the truth that everything in your life flows from being rooted in God's love. Before love is something you give, manage, or struggle with, it is something you receive. This month invites you to slow down and settle deeply into the assurance that God's love is steady, personal, and unchanging.

Being rooted means drawing nourishment from a source that does not fail. God's love is not based on performance, perfection, or proximity. It does not fluctuate with your emotions or circumstances. As you journey through February, you will be reminded that His love is the foundation of your identity, not something you must earn or maintain.

When you are rooted in God's love, your life begins to grow differently. Healing takes place without striving. Obedience flows from security rather than fear. Boundaries become healthy instead of defensive. Relationships become spaces of freedom rather than pressure. This month invites you to live from a place of assurance, allowing God's love to anchor you, strengthen you, and shape every area of your life.

February 1

Rooted and Grounded

Ephesians 3:17 (NIV)

"So that Christ may dwell in your hearts through faith. And I pray that you, being rooted and established in love,"

Devotional

Before love becomes something you extend to others, it must first be the place where you live. This verse reminds us that Christ does not visit our hearts temporarily. He dwells there. His presence is not fleeting or conditional. When Christ makes His home in your heart, love becomes the soil in which your life is meant to grow.

Being rooted in God's love means your identity is anchored beneath the surface, where storms cannot easily uproot it. Roots develop quietly over time, strengthened by consistency rather than intensity. In the same way, spiritual confidence is formed not by emotional highs, but by daily assurance that God's love is steady and secure.

Many people attempt to build their lives on approval, achievement, or relationships, only to find those foundations unstable. God invites you to build from a deeper place. When you are rooted in His love, you are no longer striving to be accepted. You are living from acceptance already given.

February begins with this invitation: let God's love be your foundation. From this place, healing can happen, obedience can grow, and love can be extended to others without fear of loss. A rooted life is not easily shaken because it is grounded in Christ Himself.

Reflection

What has your sense of worth or identity been rooted in recently?

Life Application

Take a moment today to thank God for loving you before you did anything to earn it. Let that truth shape how you move through this day.

Prayer

God, thank You for making Your home in my heart. Help me grow rooted and grounded in Your love so that my life reflects security, confidence, and trust in You. Amen.

February 2

Abiding in Love

1 John 4:16 (NLT)
"We know how much God loves us, and we have put our trust in his love. God is love, and all who live in love live in God, and God lives in them."

Devotional

To abide means to remain, to stay, to make your home in something rather than visiting it occasionally. This verse invites you into a deeper way of living where God's love is not just something you acknowledge, but something you trust and dwell in daily. Love is not simply what God gives. Love is who God is.

Many people believe God loves them in theory but struggle to trust that love in practice. They question it when they fall short, when prayers go unanswered, or when life becomes difficult. Yet Scripture reminds us that trusting God's love is foundational to living fully connected to Him. When you trust His love, you begin to rest rather than strive.

Living in love means allowing God's love to shape how you see yourself and how you respond to others. When love becomes your dwelling place, fear loses its grip, insecurity quiets, and comparison fades. You no longer live from a place of scarcity, wondering if you are enough. You live from the assurance that God is present and abiding within you.

Today, you are invited to remain in God's love. Not just when you feel close to Him, but especially when you do not. Abiding in love is a daily choice to trust what God says is true, even when emotions try to tell a different story.

Reflection

What makes it difficult for you to fully trust God's love at times?

Life Application

When doubt or insecurity arises today, pause and remind yourself that God is love and that you are living in Him.

Prayer

God, thank You for loving me so completely. Help me trust Your love and remain rooted in it each day. Teach me to live from the assurance that You are with me and within me. Amen.

February 3

Loved Before You Knew Him

Romans 5:8 (NKJV)

"But God demonstrates His own love toward us, in that while we were still sinners, Christ died for us."

Devotional

God's love did not begin when you chose Him. It began long before you were aware of Him. This verse reminds us that God's love is proactive, not reactive. He did not wait for you to get it right, clean yourself up, or prove your devotion. He moved toward you first.

Many people struggle with feeling worthy of love because they measure love by performance. They assume God's love fluctuates based on obedience, consistency, or spiritual maturity. But Scripture makes it clear that God's love was demonstrated at your worst, not your best. His love is anchored in His character, not your behavior.

Being rooted in God's love means releasing the lie that you must earn His affection. When you understand that Christ died for you while you were still far from Him, it reshapes how you see yourself and your relationship with God. Grace becomes real. Shame loses its power. Gratitude replaces striving.

Today is an invitation to rest in the truth that you are deeply loved, not because of who you are becoming, but because of who God is. Let this assurance settle your heart and remind you that your journey with God is built on love that never required perfection.

Reflection

What beliefs have you held about needing to earn God's love?

Life Application

When you find yourself striving for approval today, pause and remind yourself that God loved you before you ever loved Him.

Prayer

God, thank You for loving me before I knew You. Help me release the need to earn Your love and live confidently rooted in the grace You have already given. Amen.

February 4

Secure in His Love

John 15:9 (NIV)

"As the Father has loved me, so have I loved you. Now remain in my love."

Devotional

Security comes from knowing where you belong. In this verse, Jesus makes a profound statement about the nature of His love. He loves you with the same love He receives from the Father. That love is not fragile, conditional, or temporary. It is steady, unbroken, and secure.

Jesus invites you not just to receive His love, but to remain in it. Remaining requires intention. It means choosing to stay rooted in truth when doubt, fear, or distraction try to pull you away. When you remain in His love, you stop living as though love must be proven or protected. You begin living from a place of rest.

Many people struggle with insecurity because they measure love by how others respond to them. God's love offers a different foundation. It does not fluctuate based on your performance or circumstances. When you remain in His love, you are anchored in something unchanging.

Today, let this truth settle deeply in your heart. You are secure in God's love. You do not have to chase it or fear losing it. Remaining in His love is where peace grows and confidence takes root.

Reflection

What makes it difficult for you to remain in God's love during challenging moments?

Life Application

When insecurity surfaces today, pause and remind yourself that you are secure and held in God's love.

Prayer

Jesus, thank You for loving me as the Father loves You. Help me remain rooted in Your love and live with confidence grounded in that truth. Amen.

February 5

Resting in His Delight

Zephaniah 3:17 (NLT)

"For the Lord your God is living among you. He is a mighty savior. He will take delight in you with gladness. With his love, he will calm all your fears. He will rejoice over you with joyful songs."

Devotional

Many people understand God as powerful, holy, and sovereign, yet struggle to see Him as delighted in them. This verse gently reshapes that image. God is not distant or indifferent. He is present with you, and His love toward you is filled with joy, not reluctance or disappointment.

God's delight is not based on your performance or productivity. He delights in you because you are His. When you are rooted in God's love, you begin to understand that His affection is not something you earn, but something you receive. His presence brings calm, not pressure. His love quiets fear rather than fueling it.

Fear often grows when we believe we are barely tolerated or constantly evaluated. But God's love does the opposite. It reassures, steadies, and comforts. He rejoices over you, even in seasons when you feel uncertain or unfinished. His love meets you where you are and invites you to rest.

Today, allow yourself to sit with this truth. God delights in you. You do not need to strive for His approval or prove your worth. Being rooted in His love means learning to rest in the joy He already has over you.

Reflection

What makes it difficult for you to believe that God delights in you?

Life Application

When self-doubt or fear arises today, pause and remind yourself that God rejoices over you and calms your heart with His love.

Prayer

God, thank You for delighting in me. Help me rest in Your love and allow it to quiet my fears. Teach me to live rooted in the joy You have over my life. Amen.

February 6

Steadfast Love That Renews

Lamentations 3:22–23 (NLT)
"The faithful love of the Lord never ends. His mercies never cease. Great is his faithfulness; his mercies begin afresh each morning."

Devotional

God's love is not only deep, it is dependable. This passage reminds us that His love does not run out, wear thin, or disappear when life becomes difficult. Even in seasons marked by loss, uncertainty, or disappointment, God's faithful love remains constant. It is not interrupted by yesterday's failures or today's fatigue.

Each morning brings fresh mercy. That truth alone reshapes how you face the day. You are not carrying yesterday's mistakes into today without help. God meets you anew, offering compassion that restores and faithfulness that steadies your heart. His love renews you right where you are.

Being rooted in God's love means trusting that His faithfulness is not seasonal. It does not depend on your emotional state or spiritual consistency. His love renews you again and again, giving strength for what lies ahead without requiring perfection.

Today is an invitation to receive what God freely offers. Let His steadfast love remind you that you are not starting from scratch. You are starting from grace. Each day is held by His faithfulness, and His love is more than enough to carry you forward.

Reflection

How does knowing God's mercy is new each morning change the way you view today?

Life Application

Begin your day by thanking God for fresh mercy and intentionally releasing any guilt or discouragement from yesterday.

Prayer

God, thank You for Your faithful love and new mercies each morning. Help me trust Your steadiness and live today rooted in Your grace. Amen.

February 7

Drawn With Lovingkindness

Hosea 11:4 (NLT)
"I led Israel along with my ropes of kindness and love. I lifted the yoke from his neck, and I myself stooped to feed him."

Devotional

God's love is not forceful or harsh. It is gentle, intentional, and deeply personal. This verse paints a tender picture of a God who leads with kindness rather than control. He does not drag His people forward. He draws them closer with love.

Many people associate obedience to God with pressure or fear, but this scripture reveals a different posture. God leads by compassion. He notices burdens and responds with care. When the weight becomes too heavy, He lifts it. When strength is depleted, He stoops low to provide nourishment.

Being rooted in God's love means recognizing that His guidance is always wrapped in kindness. Even when He corrects or redirects, His heart remains gentle. His love does not push you past your limits without provision. It supports you as you grow.

Today, allow yourself to be drawn rather than driven. God's love is not rushing you or demanding perfection. It is patiently leading you, lifting burdens, and caring for you along the way. Trust the tenderness of His guidance.

Reflection

Where have you felt pressure instead of gentleness in your walk with God?

Life Application

Pay attention today to how God may be inviting you forward through kindness rather than pressure or fear.

Prayer

God, thank You for leading me with love and compassion. Help me trust Your gentle guidance and remain rooted in the kindness You show me each day. Amen.

February 8

Loved With an Everlasting Love

Jeremiah 31:3 (NKJV)

"The Lord has appeared of old to me, saying: 'Yes, I have loved you with an everlasting love; therefore with lovingkindness I have drawn you.'"

Devotional

God's love is not seasonal or temporary. This verse reminds us that His love stretches beyond time, circumstance, and human limitation. Long before you were aware of Him, God had already set His love upon you. His love did not begin at your point of faith, nor will it end when life becomes difficult.

Everlasting love means God's affection toward you does not expire. It is not reduced by mistakes or weakened by distance. His love remains steady through every chapter of your life. When you are rooted in this truth, you begin to live with greater security and peace, knowing that God's commitment to you is unchanging.

God draws you with lovingkindness, not coercion. He invites you closer through patience, mercy, and grace. Even when you wander, His love continues to pull you gently back toward Him. This drawing is an expression of care, not correction.

Today, let the truth of God's everlasting love settle your heart. You are not living on borrowed affection or temporary grace. You are deeply and permanently loved by a faithful God whose love will not let you go.

Reflection

How does knowing God's love is everlasting change the way you view your relationship with Him?

Life Application

When feelings of insecurity arise today, remind yourself that God's love for you has no expiration date.

Prayer

God, thank You for loving me with an everlasting love. Help me rest in the assurance that Your love is constant and unchanging. Draw me closer to You with Your lovingkindness. Amen.

February 9

Known and Loved

Psalm 139:1–2 (NIV)

"You have searched me, Lord, and you know me. You know when I sit and when I rise; you perceive my thoughts from afar."

Devotional

To be fully known and fully loved is one of the deepest longings of the human heart. This scripture reminds us that God knows every part of us, the visible and the hidden, the strengths and the struggles. Nothing about you is concealed from Him, yet His love remains constant.

Many people fear being truly known because they assume exposure leads to rejection. God's love offers the opposite experience. He sees your thoughts, understands your motives, and knows your fears, yet He stays. His knowledge of you does not diminish His affection. It deepens it.

Being rooted in God's love means trusting that His understanding of you is complete and compassionate. You do not have to explain yourself to Him or clean yourself up before approaching Him. God meets you with acceptance, not surprise.

Today, allow yourself to rest in the safety of being known by God. You are not misunderstood or overlooked. You are seen, understood, and deeply loved by a God who delights in every part of your journey.

Reflection

What parts of yourself do you find hardest to believe God fully knows and still loves?

Life Application

Spend time today honestly sharing your thoughts and emotions with God, trusting that His love remains unchanged.

Prayer

God, thank You for knowing me completely and loving me fully. Help me trust Your understanding and rest in the security of Your love. Amen.

February 10

Treasured and Safe

Psalm 36:7 (NLT)
"How precious is your unfailing love, O God! All humanity finds shelter in the shadow of your wings."

Devotional

God's love is not distant or abstract. It is precious, personal, and protective. This verse reminds you that His unfailing love is a place of refuge, not just a feeling to be admired.

The image of shelter under God's wings speaks to care, closeness, and safety. It is an invitation to rest, not to strive. When life feels uncertain or overwhelming, God does not ask you to prove your strength. He offers you His presence as protection.

Being treasured by God means you are seen and valued exactly where you are. His love does not waver based on performance or circumstance. It remains steady, covering you with grace and drawing you close when you need it most.

Safety in God is not the absence of difficulty. It is the assurance that you are never facing it alone. When you choose to dwell in His love, peace begins to replace fear, and trust grows stronger than worry.

Reflection
Where do you need to rest more fully in God's protection?

Life Application
When anxiety or fear arises today, pause and remind yourself that you are sheltered by God's unfailing love.

Prayer
God, thank You for Your precious and unfailing love. Help me rest in Your protection and trust that I am safe in Your care. Amen.

February 11

Rich in Mercy

Ephesians 2:4–5 (NLT)

"But God is so rich in mercy, and he loved us so much, that even though we were dead because of our sins, he gave us life when he raised Christ from the dead. It is only by God's grace that you have been saved!"

Devotional

God's love is inseparable from His mercy. This passage reminds us that God's response to brokenness was not distance or condemnation, but compassion and action. When you were at your weakest, God moved toward you with love that restores life.

Mercy means you are not treated according to your failures. It means God sees beyond your past and speaks life into places that once felt lifeless. His love does not wait for improvement before extending grace. It meets you where you are and begins the work of renewal.

Being rooted in God's love requires understanding that His mercy is abundant, not limited. You are not surviving on leftover grace or borrowed compassion. God is rich in mercy, and His love toward you is generous and intentional.

Today, let this truth reshape how you see yourself. You are not defined by what once held you back. You are alive because of God's mercy and deeply loved because of His grace. This is the foundation from which you now live.

Reflection

How does knowing God is rich in mercy change the way you view your past?

Life Application

When self-judgment or guilt surfaces today, remind yourself that God's mercy has already spoken life over you.

Prayer

God, thank You for being rich in mercy and great in love. Help me live from the freedom and life You have given me through Your grace. Amen.

February 12

Chosen and Beloved

Colossians 3:12 (NLT)

"Since God chose you to be the holy people he loves, you must clothe yourselves with tenderhearted mercy, kindness, humility, gentleness, and patience."

Devotional

Being chosen by God is not about exclusivity. It is about intentionality. This verse reminds us that God's love is personal and purposeful. You are not an afterthought or a coincidence. You are chosen and deeply loved by Him.

When you understand yourself as chosen, it reshapes how you move through the world. You no longer operate from insecurity or the need to prove your worth. Instead, you begin to live from a place of assurance. God's love becomes the starting point for how you treat others and how you respond to life.

Paul encourages believers to clothe themselves with qualities that reflect God's heart. These are not traits we force out of obligation. They flow naturally when we are rooted in the knowledge that we are loved. Love received becomes love expressed.

Today, remember that God's love for you is active and intentional. You are chosen, cherished, and invited to reflect His love through how you live. Let His love shape not only who you are, but how you show up for others.

Reflection

How does seeing yourself as chosen by God affect the way you see yourself and others?

Life Application

Choose one quality listed in this verse to intentionally practice today as a reflection of God's love in you.

Prayer

God, thank You for choosing me and loving me so deeply. Help me clothe myself with compassion and kindness as a reflection of Your love. Amen.

February 13

Loved and Called by Name

Isaiah 43:1 (NIV)
"Do not fear, for I have redeemed you; I have summoned you by name; you are mine."

Devotional

God's love is deeply personal. This verse reminds you that you are not known by circumstance, mistake, or role. You are known by name. God speaks directly to identity, not fear.

Redemption here is not distant or theoretical. It is intimate and intentional. God does not merely rescue. He claims. Being called by name means you belong to Him fully and securely, not conditionally or temporarily.

Fear loses its power when you remember who has claimed you. God's declaration, "You are mine," is both protection and promise. It affirms that your life is held by Him, even when uncertainty tries to shake your confidence.

This scripture invites you to rest in belonging rather than striving for approval. You do not have to earn what has already been spoken over you. You are loved, known, and held by God.

Reflection
Where do you need to remember that you belong to God?

Life Application
When fear surfaces today, repeat this truth: I am called by name, and I belong to God.

Prayer
God, thank You for knowing me and calling me by name. Help me live with confidence, grounded in the truth that I belong to You. Amen.

February 14

Loved First

1 John 4:19 (NIV)

"We love because he first loved us."

Devotional

Love does not begin with what you give. It begins with what you receive. This verse gently but firmly resets the order of love in your life. Before love becomes something you offer to others, it is something God has already extended to you. His love is the starting point, not the reward.

Many people feel pressure on this day to measure love by attention, affirmation, or relationships. But God's love does not fluctuate based on seasons, status, or circumstances. It is steady and initiating. He loved you first, before you responded, before you understood, and before you felt worthy.

Being rooted in God's love means recognizing that your ability to love well flows from His love toward you. When you are secure in being loved by God, you are no longer dependent on others to validate your worth. Love becomes something you share freely, not something you grasp for.

Today, let God's love reframe what love means to you. You are already loved. From that place, you can love others with freedom, sincerity, and peace, without fear of loss or rejection.

Reflection

How does knowing that God loved you first change the way you view love in your life?

Life Application

Today, remind yourself that you are already loved by God. Let that assurance guide how you interact with others and how you care for yourself.

Prayer

God, thank You for loving me first. Help me live from the security of Your love and extend that love to others with grace and confidence. Amen.

February 15

Better Than Life

Psalm 63:3 (NKJV)

"Because Your lovingkindness is better than life, my lips shall praise You."

Devotional

There are many things in life we are taught to pursue as essential: success, security, relationships, stability. Yet this verse places God's love above them all. David declares that God's lovingkindness surpasses even life itself. This is not an abstract statement. It is a testimony born out of experience, struggle, and dependence on God.

To say that God's love is better than life means it sustains you when circumstances fail to satisfy. It means His love brings meaning even when life feels uncertain or incomplete. God's love is not merely an addition to your life. It is the source that gives life its true value.

Being rooted in God's love reshapes your priorities. When His love becomes central, you are no longer driven by fear of loss or the need for constant fulfillment. Praise begins to flow naturally, not because everything is perfect, but because you are grounded in something greater than circumstances.

Today, let this truth realign your heart. God's love is not competing with the things you value. It is the foundation that allows you to enjoy them rightly. When you recognize His love as better than life, gratitude and trust begin to overflow.

Reflection

What things in your life have you been tempted to place above God's love?

Life Application

Take a moment today to thank God for His lovingkindness and intentionally place your trust in His love above all else.

Prayer

God, thank You for a love that is better than life. Help me remain rooted in Your lovingkindness and allow my life to reflect praise and trust in You. Amen.

February 16

Held in Perfect Love

1 John 4:18 (NIV)

"There is no fear in love. But perfect love drives out fear, because fear has to do with punishment. The one who fears is not made perfect in love."

Devotional

Fear often settles in quietly, shaping decisions, reactions, and expectations without being immediately noticed. This verse reveals that fear and love cannot occupy the same space fully. Where God's love is allowed to take root, fear begins to loosen its grip.

Perfect love does not mean flawless circumstances or a life without uncertainty. It means complete, mature love that reassures the heart of God's presence and care. When you are rooted in God's love, you no longer have to live guarded or braced for what might go wrong. His love provides security that fear cannot override.

Many fears are tied to rejection, loss, or punishment. God's love speaks directly against those concerns. It reassures you that you are accepted, held, and protected. As His love grows deeper in your heart, fear loses its authority and influence over how you live.

Today is an invitation to examine where fear may still be lingering. God's love is not distant or conditional. It is present and powerful enough to steady your heart. When you allow His love to remain central, fear no longer defines your path forward.

Reflection

What fears have been influencing your thoughts or decisions recently?

Life Application

When fear arises today, pause and remind yourself that you are held in God's perfect love and do not need to be afraid.

Prayer

Father, thank You for Your perfect love that drives out fear. Help me remain rooted in Your love and trust You with every concern that tries to unsettle my heart. Amen.

February 17

Compassion That Holds You

Psalm 103:13 (NIV)

"As a father has compassion on his children, so the Lord has compassion on those who fear him."

Devotional

God's love is not distant or abstract. It is compassionate and attentive. This verse draws a tender picture of God as a Father who understands His children and responds with care. His compassion is not earned through perfection; it flows from relationship.

Compassion means God notices your weakness without condemnation. He understands the weight you carry, the emotions you struggle to name, and the places where you feel tired or unsure. When you are rooted in God's love, you are not required to hide your humanity. You are met with understanding rather than judgment.

Many people confuse reverence for God with fear that keeps them distant. But this verse shows a different reality. To fear the Lord is to trust Him deeply, to honor Him, and to rely on His care. God's compassion meets those who come to Him with humility and trust.

Today, let yourself receive God's compassion. You do not have to be strong all the time. You are held by a Father whose love is gentle, patient, and sustaining. His compassion steadies your heart and reminds you that you are never alone in what you face.

Reflection

Where do you most need to receive God's compassion right now?

Life Application

When you feel overwhelmed today, pause and remind yourself that God's compassion meets you exactly where you are.

Prayer

Lord, thank You for Your compassion toward me. Help me trust Your care and remain rooted in the love that understands and sustains me each day. Amen.

February 18

Surrounded by Love

Psalm 32:10 (NLT)

"Many sorrows come to the wicked, but unfailing love surrounds those who trust the Lord."

Devotional

Life brings challenges to everyone, but this verse highlights a profound distinction for those who trust in God. While difficulties may still arise, God's unfailing love surrounds those who place their confidence in Him. His love becomes a covering that holds you steady even when circumstances feel uncertain.

Being surrounded by God's love does not mean hardship disappears. It means you are not exposed or unprotected in the midst of it. God's love wraps around you, guarding your heart and reminding you that you are never facing life alone. When you trust Him, His presence becomes your refuge.

Trust is what positions you to experience this surrounding love. It is an ongoing decision to lean into God's character rather than fear what lies ahead. As you trust Him, you begin to notice how His love sustains you through moments of difficulty and restores your hope.

Today, remember that God's love is not distant. It surrounds you on every side. When you place your trust in Him, His unfailing love becomes a constant presence, offering comfort, strength, and peace throughout your day.

Reflection

What does it look like for you to trust God more fully in your current season?

Life Application

When you feel overwhelmed today, pause and remind yourself that God's unfailing love surrounds you and is holding you steady.

Prayer

Lord, thank You for Your unfailing love that surrounds me. Help me trust You more deeply and rest in the assurance that I am always held by Your care. Amen.

February 19

Loved Beyond Measure

Ephesians 3:18–19 (NIV)

"May have power, together with all the Lord's holy people, to grasp how wide and long and high and deep is the love of Christ, and to know this love that surpasses knowledge - that you may be filled to the measure of all the fullness of God."

Devotional

God's love cannot be measured by human standards. This passage reminds us that His love extends far beyond what we can fully understand or explain. It is wide enough to reach every corner of your life, long enough to sustain you through every season, high enough to lift you above despair, and deep enough to meet you at your lowest point.

Knowing God's love is not only an intellectual exercise. It is an experience that shapes how you live, respond, and believe. Paul prays that believers would have the power to grasp this love because it takes spiritual awareness to truly receive it. God's love surpasses knowledge, yet He invites you to know it deeply through relationship.

When you are rooted in God's love, you begin to live from fullness rather than lack. His love fills the empty places, strengthens the weary parts of your heart, and reassures you that you are never operating on your own strength. You are being filled by God Himself.

Today, allow yourself to sit with the vastness of God's love. You do not need to understand it completely to be changed by it. As you open your heart to His love, He continues to fill you with peace, strength, and confidence that flows into every area of your life.

Reflection

Which aspect of God's love feels hardest for you to grasp right now?

Life Application

Take a moment today to reflect on how God's love has shown up in your life, even in ways you did not immediately recognize.

Prayer

Lord, help me grasp the depth and breadth of Your love. Fill my heart with the fullness that comes from knowing You and trusting Your love for me. Amen.

February 20

Established in Love

Ephesians 3:17 (NKJV)

"That Christ may dwell in your hearts through faith; that you, being rooted and grounded in love,"

Devotional

To be rooted and grounded in love is to live from a place of stability rather than uncertainty. This verse reminds us that Christ dwells in our hearts through faith, making His love the foundation on which everything else stands. When love is the ground beneath you, life feels less fragile and faith feels more secure.

Being grounded in love means you are not easily shaken by circumstances or opinions. God's love becomes the anchor that holds you steady when emotions fluctuate or challenges arise. You may still feel the weight of life, but you are no longer uprooted by it.

Christ dwelling in your heart is an ongoing reality, not a temporary experience. His presence shapes your thoughts, strengthens your faith, and reassures your heart. As you continue to trust Him, His love deepens your sense of belonging and purpose.

Today, let this truth encourage you. You are not drifting or standing on uncertain ground. You are established in God's love, firmly planted in a foundation that will not fail. From this place, you can move forward with confidence and peace.

Reflection

What helps you feel most grounded in God's love when life feels unsettled?

Life Application

When you feel uncertain today, pause and remind yourself that you are rooted and grounded in God's love, not in circumstances.

Prayer

Father, thank You for making Your love my foundation. Help me remain rooted and grounded in You, trusting that Your love holds me steady in every season. Amen.

February 21

Steady in His Love

Psalm 86:15 (NKJV)

"But You, O Lord, are a God full of compassion, and gracious, longsuffering and abundant in mercy and truth."

Devotional

God's love is steady, not reactive. This verse reveals the consistency of His character. He is compassionate when you are weak, gracious when you fall short, patient when growth takes time, and abundant in mercy and truth at all times. His love does not shift with circumstances or moods. It remains firm and dependable.

Many people struggle with instability in relationships because love often feels conditional or unpredictable. God's love offers a different experience. It is rooted in who He is, not in how you perform. When you understand God's nature, you begin to trust His heart even when life feels uncertain.

Being rooted in God's love means learning to rest in His patience and mercy. You do not need to rush your growth or pressure yourself to have everything figured out. God is long suffering, meaning He walks with you through the process, offering truth without withdrawing love.

Today, let yourself be reminded that God's love is not fragile. It is steady, compassionate, and trustworthy. When you place your confidence in His character, you find stability that carries you through every season.

Reflection

Which aspect of God's character brings you the most comfort right now?

Life Application

When you feel rushed or discouraged today, pause and remind yourself that God is patient, compassionate, and steady in His love toward you.

Prayer

Lord, thank You for Your compassion, patience, and mercy. Help me remain steady and rooted in Your love, trusting Your character in every season. Amen.

February 22

Love That Stays

Deuteronomy 31:6 (NIV)
"Be strong and courageous. Do not be afraid or terrified because of them, for the Lord your God goes with you; he will never leave you nor forsake you."

Devotional

One of the deepest fears people carry is the fear of being abandoned. Whether shaped by past relationships, disappointment, or loss, the thought of being left behind can quietly influence how we love, trust, and show up. This verse speaks directly to that fear with a promise that is both reassuring and firm: God does not leave.

God's love is not temporary or situational. He does not walk away when things become difficult or when faith feels fragile. His presence remains constant, even when emotions fluctuate or circumstances change. Being rooted in God's love means trusting that His nearness is not dependent on your strength or consistency.

This promise invites courage, not because challenges disappear, but because you are not facing them alone. God's love stays with you through uncertainty, fear, and transition. His presence becomes the steady ground beneath your feet when life feels unstable.

Today, let this truth settle deeply in your heart. You are not navigating this season by yourself. God is with you, and His love remains. When you trust the love that stays, fear loses its power to define your steps.

Reflection

Where have you struggled with the fear of being left or forgotten?

Life Application

When fear or insecurity surfaces today, remind yourself that God is with you and will never leave or forsake you.

Prayer

Lord, thank You for being a God who stays. Help me trust Your presence and remain rooted in the love that never leaves me. Amen.

February 23

Love That Casts Out Fear

Psalm 118:6 (NKJV)

"The Lord is on my side; I will not fear. What can man do to me?"

Devotional

Fear often grows when we feel alone or unsupported. This verse speaks directly to that vulnerability by reminding us that the Lord is present and actively for us. When God is on your side, fear loses its power to dominate your thoughts and decisions.

God's love reassures you that you are not facing life's challenges alone. His presence brings courage, not because circumstances suddenly change, but because your perspective does. Being rooted in God's love allows you to stand firm even when pressure arises from others or situations beyond your control.

Many fears are tied to the opinions, actions, or expectations of people. But God's love invites you to anchor your confidence in Him rather than external validation. When you trust that God is with you, you no longer need to live in fear of what others may say or do.

Today, let this truth strengthen your heart. God is on your side. His love surrounds you, supports you, and gives you courage to move forward without fear. When you remain rooted in His love, confidence replaces anxiety and peace steadies your steps.

Reflection

What fears tend to surface when you feel uncertain or pressured by others?

Life Application

When fear arises today, remind yourself that God is with you and on your side, allowing His love to strengthen your confidence.

Prayer

Lord, thank You for being on my side. Help me trust Your presence and remain rooted in Your love so that fear does not guide my decisions. Amen.

February 24

Marked by Love

John 13:34–35 (NIV)

"A new command I give you: Love one another. As I have loved you, so you must love one another. By this everyone will know that you are my disciples, if you love one another."

Devotional

Love is not only something you receive from God. It is also the way your faith becomes visible in the world. In this passage, Jesus makes it clear that love is the defining mark of those who belong to Him. Not performance, not perfection, and not appearance, but love.

Jesus sets the standard for love by pointing to His own example. He does not ask you to love from your own limited capacity. He invites you to love as you have been loved by Him. This kind of love is patient, sacrificial, and rooted in grace rather than convenience.

Being rooted in God's love changes how you show up in relationships. When love becomes your foundation, it shapes your responses, your boundaries, and your compassion for others. Love expressed through God's strength reflects His presence more clearly than words ever could.

Today, consider how God's love is being revealed through you. You do not have to strive to prove your faith. When you remain rooted in His love, it naturally flows outward and becomes a testimony of His work in your life.

Reflection

How does knowing that love is the defining mark of your faith challenge or encourage you?

Life Application

Look for one opportunity today to reflect God's love through patience, kindness, or grace toward someone else.

Prayer

Lord, thank You for loving me so fully. Help me remain rooted in Your love and reflect it to others in a way that honors You and draws them closer to You. Amen.

February 25

Secure in His Commitment

Deuteronomy 7:9 (NIV)

"Know therefore that the Lord your God is God; he is the faithful God, keeping his covenant of love to a thousand generations of those who love him and keep his commandments."

Devotional

God's love is not fragile or fleeting. It is covenantal, meaning it is built on commitment, faithfulness, and promise. This verse reminds us that God's love is not only felt, but established. He keeps His word, remains faithful, and does not abandon what He has chosen to love.

Being rooted in God's love means trusting His consistency, even when emotions waver or circumstances shift. God's love is not dependent on how strongly you feel it in a given moment. It is anchored in who He is. He is faithful, and His love endures beyond what you can see or fully understand.

God's covenant of love stretches across generations, reminding you that His faithfulness is bigger than a single moment or season. When you feel uncertain about the future, this truth offers reassurance. God's love is not short term. It is lasting, intentional, and secure.

Today, allow this truth to steady your heart. You are held by a faithful God whose love does not expire. When you remain rooted in His commitment, fear loses its grip and trust grows stronger with each passing day.

Reflection

How does knowing that God's love is based on faithfulness and covenant change the way you view your relationship with Him?

Life Application

When doubt or uncertainty arises today, remind yourself that God is faithful and His covenant of love toward you remains secure.

Prayer

Lord, thank You for being faithful and keeping Your covenant of love. Help me remain rooted in the assurance that Your commitment to me is unchanging and secure. Amen.

February 26

Held in Steadfast Love

Psalm 136:26 (NIV)

"Give thanks to the God of heaven. His love endures forever."

Devotional

Some truths are meant to be repeated until they settle deeply into the heart. This verse offers a simple yet powerful reminder: God's love endures forever. It does not weaken with time, diminish through failure, or disappear when life becomes difficult. His love remains steady and constant through every season.

Being rooted in God's love means anchoring yourself in what does not change. When circumstances shift and emotions fluctuate, God's enduring love becomes the foundation you stand on. It reassures you that you are not living on temporary grace or conditional affection.

Gratitude flows naturally when you recognize the permanence of God's love. Thanksgiving becomes more than a response to blessings; it becomes a posture of trust. Even when answers are delayed or clarity feels distant, you can still give thanks knowing His love remains.

Today, let this truth strengthen your confidence. God's love is not fragile. It endures forever. As you remain rooted in His love, you are held securely, today and always.

Reflection

How does knowing that God's love endures forever bring stability to your current season?

Life Application

Take a moment today to thank God specifically for the ways His love has remained consistent in your life.

Prayer

Father, thank You for Your enduring love. Help me remain rooted in the truth that Your love does not fade and that I am held securely in Your care. Amen.

February 27

Loved Without Condition

Psalm 103:11–12 (NLT)

"For his unfailing love toward those who fear him is as great as the height of the heavens above the earth. He has removed our sins as far from us as the east is from the west."

Devotional

God's love is not limited by your past or constrained by your failures. This verse reveals the vastness of His unfailing love and the completeness of His forgiveness. God does not love you cautiously or partially. He loves you fully and without condition.

The image of sins removed as far as the east is from the west speaks to permanence. God does not hold your past over you or revisit what He has already forgiven. When you are rooted in God's love, you are not defined by where you have been, but by who He says you are now.

Many people struggle to believe they are truly forgiven. Shame lingers, and self-judgment resurfaces. But God's love declares freedom. His love releases you from the weight of condemnation and invites you to live unburdened by what He has already removed.

Today, allow this truth to renew your heart. You are loved without condition and forgiven completely. God's love does not keep score. It restores, releases, and calls you forward into freedom and peace.

Reflection

What past failures or regrets have been difficult for you to release?

Life Application

When feelings of guilt or shame arise today, remind yourself that God has removed your sins and loves you fully and freely.

Prayer

Lord, thank You for Your unfailing love and complete forgiveness. Help me release the weight of the past and live rooted in the freedom Your love provides. Amen.

February 28

Nothing Can Separate You

Romans 8:38–39 (NKJV)

"For I am persuaded that neither death nor life, nor angels nor principalities nor powers, nor things present nor things to come, nor height nor depth, nor any other created thing, shall be able to separate us from the love of God which is in Christ Jesus our Lord."

Devotional

This passage is a declaration, not a question. Paul speaks with confidence that nothing in existence has the power to separate you from God's love. Not circumstances, not spiritual forces, not time, and not fear. God's love is not fragile or vulnerable. It is secure and unbreakable.

Being rooted in God's love means trusting its permanence even when life feels uncertain. Seasons change, emotions fluctuate, and challenges arise, but God's love remains untouched by any of it. It does not weaken under pressure or retreat in difficulty. It stays.

Many people wrestle with the fear that something could disqualify them from God's love. This scripture speaks directly against that fear. There is no situation, failure, or force strong enough to remove you from the love God has already given. His love is not conditional or temporary.

As this month comes to a close, let this truth anchor your heart. You are not holding onto God's love by your strength. God's love is holding onto you. Nothing can separate you from it, now or ever.

Reflection

What fears have made you question the security of God's love in your life?

Life Application

When doubt or uncertainty arises, remind yourself that nothing can separate you from God's love in Christ.

Prayer

Lord, thank You for a love that cannot be broken or taken away. Help me live confidently rooted in the truth that nothing can separate me from Your love. Amen.

February 29

A Love That Extends Beyond the Ordinary

Isaiah 54:10 (NLT)

"For the mountains may move and the hills disappear, but even then my faithful love for you will remain. My covenant of blessing will never be broken," says the Lord, who has mercy on you.

Devotional

February 29 appears only once every four years, a day set apart from the ordinary rhythm of time. It serves as a quiet reminder that not every moment fits neatly into what is expected or predictable. In the same way, God's love often meets us in places that feel uncommon, unexpected, or overlooked.

This verse reassures us that while the world around us may shift and change, God's faithful love remains steady. Mountains and hills symbolize stability, yet even those can be moved. God's love, however, is not subject to disruption or removal. It stands firm regardless of circumstance, season, or uncertainty.

Being rooted in God's love means trusting its permanence even when life feels unpredictable. Just as this extra day does not disrupt the calendar but completes it, God's love does not interrupt your life. It completes it. His covenant of peace holds you steady through moments that feel out of sync or beyond your control.

Today is a gift, a reminder that God's love extends beyond what is routine or expected. As this month comes to a close, let this truth anchor your heart. God's love is faithful, unshaken, and present in every season, even the ones that appear only once in a while.

Reflection

How does recognizing God's unchanging love affect the way you view unexpected seasons in your life?

Life Application

Take a moment today to thank God for His faithful love, especially in seasons that have felt uncertain or out of the ordinary.

Prayer

Father, thank You for a love that remains steady no matter what changes around me. Help me trust Your faithfulness and rest in the peace of knowing I am always held by Your love. Amen.

March

Cultivating Spiritual Growth

Cultivating spiritual growth requires intention, patience, and care. Just as growth in nature does not happen by accident, spiritual growth develops when we consistently tend to our relationship with God. This month invites you to pay attention to what you are allowing to take root in your heart and how God is shaping you through daily obedience and trust.

Spiritual growth is not measured by speed or visibility. It often unfolds quietly through prayer, reflection, and surrender. As God works within you, He may challenge habits, reveal new understanding, or strengthen areas that have felt weak. Cultivation requires willingness to be shaped and a commitment to remain present in the process.

Throughout March, this devotional will encourage you to nurture your faith with intention, allowing God to deepen your understanding, stretch your obedience, and produce lasting fruit. As you cultivate spiritual growth, trust that God is at work, bringing maturity, clarity, and renewal that will sustain you in every season ahead.

March 1

Preparing the Soil

Hosea 10:12 (NIV)

"Sow righteousness for yourselves, reap the fruit of unfailing love, and break up your unplowed ground; for it is time to seek the Lord, until he comes and showers his righteousness on you."

Devotional

Growth does not begin with what is visible. It begins beneath the surface, in the condition of the soil. This verse reminds us that before righteousness can be sown and fruit can be reaped, the ground must be prepared. Spiritual growth requires intentional work in the hidden places of the heart.

Unplowed ground represents areas that have been neglected, hardened, or left untouched for too long. These may be habits, attitudes, or wounds that have quietly shaped how you live and respond. Cultivating spiritual growth means allowing God to gently break up what has become resistant so new life can take root.

Seeking the Lord is the act of turning toward Him with openness and humility. It is an acknowledgment that growth cannot be forced through effort alone. True transformation happens as God works righteousness into the soil of your heart over time. When you remain willing and receptive, He brings growth that is lasting and fruitful.

As this month begins, consider what God may be inviting you to prepare. Spiritual growth is not about rushing the process, but about committing to it. When you allow God to tend to the soil of your heart, you create space for deeper faith, obedience, and renewal to grow.

Reflection

What areas of your heart may need preparation before growth can take place?

Life Application

Spend time today asking God to reveal any areas that need attention or renewal and invite Him to begin that work gently and faithfully.

Prayer

Lord, help me prepare my heart for the growth You desire to bring. Show me where I need to be open, teachable, and willing to change as I seek You more fully. Amen.

March 2

Growing Through Daily Discipline

1 Timothy 4:7–8 (NIV)
"Rather, train yourself to be godly. For physical training is of some value, but godliness has value for all things, holding promise for both the present life and the life to come."

Devotional

Spiritual growth does not happen by accident. It is cultivated through consistent, daily choices that shape how you live and respond. In this passage, Paul compares godliness to training, reminding us that growth requires intention, repetition, and commitment over time.

Discipline is often misunderstood as restrictive, but in truth it is formative. Spiritual disciplines such as prayer, time in God's Word, and intentional reflection create space for God to work deeply within you. These practices do not earn God's love, but they position your heart to receive instruction, correction, and renewal.

Just as physical training strengthens the body, spiritual discipline strengthens faith. Some days the effort feels light and rewarding, while other days it requires perseverance. Yet over time, discipline produces maturity that carries you through both ordinary moments and challenging seasons.

Today, remember that cultivating spiritual growth is not about perfection. It is about showing up consistently and trusting God to use small acts of obedience to produce lasting transformation. Each intentional step matters more than you may realize.

Reflection

Which spiritual discipline has been hardest for you to maintain consistently?

Life Application

Choose one simple spiritual practice today and commit to engaging it with intention, trusting God to use it for growth.

Prayer

Father, help me embrace discipline as a pathway to growth. Give me the desire and strength to cultivate habits that draw me closer to You each day. Amen.

March 3

Rooted Before You Rise

Colossians 2:6–7 (NLT)
"And now, just as you accepted Christ Jesus as your Lord, you must continue to follow him. Let your roots grow down into him, and let your lives be built on him. Then your faith will grow strong in the truth you were taught, and you will overflow with thankfulness."

Devotional

Spiritual growth is not built on visibility but on depth. Long before anything rises above the surface, roots must grow downward. This scripture reminds you that following Christ is not a moment but a continuing journey of being established in Him.

Roots develop quietly. They form through daily obedience, consistent trust, and choosing faith even when progress is unseen. When your life is built on Christ, strength comes from what is anchored beneath the surface, not from outward results or recognition.

As your roots grow deeper, your faith becomes steadier. You are less shaken by circumstances and more grounded in truth. Gratitude flows naturally from a life that knows where it is anchored. God strengthens what is rooted in Him.

Reflection
Where do you need deeper spiritual grounding right now?

Life Application
Choose one daily habit today that helps you grow deeper in Christ, not just move faster.

Prayer
Lord, help me grow deep roots in You. Build my life on Your truth so my faith remains strong and steady in every season. Amen.

March 4

Pruned for Growth

John 15:2 (NIV)

"He cuts off every branch in me that bears no fruit, while every branch that does bear fruit he prunes so that it will be even more fruitful."

Devotional

Growth often involves removal before it results in multiplication. This verse reminds us that pruning is not punishment. It is a purposeful act of care. God removes what hinders growth so that what remains can flourish more fully.

Pruning can feel uncomfortable because it requires letting go. God may be trimming habits, mindsets, or attachments that no longer serve His purpose in your life. Even good things can be removed if they begin to limit deeper growth. Cultivating spiritual growth means trusting God's wisdom when He chooses what must be refined.

Fruitful branches are pruned, not discarded. This truth reassures us that God's pruning is a sign of His investment, not His rejection. He sees potential for greater growth and is shaping you with care and intention.

Today, consider where God may be inviting you to release something that no longer supports your spiritual development. Trust that His pruning leads to increased fruitfulness and deeper maturity. Growth often begins with surrender.

Reflection

What might God be pruning in your life to encourage deeper spiritual growth?

Life Application

Ask God today to help you recognize and release anything that is hindering your growth, trusting His care and purpose.

Prayer

Father, help me trust You in seasons of pruning. Give me the willingness to release what You are removing so that my life may bear greater fruit for You. Amen.

March 5

Growing Through Obedience

James 1:22 (NIV)
"Do not merely listen to the word, and so deceive yourselves. Do what it says."

Devotional

Spiritual growth moves beyond understanding into action. This verse reminds us that listening alone is not enough. Growth happens when God's Word shapes how we live, not just what we know. Obedience is where faith becomes active and transformative.

Obedience is often formed in small, daily decisions. Choosing patience, extending grace, or responding with humility may seem simple, but these moments cultivate lasting growth. God uses obedience to align your heart with His will and to strengthen your spiritual maturity over time.

At times, obedience feels challenging because it requires trust. You may not always see immediate results or understand the full purpose behind God's instruction. Yet obedience positions you to experience growth that goes deeper than comfort or convenience.

Today, reflect on how God's Word is inviting you to respond. Cultivating spiritual growth means allowing truth to guide your actions. As you walk in obedience, God shapes your character and deepens your relationship with Him.

Reflection

Where is God inviting you to move from hearing His Word to living it out?

Life Application

Identify one specific way today to apply God's Word through obedience, even if it feels small or challenging.

Prayer

Lord, help me not only hear Your Word but live it out daily. Give me the courage and willingness to obey as You continue to grow my faith. Amen.

March 6

Strengthened Through Prayer

Colossians 4:2 (NIV)

"Devote yourselves to prayer, being watchful and thankful."

Devotional

Prayer is not simply a spiritual discipline. It is the place where growth is sustained. This verse calls us to devotion, not occasional engagement. Devotion implies consistency, attention, and commitment. When prayer becomes a regular part of your life, it strengthens your spiritual roots and keeps you connected to God's presence.

Being watchful in prayer means remaining spiritually alert. It invites awareness of how God is moving, what He is revealing, and where He is leading. Prayer sharpens discernment and keeps your heart aligned with God's will rather than drifting into distraction or self-reliance.

Thankfulness anchors prayer in trust. When gratitude is present, prayer shifts from obligation to relationship. It reminds you that God has already been faithful and will continue to be. Gratitude nurtures spiritual growth by keeping your heart receptive and grounded.

Today, remember that prayer is not about perfect words or long moments. It is about devotion. As you remain committed to prayer, God uses it to strengthen your faith and cultivate growth that reaches every area of your life.

Reflection

How consistent is your prayer life, and what helps or hinders that consistency?

Life Application

Set aside intentional time today to pray with focus and gratitude, even if only for a few quiet moments.

Prayer

Father, help me remain devoted to prayer. Teach me to be watchful, thankful, and consistent as You strengthen my faith through time spent with You. Amen.

March 7

Growing in Patience

James 5:7 (NLT)

"Dear brothers and sisters, be patient as you wait for the Lord's return. Consider the farmers who patiently wait for the rains in the fall and in the spring. They eagerly look for the valuable harvest to ripen."

Devotional

Growth requires patience. This verse uses the image of a farmer to remind us that fruit does not appear overnight. Farmers prepare the soil, plant the seed, and wait with expectation, trusting that growth will come in its proper time. Spiritual growth follows the same pattern.

Patience is often developed in waiting seasons. When progress feels slow or answers feel delayed, it can be tempting to grow discouraged. Yet God uses waiting to deepen trust and strengthen endurance. Cultivating spiritual growth means learning to wait with faith rather than frustration.

Just as a farmer watch over the field, you are invited to remain attentive to your heart while you wait. Patience does not mean passivity. It means trusting God's timing while continuing to show up in obedience, prayer, and faithfulness.

Today, allow patience to take root in your heart. Growth is happening, even when it is not immediately visible. When you trust God's timing, the harvest will come, and it will be worth the wait.

Reflection

Where in your life are you struggling to be patient as you wait on God?

Life Application

Practice patience today by choosing trust over frustration and reminding yourself that growth takes time.

Prayer

Lord, help me grow in patience as I wait on You. Teach me to trust Your timing and remain faithful as You continue the work You have begun in me. Amen.

March 8

Growing Through God's Word

Psalm 1:2–3 (NIV)
"Blessed is the one whose delight is in the law of the Lord, and who meditates on his law day and night. That person is like a tree planted by streams of water, which yields its fruit in season and whose leaf does not wither - whatever they do prospers."

Devotional

Spiritual growth is nourished by what you consistently take in. This passage paints a picture of a life rooted in God's Word, drawing strength and sustenance from it daily. Just as a tree depends on water to thrive, your faith depends on time spent meditating on God's truth.

Delighting in God's Word means approaching it not as an obligation, but as a source of life and renewal. When Scripture becomes part of your daily rhythm, it shapes your perspective, steadies your heart, and strengthens your faith. Over time, God's Word works quietly within you, producing fruit in its proper season.

Meditation allows truth to move from your mind into your heart. It invites reflection, application, and deeper understanding. As you meditate on God's Word, your spiritual roots grow stronger, making you resilient even in seasons of difficulty or change.

Today, consider how God's Word is feeding your growth. When you remain planted in His truth, you are sustained, strengthened, and positioned to bear fruit that reflects His work in your life.

Reflection

How regularly are you engaging with God's Word in a way that allows it to shape your heart and actions?

Life Application

Set aside intentional time today to read and reflect on Scripture, asking God to speak and guide you through His Word.

Prayer

Father, thank You for Your Word that nourishes my faith. Help me delight in Your truth and remain rooted so that my life bears fruit in every season. Amen.

March 9

Growth Requires Endurance

Hebrews 12:11 (NLT)
"No discipline is enjoyable while it is happening. It is painful. But afterward there will be a peaceful harvest of right living for those who are trained in this way."

Devotional

Lasting growth is shaped through endurance, not comfort. This verse acknowledges what many try to avoid: growth often involves discomfort. Discipline stretches you, challenges you, and requires patience when the process feels difficult.

Pain does not mean the process is failing. It often means something new is forming. God uses seasons of discipline to train your character, refine your faith, and prepare you for what lies ahead. The harvest does not appear immediately, but it is promised.

Endurance teaches you to trust the outcome even when the process is uncomfortable. Peace follows perseverance. What feels heavy now is shaping something stronger, wiser, and more grounded within you.

Reflection
Where is God asking you to endure rather than escape?

Life Application
When today feels uncomfortable, remind yourself that endurance produces lasting fruit.

Prayer
God, help me endure the process You are using to grow me. Give me strength to remain faithful and trust the harvest You are producing in my life. Amen.

March 10

Staying Faithful in Small Steps

Zechariah 4:10 (NIV)
"Who dares despise the day of small things, since the Lord rejoices to see the work begin, to see the plumb line in the hand of Zerubbabel?"

Devotional

Spiritual growth often unfolds through small, faithful steps rather than dramatic moments. This verse reminds us that God values beginnings and rejoices in progress, even when it seems modest or unnoticed. What may feel insignificant to you is meaningful to Him.

Small acts of obedience build a foundation for lasting growth. Prayer whispered in quiet moments, Scripture read consistently, and choices made with intention all contribute to spiritual maturity. God is not rushing the process. He delights in the work unfolding step by step.

It is easy to compare your growth to others or to feel discouraged when progress appears slow. Yet God measures growth differently. He looks at faithfulness, not speed. Each small step matters and contributes to the larger work He is doing within you.

Today, honor the small beginnings in your journey. Cultivating spiritual growth means trusting that God is pleased with your faithfulness and that every step forward is part of His greater plan.

Reflection

What small step of faithfulness have you been tempted to overlook or dismiss?

Life Application

Choose one small, intentional act of obedience today and offer it to God with trust and gratitude.

Prayer

Father, help me remain faithful in the small steps. Teach me to trust that You are at work even when growth feels slow or unseen. Amen.

March 11

Growing Through Surrender

Proverbs 16:3 (NKJV)
"Commit your works to the Lord, and your thoughts will be established."

Devotional

Spiritual growth is deeply connected to surrender. This verse reminds us that when we commit our plans, efforts, and intentions to the Lord, He brings clarity and direction to our thoughts. Growth does not come from striving for control, but from releasing it into God's hands.

Surrender is not passive. It is an intentional decision to trust God with the outcomes of your obedience. When you commit your works to Him, you invite His wisdom to guide your thinking and shape your perspective. Over time, surrender produces stability and peace in the way you approach life.

Many people resist surrender because it feels uncertain. Yet surrender is where growth is anchored. As you release your need to manage every detail, God establishes your thoughts with truth and purpose. He aligns your heart with His will and strengthens your faith in the process.

Today, consider what God may be asking you to place fully in His care. Cultivating spiritual growth means trusting that God is faithful to lead you as you surrender your plans, your efforts, and your expectations to Him.

Reflection

What is one area of your life where God may be inviting you to surrender control?

Life Application

Take a moment today to commit your plans and efforts to the Lord, trusting Him to establish your thoughts and guide your steps.

Prayer

Lord, help me surrender my plans and trust You with the outcome. Establish my thoughts with Your truth as I continue to grow in faith and obedience. Amen.

March 12

Steady Growth in Quiet Faithfulness

Galatians 6:9 (NKJV)
"And let us not grow weary while doing good, for in due season we shall reap if we do not lose heart."

Devotional

Spiritual growth often happens quietly, without immediate reward or recognition. This verse acknowledges the reality of weariness that can set in when obedience feels repetitive or progress seems slow. God's encouragement is clear: do not lose heart. Growth is unfolding, even when you cannot yet see the harvest.

Faithfulness requires perseverance. There are seasons when doing good feels unseen or unappreciated, yet God assures us that due season will come. Growth is not measured by quick results, but by steady commitment to what is right and honoring to God.

Weariness can tempt you to stop short of the fruit God intends to produce. Yet cultivating spiritual growth means trusting God's timing and remaining faithful even when motivation wanes. Each act of obedience contributes to a harvest that arrives at the appointed time.

Today, let this truth strengthen your resolve. Your faithfulness matters. God sees every step, every effort, and every moment you choose to remain committed. Growth is taking place, and the harvest will come as you continue forward with trust.

Reflection

Where have you felt tempted to grow weary or discouraged in your spiritual journey?

Life Application

Choose to remain faithful today, even in small ways, trusting God to bring growth and fruit in His perfect timing.

Prayer

Father, give me strength when I feel weary. Help me remain faithful and trust that You are producing growth and fruit through my obedience. Amen.

March 13

Growth Through Trust

Proverbs 3:5–6 (NIV)
"Trust in the Lord with all your heart and lean not on your own understanding; in all your ways submit to him, and he will make your paths straight."

Devotional

Spiritual growth is often tested at the point where understanding feels incomplete. This verse invites you to trust God fully, even when clarity is lacking. Growth requires releasing the need to have every answer and choosing faith over certainty.

Leaning on your own understanding can limit spiritual maturity because it keeps control centered on self. Trust shifts that center back to God. When you submit your ways to Him, you open yourself to guidance that goes beyond what you can reason or predict.

Trust deepens as you experience God's faithfulness over time. Each moment you choose reliance on Him strengthens your spiritual roots. Growth happens as trust becomes a habit rather than a reaction to crisis.

Today, consider where God may be asking you to trust Him more deeply. Cultivating spiritual growth means allowing God to lead, even when the path ahead is not fully visible. As you trust Him, He faithfully directs your steps.

Reflection

Where do you find it most difficult to trust God when understanding feels limited?

Life Application

Choose one area today where you will intentionally trust God instead of relying on your own understanding.

Prayer

Lord, help me trust You with my whole heart. Teach me to submit my ways to You and walk confidently in the paths You set before me. Amen.

March 14

Growing Through Renewal of the Mind

Romans 12:2 (NKJV)
"And do not be conformed to this world, but be transformed by the renewing of your mind, that you may prove what is that good and acceptable and perfect will of God."

Devotional

Spiritual growth is closely connected to how your mind is shaped. This verse reminds us that transformation does not begin with external change, but with internal renewal. As God renews your mind, He reshapes how you think, respond, and discern His will.

The world constantly applies pressure to conform through patterns, expectations, and distractions. Without intention, those influences can slowly shape beliefs and behavior. Cultivating spiritual growth means allowing God's truth to replace assumptions, fears, and habits that no longer align with His purpose.

Renewal is an ongoing process. God works patiently, transforming thoughts over time as you submit them to Him. As your mind is renewed, clarity increases, and discernment grows. You begin to recognize what is good, pleasing, and aligned with God's will more readily.

Today, reflect on what is shaping your thinking. Spiritual growth flourishes when you invite God to renew your mind daily. As He does, transformation follows, guiding you into deeper maturity and alignment with His purpose.

Reflection

What influences have been shaping your thoughts more than God's truth?

Life Application

Choose one thought pattern today to surrender to God, inviting Him to renew your mind with His truth.

Prayer

Father, transform my thinking through Your truth. Help me let go of patterns that no longer align with You, and shape my thoughts and actions according to Your will. Amen.

March 15

Growing Through Godly Wisdom

James 1:5 (NIV)
"If any of you lacks wisdom, you should ask God, who gives generously to all without finding fault, and it will be given to you."

Devotional

Spiritual growth often reveals the limits of our own understanding. This verse offers reassurance that wisdom is not something you must generate on your own. God invites you to ask, promising to give generously and without judgment. Growth deepens when you rely on His wisdom rather than your own.

Wisdom guides decisions, shapes responses, and strengthens discernment. As you cultivate spiritual growth, you will encounter moments where clarity feels elusive. God's invitation is simple: ask. Seeking His wisdom keeps your heart aligned with His truth and protects you from unnecessary confusion or missteps.

Asking for wisdom requires humility. It acknowledges that growth is not about having all the answers, but about trusting the One who does. When you consistently seek God's wisdom, your faith matures and your confidence rests in His guidance rather than personal certainty.

Today, remember that God delights in guiding His children. Cultivating spiritual growth means turning to Him regularly for wisdom. As you do, He faithfully provides direction that strengthens your walk and deepens your trust.

Reflection

Where do you need God's wisdom most in your life right now?

Life Application

Take time today to ask God for wisdom in a specific area, trusting Him to guide you clearly and generously.

Prayer

Lord, thank You for giving wisdom generously and without hesitation. Teach me to seek Your guidance with humility and confidence as I grow in faith and understanding. Amen.

March 16

Growing Through Perseverance

Romans 5:3–4 (NLT)
"We can rejoice, too, when we run into problems and trials, for we know that they help us develop endurance. And endurance develops strength of character, and character strengthens our confident hope of salvation."

Devotional

Spiritual growth is often shaped in moments that test endurance. This passage reminds us that trials are not wasted experiences. God uses them to develop perseverance, which strengthens character and deepens hope. Growth unfolds as you remain faithful through challenges rather than avoiding them.

Perseverance is formed when you choose to trust God in difficulty. It teaches patience, resilience, and reliance on Him. Over time, endurance transforms how you respond to adversity, grounding you in confidence rather than discouragement.

Character is the fruit of sustained faithfulness. As God shapes your character, your hope becomes steadier and more confident. Growth through perseverance produces maturity that cannot be gained through ease alone.

Today, consider how God may be using a current challenge to strengthen your endurance. Cultivating spiritual growth means trusting that even difficult seasons are producing something meaningful within you. God is at work, shaping you with purpose and care.

Reflection

How have challenges in your life contributed to your spiritual growth?

Life Application

When facing difficulty today, choose to respond with trust, reminding yourself that God is developing endurance and strength through the process.

Prayer

Father, give me strength to endure challenges with faith and hope. Use every trial to shape my character and deepen the work You are doing within me. Amen.

March 17

Growing Through Faithful Practice

Hebrews 5:14 (NIV)
"But solid food is for the mature, who by constant use have trained themselves to distinguish good from evil."

Devotional

Spiritual growth is revealed through practice, not just knowledge. This verse reminds us that maturity develops as we consistently apply what we learn. Growth happens when faith moves from theory into daily living, shaping how we discern and respond.

Maturity requires repetition. Just as physical strength grows through regular exercise, spiritual discernment develops through constant use of God's truth. Each time you choose obedience, patience, or wisdom, you are training your heart to recognize what aligns with God's will.

Growth also brings clarity. Over time, faithful practice sharpens your ability to discern what is right and pleasing to God. Decisions become less confusing as your spiritual senses are trained through consistency and trust.

Today, consider how God is inviting you to practice what you already know. Cultivating spiritual growth means showing up daily, allowing steady obedience to produce maturity that reflects God's work within you.

Reflection

Where do you sense God inviting you to practice faith more consistently?

Life Application

Choose one area today where you will intentionally apply God's truth through faithful action.

Prayer

Lord, develop discernment within me as I grow through faithful practice. Strengthen my commitment to maturity and help me walk consistently in alignment with Your will. Amen.

March 18

Growing Through Stillness

Psalm 46:10 (NKJV)
"Be still, and know that I am God; I will be exalted among the nations, I will be exalted in the earth!"

Devotional

Spiritual growth is not always driven by action. Sometimes it is formed in stillness. This verse invites you to pause, quiet your striving, and recognize God's presence and authority. Growth deepens when you learn to rest in who God is rather than constantly pushing for outcomes.

Stillness creates space for awareness. When distractions are silenced, your heart becomes more attentive to God's voice. In moments of stillness, God reminds you that He is in control, even when life feels busy or overwhelming. Trust grows as you release the need to manage every detail.

Being still does not mean disengaging from responsibility. It means anchoring your soul in God's sovereignty. As you cultivate spiritual growth, stillness becomes a discipline that strengthens faith, restores clarity, and renews perspective.

Today, allow yourself a moment of stillness before God. Let His presence steady your heart and remind you that growth flourishes when you trust Him enough to pause and listen.

Reflection

What distractions make it difficult for you to experience stillness before God?

Life Application

Set aside intentional time today to be still and focus on God's presence, even if only for a few quiet moments.

Prayer

Father, draw my heart into stillness before You. Quiet my thoughts, steady my spirit, and deepen my awareness of Your presence and power. Amen.

March 19

Growing Through Quiet Trust

Isaiah 30:15 (NIV)

"This is what the Sovereign Lord, the Holy One of Israel, says: 'In repentance and rest is your salvation, in quietness and trust is your strength, but you would have none of it.'"

Devotional

Spiritual growth is often strengthened in moments of quiet trust rather than constant motion. This verse reminds us that strength is found not in striving, but in resting and trusting God. Growth deepens when you allow yourself to slow down and depend on Him fully.

Quietness creates space for trust to develop. When you resist the urge to control outcomes or rush the process, you position your heart to receive God's guidance. Trust grows as you learn to rely on God's presence rather than your own effort or understanding.

Rest is not a sign of weakness. It is an expression of faith. Cultivating spiritual growth means recognizing when to pause, reflect, and trust that God is working even when you are not actively doing. In these moments, strength is renewed and clarity is restored.

Today, consider how God may be inviting you to trust Him more deeply through rest and quietness. Growth flourishes when you allow God to be your strength instead of striving in your own power.

Reflection

Where in your life is God inviting you to choose quiet trust over constant effort?

Life Application

Practice quiet trust today by intentionally releasing control in one area and resting in God's strength.

Prayer

Lord, teach me to find strength in quietness and trust. Help me rest in You and allow You to guide my growth with wisdom and care. Amen.

March 20

Growing Through Persevering Hope

Hebrews 6:11–12 (NLT)

"Our great desire is that you will keep on loving others as long as life lasts, in order to make certain that what you hope for will come true. Then you will not become spiritually dull and indifferent. Instead, you will follow the example of those who are going to inherit God's promises because of their faith and endurance."

Devotional

Spiritual growth is sustained by hope that perseveres. This passage reminds us that faith and endurance work together to keep the heart engaged and responsive to God. Growth slows when hope fades, but it flourishes when you remain committed over time.

Becoming spiritually dull often happens gradually, when effort gives way to complacency or discouragement. God's invitation is to stay engaged, to continue loving, trusting, and enduring. Persevering hope keeps your spirit alert and your faith active, even when the journey feels long.

Endurance does not mean forcing growth. It means staying faithful in the process. As you follow the example of those who inherited God's promises, you learn that growth is not instant, but it is certain when faith and perseverance remain present.

Today, allow hope to steady your heart. Cultivating spiritual growth means choosing to remain engaged, trusting that God is faithful to fulfill what He has promised. Your endurance is producing something meaningful and lasting.

Reflection

What helps you remain hopeful and engaged when spiritual growth feels slow?

Life Application

Identify one way today to nurture hope through faith and endurance, trusting God's promises over time.

Prayer

Father, help me persevere with hope and faith. Keep my heart engaged and my spirit attentive as You continue to cultivate growth in my life. Amen.

March 21

Growing Through God's Timing

Ecclesiastes 3:11 (NIV)

"He has made everything beautiful in its time. He has also set eternity in the human heart; yet no one can fathom what God has done from beginning to end."

Devotional

Spiritual growth unfolds according to God's timing, not ours. This verse reminds us that God works with purpose and intention, bringing beauty in the proper season. Growth may feel slow or uneven, but God is never late. He is always at work, shaping something meaningful within you.

Impatience can hinder growth when expectations do not align with God's pace. Yet cultivating spiritual growth means trusting that timing is part of God's design. He sees the full picture, even when you can only see a single moment. What feels delayed may actually be developing depth and maturity.

God has placed a longing for eternity in the human heart, which often fuels the desire for immediate clarity or completion. But growth requires faith in what cannot yet be fully understood. Trust deepens as you allow God to work beyond your limited perspective.

Today, take comfort in knowing that God is making everything beautiful in its time. Growth is not rushed or random. As you trust His timing, you position your heart to receive what He is faithfully bringing forth.

Reflection

Where have you struggled to trust God's timing in your spiritual growth?

Life Application

Practice patience today by releasing expectations and trusting that God is working beautifully in His time.

Prayer

Father, help me trust Your timing even when growth feels slow. Teach me to rest in Your wisdom and remain faithful as You shape my life according to Your purpose. Amen.

March 22

Growing Through Humility

1 Peter 5:6 (NIV)
"Humble yourselves, therefore, under God's mighty hand, that he may lift you up in due time."

Devotional

Spiritual growth is deeply connected to humility. This verse reminds us that growth does not come from elevating ourselves, but from willingly placing our lives under God's authority. Humility creates space for God to work freely, shaping us according to His purpose rather than our preferences.

Humbling yourself under God's hand means trusting His guidance even when it feels uncomfortable or unclear. It is the recognition that God's wisdom surpasses your own and that His timing is always intentional. Growth deepens as you surrender the need to control outcomes or prove worth.

God's promise in this verse is not just about humility, but about elevation in the proper season. When you allow God to lead, He lifts you in ways that are lasting and aligned with His will. Spiritual growth flourishes when humility anchors your faith.

Today, consider where humility may be inviting deeper growth in your life. As you submit yourself to God's care, trust that He is working faithfully and will lift you at the right time.

Reflection

In what area of your life might God be inviting you to grow through humility?

Life Application

Practice humility today by surrendering control in one situation and trusting God's guidance and timing.

Prayer

Lord, help me walk in humility and trust Your hand at work in my life. Teach me to surrender control and remain faithful as You cultivate growth within me. Amen.

March 23

Growing Through Teachability

Proverbs 12:1 (NLT)
"To learn, you must love discipline; it is stupid to hate correction."

Devotional

Spiritual growth requires a teachable heart. This verse speaks plainly about the importance of being open to discipline and correction. Growth cannot happen when resistance replaces humility. God often uses correction not to condemn, but to guide and refine.

Teachability means remaining willing to learn, even when truth challenges your comfort or habits. Correction exposes areas where growth is needed and invites transformation rather than shame. When you receive instruction with humility, God shapes your character with wisdom and care.

Resisting correction can stall growth, while embracing it creates space for maturity. Cultivating spiritual growth means trusting that God's instruction is rooted in love. He corrects not to discourage you, but to lead you toward greater alignment with His will.

Today, reflect on how you respond to correction. A teachable spirit allows growth to flourish. When you remain open and willing to learn, God continues to develop wisdom, discernment, and spiritual maturity within you.

Reflection

How do you typically respond when God brings correction or instruction into your life?

Life Application

When correction comes today, pause and ask God what He may be teaching you through it instead of resisting it.

Prayer

Father, give me a teachable heart. Help me receive Your instruction with humility and trust as You continue to cultivate growth in my life. Amen.

March 24

Growing Through Faithfulness

Luke 16:10 (NIV)
"Whoever can be trusted with very little can also be trusted with much, and whoever is dishonest with very little will also be dishonest with much."

Devotional

Spiritual growth is often revealed through faithfulness in ordinary moments. This verse reminds us that God values how we steward what has been placed in our care, even when it feels small or insignificant. Growth is cultivated not only in big decisions, but in daily consistency.

Faithfulness builds trust over time. When you choose integrity, diligence, and obedience in small things, God develops your character and prepares you for greater responsibility. These quiet acts of faithfulness shape your spiritual maturity more than moments of visibility ever could.

It can be tempting to overlook the importance of small responsibilities while waiting for something larger. Yet God uses everyday faithfulness to refine your heart and strengthen your walk. Cultivating spiritual growth means honoring God in the details, trusting that nothing done in obedience is wasted.

Today, reflect on how you are stewarding what God has already entrusted to you. Growth flourishes when faithfulness becomes a habit. As you remain faithful in small things, God continues to shape you for greater purpose and impact.

Reflection

Where is God calling you to practice greater faithfulness in small, everyday moments?

Life Application

Choose one small responsibility today to steward with excellence and integrity, offering it to God as an act of faithfulness.

Prayer

Lord, help me remain faithful in what You have placed in my care. Teach me to honor You in small moments as You continue to cultivate growth in my life. Amen.

March 25

Growing Through Godly Counsel

Proverbs 15:22 (NIV)
"Plans fail for lack of counsel, but with many advisers they succeed."

Devotional

Spiritual growth is not meant to happen in isolation. This verse reminds us that wisdom is often revealed through counsel and shared insight. God frequently uses trusted voices to provide clarity, correction, and encouragement along the path of growth.

Seeking counsel requires humility and discernment. It acknowledges that growth is strengthened when you are willing to learn from others who walk in faith and wisdom. Godly counsel helps guard against blind spots and reinforces truth when decisions feel complex or uncertain.

Many people struggle to ask for guidance because they fear vulnerability or dependence. Yet cultivating spiritual growth means recognizing the value of community. God designed growth to be nurtured through relationships that sharpen, support, and guide you forward.

Today, consider where God may be inviting you to seek wise counsel. Growth flourishes when you remain open to instruction and willing to receive guidance rooted in truth and love.

Reflection

Who are the trusted voices God has placed in your life to offer wisdom and guidance?

Life Application

Seek input today from a trusted, godly source when making a decision or navigating a situation that requires discernment.

Prayer

Father, thank You for placing wise counsel in my life. Help me remain humble and receptive as You continue to cultivate growth through guidance and community. Amen.

March 26

Growing by Going Deeper

Hosea 6:3 (NIV)
"Let us acknowledge the Lord; let us press on to acknowledge him. As surely as the sun rises, he will appear; he will come to us like the winter rains, like the spring rains that water the earth."

Devotional

Spiritual growth requires intentional pursuit. This verse calls us not only to acknowledge the Lord, but to press on in knowing Him. Growth deepens when faith moves beyond surface-level belief into a daily, deliberate relationship with God.

Pressing on suggests effort and consistency. It means continuing to seek God even when the journey feels repetitive or slow. Just as rain nourishes the earth over time, God's presence renews and strengthens you as you remain committed to knowing Him more deeply.

Growth does not happen overnight. It unfolds through steady pursuit and trust in God's faithfulness. When you continue pressing forward, God meets you with renewal, clarity, and strength exactly when it is needed. His presence refreshes your spirit in every season.

Today, reflect on how you are pressing on in your relationship with God. Cultivating spiritual growth means choosing depth over familiarity and pursuit over complacency. As you continue seeking Him, trust that God will faithfully meet you.

Reflection

What does pressing on in knowing God look like in your current season?

Life Application

Take one intentional step today to deepen your relationship with God through prayer, study, or quiet reflection.

Prayer

Lord, help me press on in knowing You. Draw me deeper into relationship with You and continue to renew my spirit as I grow in faith and understanding. Amen.

March 27

Growing Through Obedient Steps

Psalm 119:105 (NIV)
"Your word is a lamp for my feet, a light on my path."
Devotional

Spiritual growth often unfolds one step at a time. This verse reminds us that God's Word does not always illuminate the entire journey at once. Instead, it provides light for the next step, guiding you forward with clarity and purpose as you walk in obedience.

Obedience requires trust. It means moving forward even when you cannot see the full picture. God uses His Word to direct your steps, offering guidance precisely when it is needed. Growth deepens as you learn to rely on His instruction rather than your own understanding.

Many people hesitate to move because they want certainty before obedience. Yet cultivating spiritual growth means learning to walk by faith, trusting that God's light will continue to guide you as you follow Him. Each obedient step strengthens your confidence and deepens your relationship with Him.

Today, consider where God may be asking you to take a step of obedience. You do not need to see the entire path. Trust that His Word will light the way as you continue to grow and move forward in faith.

Reflection

Where might God be inviting you to trust His guidance for the next step rather than the full journey?
Life Application

Spend time in God's Word today and ask Him to reveal one clear step of obedience for you to take.
Prayer

Father, thank You for guiding my steps through Your Word. Help me trust You enough to walk forward in obedience, knowing You will continue to light my path. Amen.

March 28

Growing in Grace

2 Peter 3:18 (NIV)
"But grow in the grace and knowledge of our Lord and Savior Jesus Christ. To him be glory both now and forever! Amen."
Devotional

Spiritual growth is not only about learning more, but about becoming more rooted in grace. This verse reminds us that growth happens as grace and knowledge develop together. Grace keeps growth from becoming rigid, while knowledge keeps it grounded in truth.

Growing in grace means allowing God's kindness to shape how you see yourself and others. It is learning to extend the same patience and mercy you receive from God into your daily life. Growth deepens when grace leads your responses, decisions, and relationships.

Knowledge strengthens growth by anchoring faith in truth. As you continue learning who Christ is and how He works, your faith becomes steadier and more confident. Grace and knowledge together create balance, producing maturity that reflects Christ rather than performance.

Today, reflect on how God is inviting you to grow in both grace and understanding. Cultivating spiritual growth means allowing God to shape not only what you know, but how you live. As you grow, may your life point consistently back to Him.

Reflection

How have grace and knowledge worked together in your spiritual growth journey?
Life Application

Extend grace today by responding with patience and understanding in a situation where you might normally react quickly.
Prayer

Lord, help me grow in grace and in the knowledge of You. Shape my heart, my understanding, and my responses so that my life reflects Your truth and love. Amen.

March 29

Growing Through Endurance

James 1:12 (NIV)

"Blessed is the one who perseveres under trial because, having stood the test, that person will receive the crown of life that the Lord has promised to those who love him."

Devotional

Spiritual growth is often forged through perseverance. This verse reminds us that endurance is not overlooked by God. When you remain faithful under pressure, God sees your obedience and honors the strength developed through trust in Him.

Perseverance does not mean pretending that trials are easy. It means choosing to remain anchored in God even when the weight of the moment feels heavy. Growth happens when you stay committed to faith instead of retreating in discouragement or doubt.

Trials test more than patience. They reveal devotion. When you endure with love for God, your faith deepens and your spiritual foundation strengthens. God promises that perseverance produces reward, not because you earned it, but because He is faithful to those who continue to trust Him.

Today, consider how endurance is shaping your spiritual growth. What you are walking through is not wasted. God is refining your faith, strengthening your resolve, and preparing you for what lies ahead.

Reflection

What trial has required perseverance in your spiritual journey, and how has it shaped your faith?

Life Application

Choose to respond to challenges today with perseverance, trusting that God is developing strength and maturity within you.

Prayer

Father, help me persevere with faith and love for You. Strengthen me when trials feel heavy and remind me that You are working through every season to cultivate growth in my life. Amen.

March 30

Growing Through Daily Renewal

Colossians 3:10 (NLT)
"Put on your new nature, and be renewed as you learn to know your Creator and become like him."

Devotional

Spiritual growth is sustained through daily renewal. This verse reminds us that growth is not a one-time decision, but an ongoing process of becoming more like Christ. Each day offers a new opportunity to put on the nature God is forming within you.

Renewal happens as you learn to know your Creator more deeply. Growth is shaped through relationship, not pressure. As you continue walking with God, He gently reshapes your thoughts, attitudes, and responses to reflect His character. This transformation unfolds over time through consistent surrender.

Putting on a new nature requires intention. It means choosing to release old habits, mindsets, and patterns that no longer align with who God is calling you to be. Growth deepens as you allow God to renew you from the inside out, aligning your life with His truth.

Today, recognize that renewal is available to you right now. Cultivating spiritual growth means showing up each day with a willing heart, trusting that God is continually at work, shaping you into who He created you to be.

Reflection

What does daily renewal look like in your current season of spiritual growth?

Life Application

Begin today by intentionally releasing one old habit or mindset and inviting God to renew your heart and thinking.

Prayer

Father, thank You for renewing me day by day. Help me put on the new nature You are forming within me and continue growing into who You created me to be. Amen.

March 31

Rooted and Still Growing

Philippians 1:6 (NIV)
"Being confident of this, that he who began a good work in you will carry it on to completion until the day of Christ Jesus."

Devotional

Spiritual growth is a process that God Himself initiates and sustains. This verse reminds you that growth does not rest solely on your effort, discipline, or consistency. God is the One who began the work in you, and He is committed to seeing it through to completion.

There are seasons when growth feels evident and seasons when it feels quiet. Yet even in the unseen moments, God is working. Cultivating spiritual growth means trusting that progress is happening beneath the surface, even when results are not immediately visible. Roots grow deep before fruit appears.

This month has invited you to be intentional, disciplined, and patient with the process of becoming. Growth is not about perfection. It is about faithfulness and trust in the One who is shaping you. God does not abandon what He starts, and He does not rush what He is refining.

As March comes to a close, take a moment to acknowledge how far you have come. You are still growing, still learning, still becoming. And God is not finished with you yet.

Reflection

Where have you seen evidence of growth in your life this month, even if it was subtle?

Life Application

Take time today to thank God for the work He is doing in you and commit to trusting His process moving forward.

Prayer

Father, thank You for beginning a good work in me and for remaining faithful to complete it. Help me trust the process of growth and rest in the confidence that You are still working in my life. Amen.

April

Walking by Faith, Not by Sight

April invites you into a deeper trust walk with God. Walking by faith does not mean ignoring reality or denying uncertainty. It means choosing to trust God even when the path ahead is unclear, the answers are incomplete, or the outcome feels unknown. Faith is not passive. It is an active decision to rely on God's character rather than visible evidence.

This month centers on learning to follow God beyond what you can see or predict. Faith grows when you surrender the need for certainty and allow God to guide your steps one at a time. As you journey through April, you will be encouraged to trust God in transitions, decisions, waiting seasons, and moments where clarity feels just out of reach.

Walking by faith requires courage, patience, and surrender. Yet it is in this kind of trust that peace deepens and confidence grows. April reminds you that God is faithful, present, and actively leading you, even when the way forward feels uncertain. Faith is not about seeing the whole path. It is about trusting the One who does

April 1

Trusting the Unseen Path

2 Corinthians 5:7 (NIV)
"For we live by faith, not by sight."

Devotional

Walking by faith often begins when clarity ends. This verse reminds us that the life God calls us to is not driven by what we can see, predict, or control. Faith is not rooted in visible proof but in trust in God's character. When sight is limited, faith becomes the guide.

Many people struggle with faith because they want certainty before obedience. Yet God often invites us to move forward before everything makes sense. Living by faith means choosing trust even when the road ahead feels unclear or incomplete. It is believing that God is working even when evidence is not immediately visible.

Faith does not deny reality. It acknowledges uncertainty while still placing confidence in God. It says, "I do not see the full picture, but I trust the One who does." Each step taken in faith strengthens your dependence on God and deepens your relationship with Him.

As April begins, allow this truth to set the tone for the month ahead. You are not required to see every step, only to trust God with the next one. Faith grows when you choose trust over fear and obedience over hesitation.

Reflection

Where in your life are you being asked to trust God without having full clarity?

Life Application

Today, take one small step of obedience in an area where you have been waiting for certainty instead of trusting God.

Prayer

Lord, help me walk by faith and not by sight. Teach me to trust You even when the path ahead is unclear. Strengthen my heart to rely on You with confidence and peace. Amen.

April 2

Faith That Moves Forward

Psalm 37:5 (NLT)

"Commit everything you do to the Lord. Trust him, and he will help you."

Devotional

Faith is not passive waiting. It is active trust that chooses to move forward with God rather than standing still in uncertainty. This verse invites you to commit everything, not selectively, not partially, but fully, into God's care. Faith begins when you release control and place your plans, decisions, and direction into His hands.

Committing your way to the Lord requires surrender. It means trusting God not only with outcomes but with the process itself. Often, we want reassurance before obedience, but faith calls you to trust God first and allow clarity to follow. Trust is demonstrated through action, not just intention.

God's promise in this verse is not that the path will always be easy, but that He will help you. His help may come as strength, guidance, correction, or peace, but it will always be sufficient. When you trust Him, you are never walking alone.

Today's invitation is to move forward in faith. Release the pressure to figure everything out and commit your way to God. Trust that He is actively involved in every step you take and that His help will meet you exactly where you are.

Reflection

What area of your life do you need to fully commit to God instead of holding onto control?

Life Application

Write down one decision or concern you have been carrying and intentionally place it in God's hands through prayer.

Prayer

Father, I commit my ways to You today. Help me trust You fully and release my need for control. Thank You for walking with me and helping me every step of the way. Amen.

April 3

Confidence Beyond What You See

Hebrews 11:1 (NKJV)
"Now faith is the substance of things hoped for, the evidence of things not seen."

Devotional

Faith gives form to hope before anything tangible appears. This verse reminds you that faith is not wishful thinking or blind optimism. It is a confident assurance rooted in God's promises. Even when circumstances offer no visible proof, faith stands firm in what God has spoken.

Often, we wait for evidence before believing. Yet Scripture teaches that faith itself becomes the evidence. It allows you to live with expectation even when answers have not yet arrived. Faith anchors your heart to God's truth while you wait for fulfillment to unfold in His timing.

Living by faith does not mean ignoring reality. It means choosing to believe that God is at work beyond what your eyes can see. Faith gives you confidence to hope boldly, pray expectantly, and trust deeply, even in seasons of uncertainty or delay.

Today, allow faith to shape how you view your circumstances. What you cannot yet see does not mean God is absent. Faith assures you that His promises are real, active, and unfolding, even now.

Reflection

Where do you need to trust God's promises despite not seeing immediate evidence?

Life Application

Speak God's promises aloud today over an area where you are waiting, choosing faith over doubt.

Prayer

Lord, strengthen my faith when I cannot see the outcome. Help me trust Your promises and remain confident in what You are doing, even when the evidence is unseen. Amen.

April 4

Faith That Leaves a Legacy

2 Timothy 1:5 (NIV)
"I am reminded of your sincere faith, which first lived in your grandmother Lois and in your mother Eunice and, I am persuaded, now lives in you also."

Devotional

Faith is never meant to end with one generation. This verse reveals a powerful truth about legacy: sincere faith is passed down through lives that are quietly faithful, consistent, and rooted in God. Timothy's faith did not appear in isolation. It was cultivated through the example of those who walked with God before him.

Legacy is not built through grand gestures alone. It is formed in daily devotion, steady obedience, and a life anchored in God's Word. Faith lived out over time leaves an imprint that continues to speak long after moments pass and years move forward. The impact of a faithful life often reaches further than we can see.

Walking by faith means recognizing that your obedience today carries influence beyond the present. Your trust in God, your discipline in prayer, and your commitment to His Word create a foundation others can stand on. Faith that is lived sincerely becomes a testimony that continues to grow through generations.

Today invites you to honor the faith that came before you and reflect on the legacy you are building. Faith is not only about how you walk with God now, but how your walk points others toward Him in the future.

Reflection

Whose faith has influenced your walk with God, and how can you honor that legacy in your own life?

Life Application

Take a moment today to thank God for those who modeled faith before you and consider one intentional way to live out that faith for others to see.

Prayer

Father, thank You for the legacy of faith that has shaped my life. Help me walk sincerely before You and build a legacy that reflects Your love, truth, and faithfulness. Amen.

April 5

Stepping Forward with Courage

Joshua 1:9 (NLT)

"This is my command, be strong and courageous! Do not be afraid or discouraged. For the Lord your God is with you wherever you go."

Devotional

Faith often requires courage before it provides clarity. In this verse, God speaks directly to fear and hesitation, reminding Joshua that strength and courage are not optional when walking forward in obedience. Courage is not the absence of fear, but the decision to move forward despite it, trusting that God is present.

Fear has a way of magnifying uncertainty and shrinking confidence. Yet God's instruction is clear. Do not be afraid. Do not be discouraged. These are not casual suggestions. They are anchored in the promise of His presence. Wherever you go, God is already there.

Walking by faith means stepping into situations that stretch you, challenge you, and require dependence on God rather than comfort. Courage grows when you trust that God's presence is greater than any fear you face. His nearness becomes the source of your strength.

Today's reminder is simple and powerful. You are not walking alone. God is with you in every step, every transition, and every unknown. Let courage rise as you trust His presence to carry you forward.

Reflection

Where is fear trying to keep you from moving forward in faith?

Life Application

Identify one area where fear has been holding you back and take a small, courageous step forward today.

Prayer

Lord, thank You for Your constant presence in my life. Give me strength and courage to move forward in faith, trusting that You are with me wherever I go. Amen.

April 6

Obedience Before Clarity

Genesis 12:1 (NIV)

"The Lord had said to Abram, 'Go from your country, your people and your father's household to the land I will show you.'"

Devotional

Faith often begins with a call before there is clarity. God did not give Abram a map, a timeline, or a detailed explanation. He gave a command and a promise. Go. Trust Me. I will show you along the way. This is the posture of faith that walks forward without full visibility.

Obedience is rarely comfortable when answers are incomplete. Yet Scripture consistently shows that God reveals direction after obedience, not before it. Faith grows when you choose to trust God enough to move, even when the destination is still unfolding.

Abram's journey reminds us that faith is not rooted in certainty but in trust. God does not always explain the next season in advance, but He does promise His presence and guidance through it. Each obedient step becomes a foundation for the next revelation.

Today's invitation is to obey what God has already spoken. You do not need the full picture to move forward. Faith honors God by trusting Him one step at a time, knowing He will reveal what you need when the time is right.

Reflection

Where is God asking you to obey Him before giving you full clarity?

Life Application

Identify one instruction God has already placed on your heart and take a step of obedience today, trusting Him with the outcome.

Prayer

Father, help me obey You even when I do not see the full path ahead. Teach me to trust Your voice and walk forward in faith, believing You will guide me every step of the way. Amen.

April 7

When God Asks You to Trust Him

Isaiah 43:2 (NLT)

"When you go through deep waters, I will be with you. When you go through rivers of difficulty, you will not drown. When you walk through the fire of oppression, you will not be burned up; the flames will not consume you."

Devotional

Walking by faith does not mean avoiding difficulty. It means trusting God's presence in the middle of it. This verse does not promise that you will never face deep waters or hard seasons. Instead, it offers something greater: assurance that God will be with you through them.

Faith often feels most fragile when circumstances are overwhelming. In those moments, it is easy to question whether God is near or attentive. Yet Scripture reminds us that God does not abandon us in adversity. He walks with us through it, sustaining us when strength feels depleted.

Trust grows when you believe that God's presence is greater than any challenge you face. The waters may rise, and the fire may feel intense, but God's promise remains. You are not walking alone, and you will not be consumed.

Today, allow this truth to strengthen your faith. Whatever difficulty you are facing, God is present, attentive, and faithful. Trust Him not only for deliverance, but for companionship through every trial.

Reflection

Where do you need to trust God's presence rather than focusing on the difficulty in front of you?

Life Application

In a challenging moment today, pause and remind yourself that God is with you and sustaining you through it.

Prayer

Lord, thank You for being with me in every season. Help me trust Your presence when life feels overwhelming and walk forward in faith knowing You will not leave me. Amen.

April 8

Stepping Out of the Boat

Matthew 14:29 (NIV)
"Come," he said. Then Peter got down out of the boat, walked on the water and came toward Jesus.

Devotional

Faith often requires movement before comfort. Peter's step out of the boat was not logical or safe by human standards, but it was obedient. Jesus did not calm the storm before inviting Peter to come. He called Peter to trust Him in the middle of the uncertainty.

The boat represented security, familiarity, and control. Stepping out meant risk, vulnerability, and complete dependence on Jesus. Faith works the same way today. God often calls you beyond what feels safe and into spaces where trust must replace certainty.

Walking by faith does not mean ignoring fear. It means choosing obedience despite it. Peter walked on water not because the storm stopped, but because his focus was on Jesus. Faith strengthens when you keep your eyes on who called you, not on what surrounds you.

Today's reminder is simple but challenging. Faith asks you to step out when Jesus says come, even if the water looks unstable. When your focus remains on Him, faith carries you further than fear ever could.

Reflection

What step of faith might God be inviting you to take beyond your comfort zone?

Life Application

Identify one area where God is calling you to trust Him more deeply and take a small step of obedience today.

Prayer

Lord, give me the courage to step out in faith when You call me. Help me keep my eyes fixed on You and trust You beyond what feels safe or familiar. Amen.

April 9

Living by Faith Daily

Habakkuk 2:4 (NIV)
"See, the enemy is puffed up; his desires are not upright - but the righteous person will live by his faithfulness."

Devotional

Faith is not reserved for defining moments. It is meant to guide daily living. This verse contrasts pride with righteousness, reminding you that faithfulness, not self-reliance, shapes a life aligned with God.

Living by faith requires consistency more than intensity. It is choosing trust over fear in ordinary decisions and remaining faithful even when outcomes are unclear. Pride leans on self. Faith leans on God.

This scripture calls you to steady obedience. Faithfulness becomes a way of life when you depend on God daily, not only when circumstances demand it. Righteous living flows from ongoing trust, not momentary belief.

When challenges arise, faith anchors you. It keeps you grounded, focused, and aligned with God's truth. Living by faith is not about perfection. It is about persistence.

Reflection
Where is God inviting you to live by faith more consistently?

Life Application
Today, choose one decision to approach with trust rather than control.

Prayer
God, help me live by faith each day. Teach me to rely on You consistently and walk in obedience, trusting Your guidance in every step. Amen.

April 10

Trusting God in the Waiting

Psalm 27:14 (NIV)

"Wait for the Lord; be strong and take heart and wait for the Lord."

Devotional

Faith is often tested most in seasons of waiting. Waiting can feel uncomfortable, unproductive, and uncertain, especially when answers seem delayed or progress feels slow. Yet Scripture reminds us that waiting is not wasted time. It is a space where strength is formed and trust is deepened.

Waiting on the Lord requires courage. It challenges the urge to rush ahead, force outcomes, or rely on your own timing. Faith in the waiting means believing that God is working even when you cannot see immediate results. It is choosing patience over pressure and trust over anxiety.

God uses waiting seasons to shape character, refine motives, and align hearts with His will. Strength grows when you resist the temptation to move prematurely and instead remain anchored in God's promises. Waiting becomes an act of faith when you trust that God's timing is purposeful and good.

Today's reminder is to wait with expectation rather than frustration. God is not absent in the waiting. He is present, active, and faithful. Trust that His timing will reveal exactly what you need at the right moment.

Reflection

What are you waiting on God for right now, and how is that waiting challenging your faith?

Life Application

Instead of rushing for answers today, intentionally pause and ask God for strength and patience while you wait.

Prayer

Lord, help me wait on You with strength and courage. Teach me to trust Your timing and remain faithful even when answers feel delayed. Amen.

April 11

Believing Without Seeing

John 20:29 (NIV)
"Then Jesus told him, 'Because you have seen me, you have believed; blessed are those who have not seen and yet have believed.'"

Devotional

Faith often reaches its deepest expression when sight is absent. In this moment, Jesus speaks to Thomas, but His words extend far beyond that encounter. He acknowledges belief that comes from seeing, yet He highlights a deeper blessing reserved for those who choose faith without physical proof.

Believing without seeing requires trust that goes beyond evidence. It means anchoring your confidence in who God is rather than what you can observe. This kind of faith does not depend on circumstances aligning perfectly or questions being fully answered. It rests in the assurance that God is faithful and true.

Many seasons of life require this posture. You may not see how things will work out, when clarity will come, or what the next step will look like. Faith invites you to trust anyway. It asks you to believe that God is present and working even when outcomes remain hidden.

Today's reminder is that faith does not need visible confirmation to be real. Blessed are those who trust God without seeing the full picture. That trust honors God and strengthens your walk with Him in ways that certainty never could.

Reflection

Where is God inviting you to believe without needing visible proof?

Life Application

Practice trusting God today in an area where you feel uncertain, choosing belief even without clarity.

Prayer

Lord, help me believe even when I cannot see the outcome. Strengthen my faith and teach me to trust You fully, knowing that You are always faithful. Amen.

April 12

Faith Anchored in God's Character

Numbers 23:19 (NKJV)
"God is not a man, that He should lie, nor a son of man, that He should repent. Has He said, and will He not do? Or has He spoken, and will He not make it good?"

Devotional

Faith is strengthened when it is anchored in who God is, not in what circumstances suggest. This verse reminds us that God's character is unchanging and trustworthy. Unlike people, God does not speak carelessly or change His mind. What He promises, He fulfills.

When life feels uncertain, doubt often creeps in by questioning outcomes. Faith counters doubt by remembering God's nature. He is faithful, consistent, and true. Trust grows when you shift your focus from what you see happening around you to what God has already spoken.

Walking by faith means believing that God will do exactly what He said, even when timing feels delayed or the path feels unclear. His promises are not dependent on your circumstances or your feelings. They are rooted in His character.

Today's encouragement is to rest in the reliability of God. You can trust Him because He is trustworthy. Faith becomes steadier when it is anchored not in what you hope will happen, but in who God has proven Himself to be.

Reflection

Which promise of God do you need to trust more fully right now?

Life Application

Write down a promise from Scripture that reminds you of God's faithfulness and reflect on it throughout the day.

Prayer

Father, thank You for being faithful and true. Help me anchor my faith in Your character and trust that You will do what You have promised. Amen

April 13

Choosing Faith Over Fear

Isaiah 41:10 (NIV)

"So do not fear, for I am with you; do not be dismayed, for I am your God. I will strengthen you and help you; I will uphold you with my righteous right hand."

Devotional

Fear often rises when the future feels uncertain or when circumstances seem overwhelming. This verse speaks directly to those moments, offering reassurance grounded in God's presence and power. God does not minimize fear. He addresses it by reminding you who He is and how deeply involved He remains in your life.

Walking by faith requires a conscious choice to trust God's promises rather than fear's predictions. Fear focuses on what could go wrong. Faith focuses on who God is and what He has already promised to do. When fear threatens to take hold, God offers strength, help, and support.

Faith does not eliminate challenges, but it changes how you face them. Knowing that God is with you provides courage to move forward even when anxiety tries to pull you back. His presence steadies your heart and reminds you that you are not carrying the weight of uncertainty alone.

Today, let faith lead your response instead of fear. God's promise to uphold you is not conditional or temporary. You can walk forward with confidence, knowing that His strength is greater than anything you face.

Reflection

What fear has been competing with your faith lately?

Life Application

When fear surfaces today, pause and intentionally remind yourself of God's promise to strengthen and uphold you.

Prayer

Father, help me choose faith over fear. Thank You for being with me, strengthening me, and holding me steady when I feel uncertain. Amen.

April 14

Strength to Stand

2 Timothy 1:7 (NLT)
"For God has not given us a spirit of fear and timidity, but of power, love, and self-discipline."

Devotional

Fear often surfaces when uncertainty threatens your sense of control. It whispers doubt, magnifies risk, and convinces you to shrink back instead of stepping forward. Yet Scripture reminds us that fear does not originate with God. It is not something He places within you, nor is it meant to guide your decisions.

Faith draws strength from a different source. God gives power when you feel weak, love when anxiety rises, and self-discipline when emotions feel overwhelming. Choosing faith over fear means recognizing what God has already placed within you and refusing to let fear dictate your response.

Walking by faith does not mean fear never appears. It means fear no longer has authority. Faith acknowledges fear's presence but refuses to let it determine direction. When you rely on God's power rather than your own strength, courage begins to replace hesitation.

Today is an invitation to evaluate what is driving your decisions. Fear limits. Faith empowers. God has equipped you to move forward with confidence, clarity, and trust, even when circumstances feel uncertain.

Reflection

Where has fear been influencing your thoughts or decisions more than faith?

Life Application

When fear arises today, intentionally pause and remind yourself of the power, love, and self-discipline God has already given you.

Prayer

Father, thank You for equipping me with power, love, and self-discipline. Help me choose faith over fear and walk confidently in the strength You provide. Amen.

April 15

Steady in Uncertain Times

Psalm 112:7 (NIV)
"They will have no fear of bad news; their hearts are steadfast, trusting in the Lord."

Devotional

Faith does not mean the absence of unsettling information or unexpected moments. It means remaining steady when they come. This verse speaks to a heart posture that is anchored, not reactive. A steadfast heart is one that trusts God deeply, even when circumstances shift or news feels uncertain.

Uncertainty has a way of shaking confidence and stirring fear. Yet Scripture reminds us that trust in the Lord produces stability. When your confidence is rooted in God rather than outcomes, your heart learns to remain calm even when life feels unpredictable. Faith steadies you when clarity is limited.

Walking by faith means choosing trust over panic. It means allowing God's truth to guide your response instead of fear's urgency. A steadfast heart does not deny reality. It faces reality with trust in a faithful God who remains in control.

Today's invitation is to examine where your trust is anchored. When your heart is fixed on the Lord, fear loses its grip and peace begins to take hold. Trusting God allows you to stand firm, even when circumstances feel uncertain.

Reflection

What kind of news or uncertainty tends to unsettle your heart the most?

Life Application

When something unexpected arises today, pause and intentionally place your trust in God before reacting.

Prayer

Lord, help my heart remain steadfast and trusting in You. Teach me to walk by faith and respond with peace, even when uncertainty tries to shake me. Amen.

April 16

Trusting God with What You Cannot Control

Isaiah 55:8–9 (NLT)
"My thoughts are nothing like your thoughts, says the Lord. And my ways are far beyond anything you could imagine. For just as the heavens are higher than the earth,
so my ways are higher than your ways and my thoughts higher than your thoughts."

Devotional

Trust becomes most difficult when control feels necessary. This scripture reminds you that God's perspective is not limited by what you can see or understand. His ways operate from a higher vantage point, shaped by wisdom beyond human reasoning.

When life does not unfold as expected, the instinct to grasp for control can quietly replace trust. But this verse calls you to release the need to fully understand God's plan. Surrender is not giving up. It is choosing confidence in God's wisdom over reliance on your own.

God's thoughts are higher, not distant. His ways are greater, not careless. Even when outcomes feel uncertain, His direction remains purposeful and good. Trust grows when you accept that God sees what you cannot.

This scripture invites you to rest in God's sovereignty. Peace comes not from managing every detail, but from believing that God is faithfully guiding what you place in His hands.

Reflection

What are you trying to control that God is asking you to trust Him with?

Life Application

Today, intentionally release one concern you cannot control and place it in God's care.

Prayer

God, help me trust You when I do not understand. Teach me to surrender control and rest in the confidence that Your ways are higher and Your plans are good. Amen.

April 17

Faith That Follows God's Lead

Psalm 32:8 (NIV)
"I will instruct you and teach you in the way you should go; I will counsel you with my loving eye on you."

Devotional

Walking by faith means trusting that God is actively guiding your steps, not watching from a distance. This verse offers reassurance that God's leadership is personal, attentive, and rooted in love. He does not leave you to figure things out on your own. He promises instruction, direction, and care along the way.

Faith grows when you believe that God is invested in your journey. His guidance is not rushed or harsh. It is patient, intentional, and shaped by His love for you. Even when decisions feel overwhelming, God's promise remains that He will lead you in the way you should go.

Many people hesitate to move forward because they fear making the wrong choice. Yet faith is not about flawless decision making. It is about trusting God's ability to guide and correct you as you walk. His loving eye remains on you through every step.

Today's invitation is to lean into God's leadership. Instead of striving for certainty, rest in the promise that God is teaching and guiding you with care. Faith becomes steadier when you trust the One who is leading the way.

Reflection

Where do you need to trust God's guidance instead of fearing the wrong decision?

Life Application

Before making a decision today, pause and ask God to instruct and guide you, trusting His loving care.

Prayer

Father, thank You for guiding me with Your wisdom and love. Help me trust Your leadership and follow You faithfully as I walk forward in faith. Amen.

April 18

Faith That Rests in God's Care

1 Peter 5:7 (NLT)

"Give all your worries and cares to God, for he cares about you."

Devotional

Walking by faith is not only about moving forward. It is also about learning to rest. This verse invites you to release the weight you have been carrying and place it into God's hands. Faith acknowledges that you were never meant to manage every concern on your own.

Worry often grows when you try to hold responsibility for things beyond your control. Faith responds differently. It trusts that God is attentive, compassionate, and deeply invested in your life. Casting your cares on Him is an act of surrender that says, "I trust You to handle what I cannot."

Resting in God's care does not mean ignoring challenges or responsibilities. It means choosing to rely on God's strength rather than exhausting your own. Faith deepens when you learn to release anxiety and allow God's peace to steady your heart.

Today's reminder is gentle but powerful. You are not alone in your concerns. God cares about every detail of your life. When you place your worries in His hands, faith creates space for peace, rest, and renewed trust.

Reflection

What worries or concerns do you need to release to God today?

Life Application

Take a few moments today to intentionally give your worries to God through prayer, trusting His care and attention.

Prayer

Lord, thank You for caring so deeply about me. Help me release my worries to You and trust that You are holding every concern with love and wisdom. Amen.

April 19

Trusting God When You Feel Unsteady

Psalm 55:22 (NIV)
"Cast your cares on the Lord and he will sustain you; he will never let the righteous be shaken."

Devotional

Faith is often tested when life feels unstable. Uncertainty, pressure, and unanswered questions can leave you feeling unsteady, unsure of how to move forward. This verse offers reassurance that when you place your burdens in God's hands, He provides the strength you need to stand firm.

Trusting God does not mean pretending everything is fine. It means choosing to rely on Him even when your footing feels uncertain. God promises not only to receive what you give Him, but to sustain you through the weight of it. His support steadies you when circumstances threaten to shake your confidence.

Walking by faith means believing that God is actively holding you up, even when you feel weak. His sustaining power does not depend on your strength or clarity. It rests on His faithfulness and commitment to care for you.

Today's encouragement is to release what has been weighing you down. Trust that God is able to sustain you and keep you steady, even when life feels unpredictable.

Reflection

What burden has been making you feel unsteady or shaken lately?

Life Application

Identify one concern you have been carrying and intentionally place it in God's hands through prayer today.

Prayer

Father, thank You for sustaining me when I feel unsteady. Help me trust You with my burdens and walk forward in faith, confident that You will hold me firm. Amen.

April 20

Trusting God with the Outcome

Romans 8:28 (NLT)

"And we know that God causes everything to work together for the good of those who love God and are called according to his purpose for them."

Devotional

Walking by faith means trusting God not only with your steps, but also with the outcome. This verse does not promise that everything you experience will feel good or make sense in the moment. Instead, it offers assurance that God is actively at work, weaving every detail into His greater purpose.

Faith becomes necessary when outcomes are uncertain. You may not understand how a situation will resolve or why certain things unfold the way they do. Yet faith rests in the confidence that God sees the full picture and is working for your good, even when circumstances appear fragmented.

Trusting God with the outcome requires surrender. It means releasing the need to control results and choosing to believe that God's purpose is unfolding beyond what you can see. Faith grows as you learn to place confidence in God's ability to redeem and restore every situation.

Today's reminder is to rest in God's promise. What feels unresolved today is not finished in God's hands. Trust that He is working faithfully, bringing purpose and good from every part of your journey.

Reflection

What outcome are you struggling to trust God with right now?

Life Application

Identify one situation where you have been focused on the result and intentionally release it to God in prayer today.

Prayer

Father, help me trust You with the outcomes I cannot control. Strengthen my faith as I rely on Your promise to work all things together for good. Amen.

April 21

Watching for God at Work

Micah 7:7 (NIV)
"But as for me, I watch in hope for the Lord, I wait for God my Savior; my God will hear me."

Devotional

Faith is not just about moving forward. Sometimes it is about watching, waiting, and trusting that God is actively at work even when progress feels slow. This verse reflects a posture of expectation rather than frustration. It chooses hope while waiting and confidence while trusting God's timing.

Waiting can feel uncomfortable because it asks you to resist rushing ahead. Yet faith learns to remain attentive and expectant, believing that God is listening and responding even when answers are delayed. Watching in hope means staying spiritually alert, trusting that God's presence has not diminished.

Faith grows in the waiting because it teaches dependence. Instead of relying on immediate results or visible signs, you learn to trust God's character. Waiting becomes an act of worship when you believe that God hears you and is faithfully working on your behalf.

Today's reminder is to shift your focus from what has not happened yet to who God is. Watch in hope. Wait with trust. God hears you, and His response will come at the right time.

Reflection

Where is God asking you to wait with hope instead of rushing for answers?

Life Application

Practice waiting intentionally today by choosing prayer and trust over anxiety or impatience.

Prayer

Father, help me wait with hope and trust You fully. Strengthen my faith as I watch for You at work and rest in the assurance that You hear me. Amen.

April 22

Faith That Listens for God's Voice

John 10:27 (NIV)
"My sheep listen to my voice; I know them, and they follow me."

Devotional

Walking by faith requires learning how to listen. This verse reminds you that faith is not only about trusting God's direction, but about recognizing His voice. God desires a relationship where guidance flows from connection, not confusion. When you know His voice, following Him becomes a response of trust rather than fear.

Many people struggle with faith because they expect God to speak loudly or dramatically. Yet God often speaks through Scripture, prayer, wise counsel, and quiet nudges of the Spirit. Faith grows as you become familiar with how God communicates and learn to respond with obedience.

Listening requires intentional stillness. When life is busy or decisions feel urgent, it can be tempting to act quickly without seeking God's voice. Faith slows down long enough to listen before moving forward. It trusts that God's guidance is personal, purposeful, and loving.

Today's encouragement is to lean into relationship rather than rushing for answers. God knows you, and He is speaking. Faith deepens when you listen closely and choose to follow where He leads.

Reflection

What distractions make it difficult for you to listen for God's voice?

Life Application

Create intentional quiet time today to listen for God's guidance through prayer or Scripture.

Prayer

Lord, help me recognize Your voice and follow You with trust. Teach me to listen carefully and respond faithfully as You lead me forward. Amen.

April 23

Faith That Perseveres

Hebrews 10:23 (NIV)
"Let us hold unswervingly to the hope we profess, for he who promised is faithful."

Devotional

Faith is often revealed not in how enthusiastically you begin, but in how firmly you hold on. This verse encourages perseverance rooted in hope, reminding you that faith is sustained by God's faithfulness, not your own strength. Holding unswervingly means choosing trust even when circumstances tempt you to let go.

There are seasons when faith feels effortless and seasons when it feels demanding. In moments of delay, disappointment, or discouragement, perseverance becomes an act of worship. Faith that perseveres refuses to be swayed by what is seen or felt and instead anchors itself in God's promises.

Hope remains steady when it is tied to who God is rather than what is happening. God's faithfulness does not fluctuate with circumstances. When you hold tightly to hope, you are declaring that God's promises are reliable, even when outcomes remain uncertain.

Today's encouragement is to remain firm in your trust. Do not loosen your grip on hope. God is faithful, and what He has promised, He will bring to completion in His perfect timing.

Reflection

What promise of God are you being challenged to hold onto right now?

Life Application

When discouragement surfaces, intentionally remind yourself of God's faithfulness by recalling a promise He has made.

Prayer

Father, help me hold firmly to the hope I have in You. Strengthen my faith to persevere and trust Your faithfulness in every season. Amen.

April 24

Faith That Chooses Trust

Psalm 56:3 (NIV)
"When I am afraid, I put my trust in you."

Devotional

Fear is a natural human response, but faith is a deliberate choice. This verse does not deny the presence of fear. Instead, it models a faithful response to it. When fear arises, trust becomes the anchor that steadies the heart. Faith does not wait for fear to disappear. It chooses trust in the middle of it.

Walking by faith means acknowledging fear without allowing it to lead. Trust shifts your focus from what feels threatening to who God is. It reminds you that God is greater than the situation you face and present in every moment of uncertainty.

Choosing trust is an act of surrender. It places confidence in God rather than circumstances, emotions, or outcomes. Each time you choose trust, your faith grows stronger and fear loses its grip.

Today's invitation is simple and powerful. When fear shows up, choose trust. Let your response to uncertainty be anchored in faith, knowing that God is faithful and attentive to your needs.

Reflection

What situations tend to trigger fear for you, and how do you usually respond?

Life Application

When fear arises today, pause and intentionally place your trust in God through prayer.

Prayer

Lord, help me choose trust when fear surfaces. Teach me to place my confidence in You and walk forward in faith, knowing that You are always with me. Amen.

April 25

Faith That Releases Control

Proverbs 16:9 (NLT)
"We can make our plans, but the Lord determines our steps."

Devotional

Walking by faith requires releasing the illusion of control. This verse acknowledges that planning is not wrong, but it reminds us that ultimate direction belongs to God. Faith recognizes the difference between preparation and control and learns to trust God with the outcome.

Many people struggle with faith because they want certainty before surrender. Yet God often invites you to move forward without knowing every detail. When you trust Him with your steps, you allow Him to guide you beyond your limited perspective and into His greater purpose.

Releasing control does not mean abandoning responsibility. It means holding your plans loosely and remaining open to God's redirection. Faith grows when you trust that God's guidance is wiser than your expectations and His timing is better than your urgency.

Today's encouragement is to place your plans in God's hands. Trust that He is guiding your steps with care and intention, even when the path looks different than you imagined.

Reflection

What plans or expectations are you holding onto too tightly right now?

Life Application

Offer your plans to God in prayer today and ask Him to direct your steps according to His will.

Prayer

Father, help me release control and trust You with my plans. Teach me to walk by faith, knowing that You are guiding my steps with wisdom and love. Amen.

April 26

Faith That Walks in Obedience

Luke 11:28 (NIV)

"He replied, 'Blessed rather are those who hear the word of God and obey it.'"

Devotional

Faith is more than belief. It is expressed through obedience. This verse reminds us that blessing is found not only in hearing God's Word, but in responding to it. Walking by faith means allowing God's truth to shape your actions, not just your understanding.

Obedience often requires trust, especially when God's instructions challenge your comfort or expectations. Faith chooses to act on what God has revealed, even when the outcome is uncertain. Each step of obedience strengthens your reliance on God and deepens your walk with Him.

Many people want faith to feel safe and predictable. Yet obedience calls you beyond familiarity and into trust. It asks you to believe that God's ways are good and His guidance is purposeful, even when the full picture is not clear.

Today's encouragement is to examine how you respond to God's Word. Faith comes alive when belief is paired with action. Obedience is not a burden. It is a pathway to blessing and deeper trust in God.

Reflection

Where might God be calling you to obey Him more fully right now?

Life Application

Identify one truth from Scripture that God has placed on your heart and intentionally live it out today.

Prayer

Father, help me walk in obedience to Your Word. Strengthen my faith as I trust You enough to act on what You have revealed. Amen.

April 27

Faith That Holds Firm

Ephesians 6:13 (NIV)
"Therefore put on the full armor of God, so that when the day of evil comes, you may be able to stand your ground, and after you have done everything, to stand."

Devotional

Walking by faith does not mean life will be free from resistance. This verse acknowledges that challenges will come, yet it also reminds you that God has already provided what you need to remain standing. Faith holds firm not because circumstances are easy, but because God equips you to endure.

Standing firm requires preparation and trust. The armor of God represents spiritual readiness, reminding you that faith is strengthened through intentional reliance on God. When difficulties arise, faith allows you to remain grounded rather than overwhelmed.

Faith that holds firm understands that endurance is part of the journey. You may face moments when progress feels slow or opposition feels strong, but standing your ground is an act of faith. It declares trust in God's protection and strength, even when the struggle continues.

Today's encouragement is to remain steady. After you have done all you know to do, trust God enough to stand firm. Faith does not quit when things get hard. It remains rooted, confident that God is with you and sustaining you through every challenge.

Reflection

Where do you need God's strength to help you stand firm right now?

Life Application

Pray today for spiritual strength and endurance as you trust God to help you remain steady in challenging situations.

Prayer

Father, thank You for equipping me to stand firm through every challenge. Strengthen my faith and help me trust You as I remain grounded in Your truth. Amen.

April 28

Faith That Stands When Answers Are Delayed

Lamentations 3:31–33 (NLT)
"For no one is abandoned by the Lord forever.
Though he brings grief, he also shows compassion because of the greatness of his unfailing love. For he does not enjoy hurting people or causing them sorrow."

Devotional

Faith is often tested in seasons when answers are delayed and clarity feels distant. In those moments, it can be tempting to believe that God has forgotten or withdrawn. This passage reminds you that God's silence does not equal abandonment. His compassion remains active even when circumstances are difficult.

God's faithfulness is not measured by immediate relief but by His enduring presence. Though hardship may come, it is never His final word. Faith allows you to trust that God's love is working beneath the surface, shaping and sustaining you through every season.

Waiting can be painful, especially when prayers feel unanswered. Yet Scripture assures us that God's heart is compassionate and purposeful. He does not delight in suffering, and He does not abandon those who trust Him. Faith holds onto this truth when emotions waver.

Today's encouragement is to remain confident in God's unfailing love. Even when answers are delayed, His compassion surrounds you. Faith stands firm, trusting that God is still working for your good.

Reflection

Where are you struggling to trust God because answers feel delayed?

Life Application

When impatience arises today, remind yourself of God's compassion and choose to trust His timing.

Prayer

Father, help me trust You when answers are delayed. Strengthen my faith and remind me of Your compassion and unfailing love in every season. Amen.

April 29

Faith That Remains Steady

Hebrews 13:8 (NIV)
"Jesus Christ is the same yesterday and today and forever."

Devotional

One of the greatest anchors of faith is knowing that God does not change. Circumstances shift, emotions fluctuate, and seasons come and go, but Jesus remains the same. This verse offers stability in a world that often feels unpredictable. Faith grows when it is rooted in the unchanging nature of Christ.

Walking by faith becomes difficult when life feels inconsistent. Yet God's character remains steady even when your surroundings are not. His promises do not expire, His presence does not fade, and His faithfulness does not waver. Trusting God means relying on who He is, not what you see.

Faith that remains steady learns to return to this truth repeatedly. When doubt arises or fear creeps in, remembering God's unchanging nature brings peace and confidence. You are not trusting a temporary solution or a shifting foundation. You are trusting a faithful Savior.

Today's reminder is to anchor your faith in what does not change. When everything else feels uncertain, Jesus remains constant. Faith stands firm when it is built on His enduring truth.

Reflection

How does knowing that Jesus never changes affect the way you view your current circumstances?

Life Application

When uncertainty arises today, intentionally remind yourself that God's character and promises remain the same.

Prayer

Lord, thank You for being constant and faithful in every season. Help me anchor my faith in You and trust You fully, knowing that You never change. Amen.

April 30

Walking Forward by Faith

2 Corinthians 4:18 (NIV)
"So we fix our eyes not on what is seen, but on what is unseen, since what is seen is temporary, but what is unseen is eternal."

Devotional

Walking by faith requires a shift in focus. This verse reminds you that what you see in front of you is not the full story. Circumstances, challenges, and seasons change, but God's eternal work remains steady and purposeful. Faith learns to look beyond the temporary and trust in what God is doing beneath the surface.

It is easy to become consumed by what feels urgent or visible. Faith calls you to lift your gaze and remember that God's promises extend beyond the present moment. What you see today does not define the outcome of your journey. God is always working toward something greater than what is immediately apparent.

Faith grows when you intentionally fix your eyes on eternal truth rather than temporary situations. This perspective brings peace in uncertainty and confidence in transition. When your focus remains on God's unseen work, fear loses its grip and trust deepens.

As April comes to a close, reflect on how faith has shaped your steps this month. You may not see everything clearly yet, but God is faithful. Continue walking forward by faith, trusting that what He is doing will endure far beyond what you can see.

Reflection

What temporary situation has been demanding your focus instead of God's eternal truth?

Life Application

Take time today to realign your focus by praying and reflecting on God's promises rather than your current circumstances.

Prayer

Father, help me fix my eyes on what is eternal and not be consumed by what is temporary. Strengthen my faith as I continue walking forward, trusting You beyond what I can see. Amen.

May

Choosing Joy in Every Season

Joy is not the absence of hardship, nor is it dependent on circumstances aligning perfectly. Biblical joy is rooted in trust, perspective, and the assurance of God's presence regardless of what unfolds. This month invites you to redefine joy, not as fleeting happiness, but as a steady posture of the heart anchored in God's faithfulness.

As you journey through May, you will explore how joy can coexist with uncertainty, grief, waiting, and growth. You will be reminded that joy is not something you manufacture, but something you cultivate as you remain connected to God. Choosing joy becomes a daily decision to trust God's goodness, even when life feels heavy or unclear.

Joy does not ignore reality. It transforms how you walk through it. This month will encourage you to embrace joy as strength, surrender, and quiet confidence, knowing that God is present in every season you face.

May 1

Joy That Is Rooted, Not Reactive

Nehemiah 8:10 (NKJV)

"...Do not sorrow, for the joy of the Lord is your strength."

Devotional

Joy is often misunderstood as an emotional response to favorable circumstances. But Scripture presents joy as something far deeper and far more stable. In this moment in Nehemiah, the people were not celebrating ease or abundance. They were standing in repentance and reverence before God. Yet they were reminded that joy, specifically the joy that comes from the Lord, was their strength.

Biblical joy does not deny sorrow. It exists alongside it. Joy rooted in God draws strength not from what is happening around you, but from who God is and where your trust is placed. When joy is rooted in the Lord, it becomes resilient. It sustains you when emotions fluctuate and circumstances feel uncertain.

Many people look for joy in outcomes, relationships, or seasons of ease. But those sources are fragile. God's joy is different. It strengthens you from the inside out. It gives endurance when life feels heavy and clarity when emotions threaten to overwhelm.

Today marks an invitation to reframe how you understand joy. Joy is not something you wait for after everything improves. It is a strength you receive when you remain anchored in God, regardless of what the day brings.

Reflection

Where have you been looking for joy that may be dependent on circumstances rather than God?

Life Application

When challenges arise today, remind yourself that God's joy is available to strengthen you even in difficult moments.

Prayer

Father, thank You that Your joy is my strength. Help me root my joy in You rather than my circumstances and trust You to sustain me through every season. Amen.

May 2

Joy Found in God's Presence

Psalm 16:11 (NIV)
"You make known to me the path of life; you will fill me with joy in your presence, with eternal pleasures at your right hand."

Devotional

Joy is often pursued in experiences, achievements, or relationships, yet Scripture reminds us that true joy is found in God's presence. This verse points to a joy that is not temporary or circumstantial but deeply rooted in relationship with God. When you draw near to Him, joy follows naturally, not as an effort, but as a result of connection.

God's presence provides direction and clarity. As He reveals the path of life, He also fills your heart with joy. This joy does not depend on perfection or ease. It flows from knowing that you are walking with God, guided by His wisdom and sustained by His closeness.

Many people feel depleted because they seek joy apart from God. Yet lasting joy is cultivated by spending time with Him, listening for His voice, and resting in His presence. Joy grows when your life is aligned with God's path rather than driven by constant striving.

Today's reminder is simple and powerful. When you prioritize God's presence, joy becomes a natural overflow. As you walk closely with Him, He fills your heart with a joy that strengthens and sustains you in every season.

Reflection

How often do you intentionally seek God's presence when you are searching for joy?

Life Application

Set aside intentional time today to be in God's presence through prayer or Scripture, allowing His joy to fill your heart.

Prayer

Lord, thank You for the joy that comes from being in Your presence. Help me seek You daily and walk the path You have set before me with a joyful heart. Amen.

May 3

Choosing Joy on Purpose

1 Thessalonians 5:16 (NLT)
"Always be joyful."

Devotional

Joy is not always a natural reaction, but it can be a deliberate decision. This short yet powerful instruction does not come with conditions or explanations. It simply calls you to choose joy. That invitation reminds you that joy is not something you wait for circumstances to create. It is something you cultivate intentionally.

Choosing joy does not mean ignoring pain, disappointment, or fatigue. It means refusing to allow those realities to have the final word. Joy becomes a posture of trust that says God is still good, still present, and still at work even when life feels heavy or unclear.

There will be days when joy feels easy and days when it feels costly. On harder days, joy may look quieter and more resilient than expressive. It may show up as gratitude, endurance, or hope held firmly rather than happiness felt immediately. Joy grows as you consistently choose it, even when emotions lag behind.

Today's reminder is simple but profound. Joy is available to you, not because everything is perfect, but because God is faithful. Choosing joy is an act of trust that strengthens your heart and steadies your walk through every season.

Reflection

What makes choosing joy difficult for you on certain days?

Life Application

Identify one intentional way you can choose joy today, even if circumstances are not ideal.

Prayer

Father, help me choose joy regardless of my circumstances. Teach me to trust You and cultivate joy as a steady posture of my heart. Amen.

May 4

Joy That Remains Steady

John 15:11 (NIV)
"I have told you this so that my joy may be in you and that your joy may be complete."

Devotional

Joy that endures is not something you generate on your own. Jesus makes it clear that true joy comes from remaining connected to Him. This joy is not fragile or fleeting. It is a joy He gives, designed to be complete and sustaining through every season.

Many people search for joy through external changes, hoping circumstances will improve before joy arrives. Yet Jesus offers joy that is rooted in relationship, not conditions. When His joy lives within you, it becomes steady rather than situational.

Enduring joy grows as you walk closely with Christ, allowing His truth to shape your perspective and His presence to strengthen your heart. This joy does not disappear when life feels uncertain. It remains because its source does not change.

Today's reminder is that joy is not something you have to chase. It is something you receive as you stay connected to Jesus. His joy is meant to live in you fully, strengthening you in every season you face.

Reflection

What has been competing with your connection to Jesus and affecting your sense of joy?

Life Application

Make space today to reconnect with Christ through prayer or Scripture, allowing His joy to fill and steady your heart.

Prayer

Lord, thank You for the joy You give that is complete and lasting. Help me remain connected to You so that Your joy can strengthen me in every season. Amen.

May 5

Joy That Comes from Gratitude

1 Thessalonians 5:18 (NIV)
"Give thanks in all circumstances; for this is God's will for you in Christ Jesus."

Devotional

Gratitude has a powerful way of shaping joy. This verse does not instruct you to be thankful *for* every circumstance, but *in* every circumstance. That distinction matters. Gratitude is not denial of difficulty. It is a choice to recognize God's presence and faithfulness regardless of what you are facing.

Joy often grows when gratitude leads the way. When you intentionally thank God in the middle of uncertainty, frustration, or waiting, your perspective begins to shift. Gratitude opens your eyes to what God is doing instead of focusing solely on what feels lacking or unresolved.

Choosing gratitude requires humility and trust. It acknowledges that God is still at work, even when life does not look the way you expected. Gratitude anchors joy by reminding you that God's goodness is not limited by circumstances. His will is that you remain connected to Him through thanksgiving.

Today's encouragement is to practice gratitude deliberately. As you give thanks, joy begins to rise quietly but steadily within you. Gratitude does not change every situation, but it changes how you walk through it.

Reflection

What circumstance in your life feels hardest to be thankful in right now?

Life Application

Pause today and thank God for one specific thing in a challenging area of your life.

Prayer

Father, help me choose gratitude in every circumstance. Teach me to give thanks and trust that You are present and working, even when life feels difficult. Amen.

May 6

Joy That Is Sustained by Hope

Romans 12:12 (NLT)
"Rejoice in our confident hope. Be patient in trouble, and keep on praying."

Devotional

Joy is sustained when it is tied to hope rather than circumstances. This verse connects joy, patience, and prayer, showing how they work together in seasons of difficulty. Joy is not isolated from hardship. It is strengthened by hope that looks beyond present challenges.

Hope gives joy endurance. When you trust that God is at work and that His promises remain true, joy becomes resilient instead of fragile. Even in trouble, hope allows you to rejoice, not because everything feels good, but because God is faithful.

Patience and prayer keep joy grounded. Patience reminds you that growth and change take time. Prayer keeps your heart connected to God when emotions fluctuate. Together, they guard joy from being overwhelmed by frustration or fear.

Today's encouragement is to allow hope to sustain your joy. When you rejoice in confident hope, you are choosing to trust God's goodness even before circumstances change. That trust becomes a steady source of strength.

Reflection

Where do you need to reconnect joy with hope instead of circumstances?

Life Application

Practice rejoicing today by reminding yourself of a promise from God that gives you hope.

Prayer

Father, help me rejoice in confident hope. Strengthen my patience, deepen my prayer life, and sustain my joy as I trust You in every season. Amen.

May 7

Joy That Grows Through Trust

Proverbs 17:22 (NLT)
"A cheerful heart is good medicine, but a broken spirit saps a person's strength."

Devotional

Joy has a quiet but powerful effect on the heart. Scripture reminds us that joy is not only emotional, it is restorative. A cheerful heart strengthens you from the inside out, while discouragement slowly drains your energy and resolve. Joy, when nurtured, becomes a source of renewal.

Trust plays a vital role in sustaining joy. When you trust God with your concerns, burdens, and uncertainties, joy is given room to grow. It does not erase hardship, but it softens its impact. Trust allows joy to function as healing rather than avoidance.

Many people underestimate the spiritual importance of joy. Yet God understands how closely joy and strength are connected. When joy is cultivated through trust, it becomes a form of resilience. It helps you endure challenges with steadiness instead of exhaustion.

Today's reminder is to guard your heart. Choose trust over discouragement and allow joy to restore what feels worn down. A joyful heart strengthens you for the journey ahead.

Reflection

How does discouragement affect your joy and energy when you are under pressure?

Life Application

Intentionally choose one activity today that encourages joy and strengthens your heart.

Prayer

Father, help me trust You deeply and cultivate joy in my heart. Restore my strength and renew my spirit as I walk with You each day. Amen.

May 8

Joy for Today

Psalms 118:24 (NIV)
"This is the day the Lord has made; let us rejoice and be glad in it."

Devotional

Joy is often postponed. Many people wait for better circumstances, clearer answers, or future milestones before allowing themselves to rejoice. This verse gently redirects that thinking. It reminds you that joy is available today, not because everything is perfect, but because God has given you this day.

Choosing joy today is an act of faith. It acknowledges that God is present in the now, not only in what is coming next. Rejoicing becomes a decision to honor God's goodness in the present moment rather than delaying gratitude until life feels easier.

Joy for today does not minimize real challenges. It reframes how you walk through them. When you choose to rejoice, you are recognizing God's sovereignty over your time and trusting that each day carries purpose, even when it feels ordinary or demanding.

Today's invitation is simple but intentional. Receive this day as a gift from God. Allow joy to meet you where you are, knowing that rejoicing today strengthens your heart for whatever tomorrow holds.

Reflection

What keeps you from fully embracing joy in the present moment?

Life Application

Intentionally thank God for this day and choose one way to rejoice before the day ends.

Prayer

Father, thank You for this day You have given me. Help me choose joy right where I am and trust that You are present in every moment. Amen.

May 9

Joy That Strengthens Others

Proverbs 12:25 (NLT)
"Worry weighs a person down; an encouraging word cheers a person up."

Devotional

Joy is not meant to be held quietly or privately. It is something that strengthens not only your own heart but the hearts of others as well. This verse reminds us that words carry weight. They can either deepen discouragement or lift someone toward hope. When joy guides your words, it becomes a source of strength beyond yourself.

Many people around you are quietly carrying worry, pressure, or fatigue. An encouraging word, spoken with sincerity and compassion, can restore joy in moments when heaviness feels overwhelming. Joy expressed through encouragement becomes an extension of God's care and presence.

Choosing to encourage others requires awareness and intention. It means allowing joy to influence how you speak, listen, and respond. When joy is shared, it multiplies. It softens hearts, builds connection, and reminds others that they are seen and valued.

Today's reminder is that your joy has purpose beyond your own experience. Let it flow outward. An encouraging word, offered with kindness, may be exactly what someone needs to regain strength and hope.

Reflection

Who in your life may need encouragement right now?

Life Application

Offer a sincere word of encouragement to someone today and allow joy to guide your interaction.

Prayer

Father, help me use my words to bring encouragement and joy to others. Let my heart be guided by Your compassion as I strengthen those around me. Amen.

May 10

Joy That Comes from Trusting God's Timing

Ecclesiastes 3:11 (NLT)

"Yet God has made everything beautiful for its own time. He has planted eternity in the human heart, but even so, people cannot see the whole scope of God's work from beginning to end."

Devotional

Joy often wavers when life feels out of sync with your expectations. Waiting seasons, unanswered prayers, and delayed outcomes can challenge your sense of peace. This verse reminds you that God's timing is intentional and purposeful, even when you cannot see how everything fits together.

Trusting God's timing requires faith that extends beyond the present moment. It acknowledges that God is working on a broader timeline than you can perceive. Joy grows when you believe that God is shaping something beautiful, even while the process feels incomplete.

Many people struggle to rejoice while waiting because they want clarity before contentment. Yet Scripture teaches that joy is cultivated by trusting God's wisdom rather than demanding full understanding. God's work is unfolding, even when progress feels slow or hidden.

Today's encouragement is to release the pressure to have everything figured out. Trust that God's timing is good and His work is purposeful. Joy becomes steadier when you believe that what God is doing will reveal its beauty in time.

Reflection

Where are you struggling to trust God's timing right now?

Life Application

Practice patience today by surrendering a waiting area to God and choosing to trust His timing.

Prayer

Father, help me trust Your timing even when I cannot see the full picture. Strengthen my faith and help me choose joy while I wait. Amen.

May 11

Joy That Comes in the Morning

Psalms 30:5 (NIV)

"Weeping may stay for the night, but rejoicing comes in the morning."

Devotional

Joy does not deny that seasons of sorrow exist. This verse acknowledges the reality of pain while offering hope that it does not have the final word. Night represents moments of heaviness, loss, or discouragement, but morning symbolizes renewal, restoration, and God's faithful timing.

God allows seasons to change, and with each new morning comes the promise of His mercy and presence. Joy may feel distant during the night, but it is never absent from God's plan. Faith holds onto the truth that God is working even while you wait for the morning to come.

Joy that comes in the morning teaches you to trust God through the dark moments. It invites patience, endurance, and hope. When you believe that rejoicing is coming, you can endure the night without losing heart.

Today's encouragement is to hold onto hope. Whatever season you are in, trust that God is faithful to bring renewal. Morning is coming, and with it, joy that restores and strengthens your heart.

Reflection

What season of waiting or difficulty are you trusting God to bring you through?

Life Application

When discouragement surfaces today, remind yourself that God's joy is coming and His faithfulness remains.

Prayer

Father, thank You for the promise that joy comes in the morning. Help me trust You through every season and remain hopeful as I wait for renewal. Amen.

May 12

Joy That Is Strengthened by Peace

Isaiah 26:3 (NLT)
"You will keep in perfect peace all who trust in you, all whose thoughts are fixed on you."

Devotional

Joy and peace are deeply connected. When your mind is anchored in trust, peace settles your heart and joy finds room to grow. This verse reveals that peace is not accidental. It is the result of a focused trust in God. Where your thoughts remain, your emotional strength follows.

Distraction, worry, and fear often pull attention away from God, weakening both peace and joy. But when your thoughts are fixed on Him, stability returns. Trusting God does not remove challenges, but it changes how you experience them. Peace becomes a guard that protects joy from being overwhelmed.

Joy strengthened by peace is steady rather than fragile. It is not dependent on circumstances improving or emotions staying calm. It grows as you continually redirect your thoughts toward God's faithfulness and presence.

Today's encouragement is to examine where your mind has been dwelling. Fixing your thoughts on God invites peace to settle in, and where peace remains, joy is strengthened and sustained.

Reflection

What thoughts most often disrupt your peace and joy?

Life Application

When anxious thoughts arise today, intentionally redirect your focus toward God through prayer or Scripture.

Prayer

Lord, help me fix my thoughts on You. Thank You for the peace You provide and the joy that grows as I trust You fully. Amen.

May 13

Joy That Is Produced by the Spirit

Galatians 5:22 (NIV)
"But the fruit of the Spirit is love, joy, peace, forbearance, kindness, goodness, faithfulness."

Devotional

Joy is not something you force or manufacture through effort. Scripture teaches that joy is cultivated by the Spirit of God working within you. This kind of joy does not depend on circumstances, energy levels, or emotional highs. It develops as you remain connected to God and allow His Spirit to shape your life.

Many people try to generate joy by changing external conditions, but lasting joy grows from internal transformation. When the Spirit is allowed to lead, joy takes root and strengthens over time. It deepens as trust is established and dependence on God increases.

Spiritual growth and joy are closely connected. As you walk with God, His Spirit nurtures qualities that steady your heart and anchor your emotions. Joy formed by the Spirit is resilient. It remains present even when life feels uncertain or challenging.

Today's encouragement is to focus less on producing joy and more on remaining aligned with God. As you walk in step with His Spirit, joy will continue to grow, shaping how you experience every season.

Reflection

What areas of your life need more openness to the work of the Holy Spirit?

Life Application

Invite the Holy Spirit to guide your thoughts and actions today, trusting Him to produce joy within you.

Prayer

Father, thank You for the work of Your Spirit in my life. Help me remain connected to You so that joy can grow naturally within my heart. Amen.

May 14

Joy That Calms the Anxious Heart

Psalm 94:19 (NLT)
"When doubts filled my mind, your comfort gave me renewed hope and cheer."

Devotional

Joy does not require the absence of anxiety. This verse acknowledges that doubt and anxious thoughts can crowd the mind, yet it also reveals where relief is found. God's comfort has the power to quiet inner turmoil and restore joy even when emotions feel unsettled.

An anxious heart often tries to resolve everything at once. Joy invites a different response. It allows God's comfort to meet you in the middle of uncertainty and bring calm where tension has been building. God does not dismiss your worries. He meets them with reassurance and care.

Joy that calms the heart grows as you bring your thoughts honestly before God. When you allow Him to comfort you, heaviness begins to lift. Hope returns, not because circumstances have changed, but because God's presence steadies your inner world.

Today's encouragement is to let God minister to your anxious thoughts. His comfort brings renewal, and where His comfort rests, joy quietly follows.

Reflection

What anxious thoughts have been filling your mind lately?

Life Application

Pause today and invite God to comfort you in moments of anxiety, allowing His peace to restore your joy.

Prayer

Father, thank You for meeting me with comfort when my mind feels overwhelmed. Calm my anxious thoughts and restore joy and hope within my heart. Amen.

May 15

Joy That Is Chosen Daily

Deuteronomy 30:19 (NLT)
"Today I have given you the choice between life and death, between blessings and curses. Now I call on heaven and earth to witness the choice you make. Oh, that you would choose life, so that you and your descendants might live!"

Devotional

Joy is not something that happens once and remains untouched. It is a daily choice that shapes how you experience life. This verse speaks to the power of choice, reminding you that life and blessing are available, but they must be intentionally chosen. Joy follows the same pattern. It grows when you choose it again and again.

Choosing joy does not ignore reality. It acknowledges that every day presents options for how you will respond. You can dwell on what is missing, frustrating, or uncertain, or you can choose a posture that leans toward life, trust, and hope. Joy develops as you consistently choose what leads toward God's truth and goodness.

Daily choices matter more than isolated moments. Joy deepens as you align your thoughts, words, and actions with what brings life. When joy is chosen daily, it becomes a steady companion rather than a fleeting emotion.

Today's encouragement is to recognize the power of your choices. Joy is cultivated one decision at a time. When you choose life, joy follows and strengthens every step of your journey.

Reflection

What daily choices influence your ability to experience joy?

Life Application

Identify one small decision today where you can intentionally choose joy and life over discouragement.

Prayer

Father, help me choose joy daily. Guide my decisions so that they lead toward life, trust, and hope in You. Amen.

May 16

Joy That Is Strengthened Through Praise

Psalm 63:3 (NIV)
"Because your love is better than life, my lips will glorify you."

Devotional

Praise has a way of strengthening joy, even when circumstances feel heavy. This verse reflects a heart that recognizes God's love as greater than anything else life can offer. When praise becomes a response rather than a reaction, joy begins to rise from a place deeper than emotion.

Joy is often weakened when focus remains on what is lacking or difficult. Praise shifts attention back to who God is and how faithful He has been. As you glorify God, your heart is reminded of His goodness, and joy is renewed from the inside out.

Praising God does not require everything to be going well. It is an act of faith that declares trust in God's love regardless of current conditions. Joy grows when praise becomes a regular part of your walk, anchoring your heart in truth rather than circumstance.

Today's encouragement is to let praise lead your posture. As you glorify God, joy is strengthened, perspective is restored, and your heart is reminded that His love truly is better than life.

Reflection

How does praise influence your ability to experience joy during challenging moments?

Life Application

Take time today to praise God intentionally, whether through prayer, worship, or gratitude, allowing joy to be renewed.

Prayer

Lord, thank You for Your love that is better than life. Help me cultivate praise in every season and allow joy to be strengthened as I glorify You. Amen.

May 17

Joy That Rises from Contentment

Philippians 4:11 (NIV)
"I am not saying this because I am in need, for I have learned to be content whatever the circumstances."

Devotional

Joy becomes steadier when it is grounded in contentment rather than comparison. This verse reflects a learned posture, not a natural one. Contentment is shaped through experience as trust in God deepens. It is not dependent on having more, but on resting in what God has already provided.

Many people struggle with joy because they continually measure their lives against what they believe is missing. Contentment redirects that focus. It teaches you to notice God's faithfulness in every season, whether you are walking through abundance or lack. Joy strengthens when gratitude replaces striving.

Learning contentment does not mean settling for less than God's best. It means trusting God's provision without allowing dissatisfaction to erode your peace. Joy that rises from contentment is steady and enduring. It holds you firm when circumstances fluctuate.

Today's encouragement is to practice contentment with intention. As you learn to rest in God's provision, joy becomes less fragile and more established, supporting you through every season.

Reflection

What circumstances make it difficult for you to feel content?

Life Application

Practice contentment today by thanking God for what He has already provided rather than focusing on what feels missing.

Prayer

Father, help me learn contentment in every season. Teach me to trust Your provision and allow joy to grow as I rest in You. Amen.

May 18

Joy That Is Renewed by God's Faithfulness

Psalms 36:5 (NIV)
"Your love, Lord, reaches to the heavens, your faithfulness to the skies."

Devotional

Joy is renewed when you remember how faithful God truly is. This verse paints a picture of God's faithfulness as vast and unending, stretching far beyond what you can see or measure. When life feels uncertain, reflecting on God's consistent character restores joy and confidence.

Faithfulness means God remains dependable in every season. He does not change His posture toward you based on circumstances or emotions. Joy grows when you anchor your heart in the truth that God's love and faithfulness are always present, even when outcomes feel unclear.

Remembering God's faithfulness helps shift your focus from what feels unstable to what is secure. As you reflect on how God has carried you before, joy is renewed in the present. His faithfulness becomes a steady source of strength and reassurance.

Today's encouragement is to pause and reflect on God's track record in your life. Let memories of His faithfulness renew your joy and remind you that He will continue to be faithful in every season ahead.

Reflection

How has God shown His faithfulness to you in past seasons?

Life Application

Take time today to reflect on a moment when God was faithful and allow that memory to renew your joy.

Prayer

Lord, thank You for Your unfailing love and faithfulness. Renew my joy as I remember how You have carried me through every season. Amen.

May 19

Joy That Grows Through Perseverance

Psalm 126:5 (NIV)

"Those who sow with tears will reap with songs of joy."

Devotional

Joy does not always appear at the beginning of a journey. Sometimes it grows quietly through perseverance, patience, and faithfulness in hard seasons. This verse acknowledges that tears are real and seasons of difficulty are part of life. Yet it also promises that sorrow is not the end of the story.

Perseverance requires trust that God is working even when progress feels slow or painful. Sowing with tears means continuing to show up, obey, pray, and trust God despite disappointment or fatigue. Joy grows when faith refuses to quit in the middle of difficulty.

Many people expect joy to come before the work is done. Scripture shows us that joy often follows faithfulness. As you remain committed to God through challenging seasons, joy emerges as a harvest produced by trust and endurance.

Today's encouragement is to keep sowing. Do not lose heart in seasons that feel heavy. God sees every tear, every prayer, and every act of faithfulness. Joy is growing, even when you cannot see it yet.

Reflection

Where have you been sowing faithfully despite feeling discouraged or weary?

Life Application

Choose to remain faithful today in one area where perseverance feels difficult, trusting God with the outcome.

Prayer

Father, help me persevere through difficult seasons. Strengthen my faith as I trust You to bring joy from every place of faithfulness. Amen.

May 20

Joy That Is Anchored in God's Word

Psalm 119:111 (NIV)
"Your statutes are my heritage forever; they are the joy of my heart."

Devotional

Joy becomes lasting when it is anchored in something unchanging. This verse reveals that God's Word is not simply guidance for living, but a source of deep and enduring joy. When Scripture shapes your heart, joy is no longer dependent on circumstances or emotions. It becomes rooted in truth.

God's Word provides clarity when life feels confusing and stability when emotions fluctuate. As you engage with Scripture, it reminds you of who God is and who you are in Him. Joy grows as your heart aligns with God's promises rather than the uncertainty around you.

Many people look for joy in temporary experiences, but God offers joy that endures through His Word. When Scripture becomes your heritage, it grounds you, strengthens you, and fills your heart with confidence and peace.

Today's encouragement is to lean into God's Word. Allow it to shape your perspective and steady your emotions. As you treasure His truth, joy will continue to take root and grow within you.

Reflection

How does spending time in God's Word influence your sense of joy?

Life Application

Spend intentional time today reading Scripture and allow God's truth to anchor your heart in joy.

Prayer

Father, thank You for Your Word that brings joy to my heart. Help me treasure Your truth and allow it to shape how I live and trust You each day. Amen.

May 21

Joy That Comes from Serving Others

Acts 20:35 (NIV)

"In everything I did, I showed you that by this kind of hard work we must help the weak, remembering the words the Lord Jesus himself said: 'It is more blessed to give than to receive.'"

Devotional

Joy often deepens when your focus shifts from yourself to others. This verse reminds us that there is a unique blessing found in giving, serving, and helping those in need. Joy grows when love is expressed through action rather than held only as intention.

Serving others does not diminish you. It enriches you. When you choose generosity, compassion, and humility, joy follows naturally. God designed joy to flow outward, not remain contained. Serving becomes a pathway through which joy multiplies.

Many people search for joy through self-fulfillment, yet Scripture reveals that joy is often discovered in selflessness. Helping others aligns your heart with God's love and reminds you that your life carries purpose beyond your own needs.

Today's encouragement is to look for opportunities to serve. Whether through kindness, encouragement, or practical support, your service can become a source of joy for both you and those around you.

Reflection

How does serving others affect your sense of joy and purpose?

Life Application

Intentionally serve someone today, trusting that joy will grow as you give of yourself.

Prayer

Father, help me find joy through serving others. Teach me to give generously and love selflessly as I follow the example of Jesus. Amen.

May 22

Joy That Comes from God's Truth

Psalms 19:8 (NIV)

"The precepts of the Lord are right, giving joy to the heart. The commands of the Lord are radiant, giving light to the eyes."

Devotional

Joy is strengthened when your heart is aligned with truth. This verse reminds us that God's truth is not restrictive or burdensome. It is right, life-giving, and illuminating. When God's Word guides your steps, joy follows because truth brings clarity and direction.

Confusion often drains joy. When you are unsure of what to believe or which path to take, heaviness can settle in. God's truth cuts through uncertainty and brings light to areas that feel dark or unclear. Joy grows as your heart rests in what God says rather than what circumstances suggest.

Walking in God's truth does not remove challenges, but it changes how you face them. His Word steadies your emotions and sharpens your perspective. When truth anchors your heart, joy becomes a natural response rather than a forced effort.

Today's encouragement is to let God's truth shape your thinking. As you embrace what He says, joy rises quietly and confidently, bringing light and peace to your inner life.

Reflection

How does God's truth influence your ability to experience joy?

Life Application

Spend time today reflecting on a truth from Scripture that brings clarity and joy to your heart.

Prayer

Father, thank You for Your truth that brings joy and light to my life. Help me walk in Your Word and allow joy to grow as I trust You more deeply. Amen.

May 23

Joy That Is Rooted in Hope

Romans 15:13 (NIV)
"May the God of hope fill you with all joy and peace as you trust in him, so that you may overflow with hope by the power of the Holy Spirit."

Devotional

Joy and hope are deeply intertwined. This verse reveals that joy does not stand alone. It is filled, sustained, and strengthened by trust in God. As you place your confidence in Him, joy and peace begin to rise, not as fleeting emotions, but as steady anchors for your heart.

Hope reminds you that God's story is still unfolding. When trust is present, joy grows even when circumstances feel uncertain. God is described here as the God of hope, emphasizing that hope originates with Him and flows into your life through relationship and trust.

Joy rooted in hope becomes resilient. It does not disappear when challenges arise or plans shift. Instead, it overflows as the Holy Spirit empowers you to believe God's promises and trust His faithfulness beyond what you can see.

Today's encouragement is to lean into trust. As you do, allow God to fill you with joy and peace. Hope will rise, not because everything is resolved, but because God is present and powerful in every season.

Reflection

How does trusting God influence your ability to experience joy and hope?

Life Application

Place a current concern in God's hands today and intentionally choose to trust Him, allowing joy and hope to grow.

Prayer

Father, thank You for being the God of hope. Fill me with joy and peace as I trust You, and help me overflow with hope through Your Spirit. Amen.

May 24

Joy That Is Found in God's Nearness

Psalm 145:18 (NIV)
"The Lord is near to all who call on him, to all who call on him in truth."

Devotional

Joy often feels distant when life feels heavy or overwhelming. Yet this verse offers a reassuring truth. God is not far off or detached from your experience. He is near, attentive, and responsive to those who call on Him sincerely. His nearness becomes a steady source of comfort and joy.

Calling on God in truth means approaching Him honestly, without pretense or performance. When you invite God into your reality, joy begins to rise not because circumstances instantly change, but because you are no longer walking alone. God's presence brings reassurance and peace to your heart.

Joy that flows from God's nearness is gentle and grounding. It reminds you that you are seen, heard, and held by a faithful God. His closeness strengthens you when emotions fluctuate and restores confidence when uncertainty creeps in.

Today's encouragement is to call on God openly and sincerely. As you do, trust that He is near. Where God's presence is acknowledged, joy quietly takes root and grows.

Reflection

How does knowing that God is near affect your sense of joy?

Life Application

Take a moment today to call on God honestly, trusting that His presence is close and attentive.

Prayer

Father, thank You for being near to me. Help me call on You with honesty and trust, and allow joy to grow as I rest in Your presence. Amen.

May 25

Joy That Is Strengthened by Community

Ecclesiastes 4:9 (NIV)
"Two are better than one, because they have a good return for their labor."

Devotional

Joy is not meant to be carried alone. God designed you for connection, and Scripture affirms that shared effort and shared life produce greater strength and reward. When joy is nurtured within community, it becomes more resilient and sustaining.

Isolation often weakens joy. When you try to carry burdens alone, discouragement can quietly take root. Community offers support, perspective, and encouragement that restores strength when you feel weary. Joy grows when it is shared, spoken, and reinforced by others walking alongside you.

God uses relationships to remind you that you are not meant to navigate life independently. Healthy community sharpens faith, lightens burdens, and multiplies joy. When you allow others into your journey, joy becomes steadier because it is supported by connection.

Today's encouragement is to value the gift of community. Whether through friendship, fellowship, or shared purpose, God strengthens joy through relationships that walk with you, pray with you, and grow alongside you.

Reflection

How has community strengthened or supported your joy in past seasons?

Life Application

Reach out to someone today for connection, encouragement, or shared prayer, allowing joy to grow through relationship.

Prayer

Father, thank You for the gift of community. Help me value connection and allow joy to be strengthened through relationships You have placed in my life. Amen.

May 26

Joy That Is Experienced Through Trust

Psalm 34:8 (NLT)
"Taste and see that the Lord is good. Oh, the joys of those who take refuge in him!"

Devotional

Joy deepens when it moves from belief to experience. This verse invites you not just to know that God is good, but to encounter His goodness personally. Joy becomes real when trust shifts from theory into lived relationship with God.

Taking refuge in God means choosing Him as your place of safety and confidence. It is an intentional act of trust that says God is reliable even when circumstances feel uncertain. Joy grows when you rely on God rather than your own strength or understanding.

Experiencing God's goodness often requires openness and surrender. When you trust Him fully, you begin to recognize joy in moments that once felt ordinary or overlooked. God reveals His goodness through provision, peace, guidance, and presence.

Today's encouragement is to lean into trust. As you take refuge in God, joy follows naturally. God's goodness is not distant or abstract. It is meant to be experienced and enjoyed as you walk closely with Him.

Reflection

What does it look like for you to take refuge in God during challenging moments?

Life Application

Identify one area today where you can choose trust over worry and allow God's goodness to meet you there.

Prayer

Father, thank You for Your goodness. Help me trust You more deeply and experience the joy that comes from taking refuge in You. Amen.

May 27

Joy That Is Renewed Daily

Lamentations 3:23 (KJV)

"They are new every morning: great is thy faithfulness."

Devotional

Joy does not have to be sustained by yesterday's strength. This verse reminds us that God meets each day with fresh provision. His faithfulness does not carry over out of obligation. It shows up new, intentional, and fully present every morning.

Some days require renewed joy because the weight of life feels heavy or repetitive. God does not ask you to rely on old grace for new challenges. He supplies exactly what you need for today. When you wake up, joy is available again, not because circumstances have changed, but because God remains faithful.

Daily renewal invites you to release comparison and regret. Yesterday's joy does not determine today's capacity. God's faithfulness resets your heart each morning, allowing you to move forward without carrying emotional residue from the day before.

Today's encouragement is to receive what God is offering now. Joy does not have to be chased or recreated. It is renewed as you recognize God's faithfulness meeting you in this moment.

Reflection

How does knowing God's faithfulness is renewed daily affect how you approach today?

Life Application

Begin today by acknowledging God's faithfulness and intentionally receiving the joy He offers for this day alone.

Prayer

Lord, thank You for Your faithfulness that meets me every morning. Help me receive the joy You provide today and trust You for what lies ahead. Amen.

May 28

Joy That Is Sustained by Gratitude

Psalm 92:1 (NLT)
"It is good to give thanks to the Lord, to sing praises to the Most High."

Devotional

Gratitude is not just a response. It is a rhythm that sustains joy over time. This verse reminds us that thanksgiving is good for the soul. It aligns your heart with truth and lifts your focus toward God rather than circumstances.

Joy fades when gratitude is absent. When attention stays fixed on what is missing or delayed, joy quietly drains away. Gratitude redirects your heart, helping you recognize God's faithfulness woven through everyday moments. As thanksgiving becomes a habit, joy gains staying power.

Giving thanks is also an act of worship. It acknowledges God's sovereignty, goodness, and presence. When gratitude rises, joy follows because your heart is anchored in who God is rather than what life feels like.

Today's encouragement is to let gratitude lead. As you intentionally thank God, joy will be sustained, not because everything is perfect, but because your heart is rightly aligned with Him.

Reflection

How does practicing gratitude affect your perspective and emotional well-being?

Life Application

Pause today to thank God intentionally, allowing gratitude to steady and sustain your joy.

Prayer

Father, thank You for the goodness of gratitude. Help me cultivate a thankful heart and allow joy to remain strong as I praise You daily. Amen

May 29

Joy That Is Released Through Praise

Hebrews 13:15 (NKJV)
"Therefore by Him let us continually offer the sacrifice of praise to God, that is, the fruit of our lips, giving thanks to His name."

Devotional

Praise has a unique way of unlocking joy, especially when circumstances do not naturally invite it. This verse reminds us that praise is sometimes a sacrifice, not because God demands it, but because it requires trust. When praise rises in difficult moments, joy is released from a deeper place.

Joy is often strengthened when praise becomes a choice rather than a reaction. Praising God shifts your focus from what feels heavy to who God is. It realigns your heart with truth and reminds you that God remains worthy, faithful, and present regardless of what you are facing.

Offering praise continually does not mean ignoring pain or pretending everything is fine. It means choosing to honor God even when emotions are mixed. That choice creates space for joy to return, not as a surface emotion, but as a steady confidence rooted in faith.

Today's encouragement is to lift praise intentionally. As you give thanks and honor God with your words, joy will follow, not because circumstances change, but because your heart is anchored in Him.

Reflection

How does praise influence your ability to experience joy during challenging seasons?

Life Application

Take a moment today to praise God aloud, especially in an area where joy feels strained.

Prayer

Father, help me offer praise continually. Teach me to honor You with my words and allow joy to rise as my heart stays anchored in You. Amen.

May 30

Joy That Carries You Forward

2 Corinthians 13:11 (NIV)
"Finally, brothers and sisters, rejoice. Strive for full restoration, encourage one another, be of one mind, live in peace. And the God of love and peace will be with you."

Devotional

As the month comes to a close, this verse offers both instruction and reassurance. Joy is not presented as a fleeting feeling, but as a posture that shapes how you move forward. Rejoicing here is paired with restoration, encouragement, unity, and peace. Joy becomes something that steadies your steps as you continue your journey.

Joy that carries you forward is not passive. It is intentional and practiced. It shows up when you choose restoration over resentment, encouragement over silence, and peace over division. These choices create an environment where joy can remain present and active in your life.

God's promise is clear. When you walk in these postures, His presence goes with you. The God of love and peace does not stand at a distance. He walks alongside you, guiding you into what comes next. Joy becomes the companion that helps you transition with confidence rather than fear.

Today's encouragement is to step forward with joy. Let what you have learned this month shape how you move ahead. Joy does not end here. It strengthens you for what is coming and reminds you that God is with you as you continue forward.

Reflection

How can joy help guide the way you move into what comes next?

Life Application

Choose one intentional action today that reflects joy through restoration, encouragement, or peace as you prepare for the next season.

Prayer

Father, help me move forward with joy. Guide my heart toward restoration, unity, and peace, and remind me that You are with me as I step into what comes next. Amen.

May 31

Joy That Is Complete in Christ

1 Peter 1:8 (NLT)
"You love him even though you have never seen him. Though you do not see him now, you trust him; and you rejoice with a glorious, inexpressible joy."

Devotional

This verse captures the essence of joy that transcends circumstance. It reminds you that joy is not dependent on what you see, understand, or control. It is rooted in relationship. Even without physical sight, trust in Christ produces a joy that is deep, radiant, and enduring.

Inexpressible joy does not mean life is free from difficulty. It means joy runs deeper than difficulty. When your trust is anchored in Christ, joy becomes a steady presence rather than a fleeting feeling. It flows from knowing who He is and believing that He is faithful, even when answers are not immediate.

As this month comes to a close, this verse invites you to reflect on how joy has been reshaped in your heart. Joy is no longer something you chase or manufacture. It is something that grows as trust deepens and love matures.

Today's encouragement is to rest in this truth. Your joy does not come from what you see ahead, but from who you trust. That joy is complete, sustaining, and secure in Christ.

Reflection

How has your understanding of joy changed as your trust in Christ has grown?

Life Application

Take time today to thank God for the joy that comes from trusting Him, even when the path ahead is unclear.

Prayer

Lord, thank You for the joy that comes from trusting You. Help me continue walking in a joy that is rooted in love, faith, and confidence in who You are. Amen.

June

Boldness Through Christ

Boldness is often misunderstood. It is not confidence in your own strength, personality, or ability. True boldness is rooted in Christ and grows from trust in who He is and what He has already placed within you. June invites you to explore what it means to walk forward with courage that does not rely on certainty, but on obedience and faith.

Many people hesitate when God calls them to step forward. Fear, doubt, and past experiences can make bold obedience feel risky or uncomfortable. This month will gently challenge those hesitations by reminding you that boldness is not about having all the answers. It is about trusting that God goes with you, strengthens you, and equips you for each step as you take it.

As you move through these days, you will be encouraged to release fear, grow in confidence through Christ, and take faithful steps toward the life God is inviting you into. Boldness through Christ is not reckless or forced. It is steady, rooted, and anchored in the assurance that God's power is made perfect even in moments of weakness.

June 1

Boldness Begins with Trust

Hebrews 4:16 (NIV)

"Let us then approach God's throne of grace with confidence, so that we may receive mercy and find grace to help us in our time of need."

Devotional

Boldness in Christ does not begin with action. It begins with trust. This verse invites you to approach God with confidence, not because you are strong or certain, but because God is gracious and welcoming. Boldness grows when you believe you are invited, not tolerated, in God's presence.

Many people hesitate to approach God honestly because they fear judgment, disappointment, or rejection. Yet Scripture makes it clear that God's throne is marked by grace. Confidence here is not arrogance. It is assurance rooted in relationship. When you trust God's heart toward you, boldness begins to take shape.

Approaching God with confidence allows you to receive what you actually need. Mercy for what is behind you. Grace for what lies ahead. Boldness is sustained when you stop trying to carry everything alone and instead bring your weakness, questions, and uncertainty before God.

Today's encouragement is to take that first step. Come to God honestly and confidently. As you trust His grace to meet you, boldness will begin to rise, steady and secure, rooted not in yourself but in Him.

Reflection

What makes it difficult for you to approach God with confidence?

Life Application

Take a moment today to bring a specific need or concern before God, trusting His grace to meet you there.

Prayer

Father, thank You for inviting me to come to You with confidence. Help me trust Your grace and mercy and allow boldness to grow as I depend on You. Amen.

June 2

Courage Strengthened by God's Power

2 Timothy 1:7 (NIV)
"For the Spirit God gave us does not make us timid, but gives us power, love and self-discipline."

Devotional

Boldness through Christ begins internally before it ever shows up externally. This verse reminds you that fear is not your default setting. God has already placed within you a Spirit marked by power, love, and self-control. Courage is not something you have to manufacture. It is something you are invited to walk in.

Fear often convinces you that hesitation is wisdom. God's Word gently challenges that lie. The Spirit within you equips you to move forward with clarity and confidence, even when circumstances feel uncertain. Boldness grows as you trust what God has already deposited in you.

Power enables action, love anchors motivation, and self-discipline provides steadiness. Together, they create a courage that is balanced, grounded, and purposeful. This kind of boldness does not rush ahead recklessly or shrink back in fear. It moves forward with intention and trust.

Today's encouragement is to recognize what God has already given you. You are not lacking courage. You are learning to walk in it. As you trust the Spirit at work within you, boldness will continue to rise.

Reflection

Which aspect of God's Spirit - power, love, or self-discipline do you need to lean into most right now?

Life Application

Choose one situation today where you will respond with courage, trusting the Spirit God has placed within you.

Prayer

Father, thank You for the Spirit You have given me. Help me walk in power, love, and self-discipline as I grow in boldness through You. Amen.

June 3

Boldness Grows Through Obedience

Deuteronomy 31:6 (NIV)
"Be strong and courageous. Do not be afraid or terrified because of them, for the Lord your God goes with you; he will never leave you nor forsake you."

Devotional

Boldness through Christ is often revealed through obedience. This verse was spoken at a moment of transition and uncertainty, when courage was required to move forward. God did not promise the absence of difficulty. He promised His presence. Obedience becomes possible when you trust that God goes with you into what feels unfamiliar.

Fear often surfaces when obedience requires movement without full clarity. Yet Scripture reminds you that God does not abandon you when you step out in faith. Boldness grows as you choose obedience over comfort, trusting that God remains faithful to walk beside you.

Being strong and courageous does not mean suppressing fear. It means refusing to let fear dictate your obedience. When you obey God despite uncertainty, confidence begins to form. Each obedient step strengthens your trust and deepens your courage.

Today's encouragement is to obey even when the outcome is unclear. God's presence does not depend on your certainty. As you walk in obedience, boldness will continue to grow, rooted in the assurance that God will not leave you.

Reflection

Where is God asking you to obey even though the path ahead feels uncertain?

Life Application

Take one step of obedience today in an area where fear has caused hesitation, trusting God's presence with you.

Prayer

Lord, help me walk in obedience with courage. Remind me that You go with me and will never leave or forsake me as I trust You. Amen.

June 4

Boldness Is Built in the Secret Place

Psalm 27:1 (NIV)
"The Lord is my light and my salvation - whom shall I fear?
The Lord is the stronghold of my life - of whom shall I be afraid?"

Devotional

Boldness through Christ is not developed in public moments alone. It is formed in the quiet places where fear is faced honestly and faith is strengthened privately. This verse reveals that courage flows from knowing who God is long before challenges appear.

When God is your light, confusion loses its power. When He is your salvation, fear no longer has the final word. Boldness grows as you learn to anchor your confidence in God rather than in outcomes or approval. The secret place becomes the foundation where courage is shaped.

Many people wait to feel bold before stepping forward. Scripture shows the opposite. Boldness is built as you spend time with God, allowing His presence to steady your heart. When fear arises, what you have cultivated in private will sustain you in public.

Today's encouragement is to return to the secret place. Spend time with God, not to perform, but to be strengthened. As you grow confident in who He is, boldness will naturally follow.

Reflection

Where do you need to spend more time with God to strengthen your confidence?

Life Application

Set aside intentional quiet time today to sit with God and allow His presence to steady your heart.

Prayer

Father, thank You for being my light and my salvation. Strengthen me in Your presence and build boldness in my heart as I trust You more deeply. Amen.

June 5

Boldness That Comes Through Prayer

Acts 4:29 (NIV)
"Now, Lord, consider their threats and enable your servants to speak your word with great boldness."

Devotional

Boldness through Christ is often birthed in prayer. In this verse, the believers did not ask God to remove opposition or make their circumstances easier. They asked for boldness. Their confidence was rooted in God's power, not in a change of environment.

Prayer shifts your focus from fear to faith. When you bring your concerns honestly before God, boldness begins to rise because you are no longer relying on your own strength. Prayer reminds you that God is aware, present, and actively involved in what you are facing.

Speaking God's word with boldness requires trust. It means choosing obedience even when resistance exists. Prayer strengthens that trust by aligning your heart with God's purpose and reminding you that He equips those He calls.

Today's encouragement is to pray boldly. Bring your concerns to God and ask Him for courage rather than comfort. As you do, boldness will grow, grounded in the confidence that God hears and responds.

Reflection

How does prayer influence your courage when facing difficult situations?

Life Application

Pray intentionally today for boldness in one area where fear has been holding you back.

Prayer

Lord, help me approach You honestly and boldly. Give me the courage to speak and live according to Your truth as I trust You more deeply. Amen.

June 6

Boldness That Comes from Being Heard

Psalm 138:3 (NIV)

"When I called, you answered me; you greatly emboldened me."

Devotional

Boldness through Christ grows when you trust that God hears you. This verse connects courage directly to answered prayer. The psalmist does not describe boldness as something he produced on his own. It came as a response to calling on God and receiving assurance that he was heard.

When you know God listens, fear begins to lose its grip. Being heard by God strengthens your inner confidence and steadies your heart. Boldness rises not because circumstances immediately change, but because your trust in God deepens.

Many people hesitate to act boldly because they feel unseen or unheard. Scripture reminds you that God is attentive and responsive. His answers may not always look the way you expect, but His presence emboldens you from the inside out.

Today's encouragement is to call on God with confidence. As you trust that He hears you, boldness will continue to grow, anchored in relationship rather than outcome.

Reflection

How does knowing God hears you affect your confidence and courage?

Life Application

Bring a concern honestly to God today and trust that He hears you and responds with strength.

Prayer

Father, thank You for hearing me when I call. Strengthen my heart and embolden me as I trust You more deeply. Amen.

June 7

Boldness Strengthened by God's Grip

Micah 3:8 (NIV)
"But as for me, I am filled with power, with the Spirit of the Lord, and with justice and might, to declare to Jacob his transgression, to Israel his sin."

Devotional

Boldness does not come from personality or position. It comes from being filled by the Spirit of the Lord. This verse makes it clear that strength is not self-generated. It is given. God's grip on your life is what empowers you to stand firm, speak truth, and move forward with courage.

The power described here is not aggressive or self-serving. It is grounded in justice and guided by God's purpose. When the Spirit strengthens you, boldness becomes obedience rather than bravado. You are able to say what needs to be said and do what needs to be done, even when it feels uncomfortable.

God's grip steadies you when fear tries to weaken your resolve. You do not have to manufacture confidence. When you rely on the Spirit, strength rises from trust, not effort. Boldness grows when you remember whose power is at work within you.

Reflection
Where do you need to rely more on God's strength instead of your own?

Life Application
Today, step into one situation with confidence, trusting that God's Spirit is strengthening you.

Prayer
God, thank You for filling me with Your Spirit and strength. Help me rely on Your power, not my own, as I walk boldly in obedience to You. Amen.

June 8

Boldness That Rises When Fear Tries to Speak

Psalm 56:3 (NIV)
"When I am afraid, I put my trust in you."

Devotional

Boldness through Christ does not deny fear. It confronts it with trust. This verse does not shame fear or pretend it does not exist. Instead, it shows you what to do when fear arises. Boldness begins when trust replaces panic and faith interrupts uncertainty.

Fear often tries to speak louder than truth. It whispers hesitation, doubt, and worst-case scenarios. Trust shifts the focus away from fear and back to God. Boldness grows when you choose to trust God even while fear is present rather than waiting for fear to disappear.

This verse reminds you that trust is an intentional response. You decide where your confidence will rest. When fear shows up, you can choose to anchor yourself in God's character and faithfulness. That choice strengthens boldness one moment at a time.

Today's encouragement is to name your fear and place it before God. Trust does not require certainty. It requires surrender. As you place your trust in Him, boldness will rise quietly and steadily within you.

Reflection

What fear do you need to intentionally place in God's hands today?

Life Application

When fear surfaces today, pause and choose to trust God rather than reacting to the fear.

Prayer

Father, when fear arises, help me place my trust in You. Strengthen my heart and grow boldness within me as I rely on You. Amen.

June 9

Boldness Strengthened from the Inside Out

Ephesians 6:10 (NIV)

"Finally, be strong in the Lord and in his mighty power."

Devotional

Boldness through Christ is not rooted in self-effort. It is strengthened from the inside out through dependence on God's power. This verse reminds you that strength is not something you generate. It is something you receive as you remain connected to the Lord.

Many people attempt to walk boldly by pushing themselves harder or relying on determination alone. Scripture redirects that approach. True strength flows from the Lord and His power, not from personal resolve. Boldness becomes sustainable when it is anchored in God rather than in your own capacity.

Being strong in the Lord requires intentional reliance. It means recognizing your limitations and trusting God's might to carry you through what you cannot handle alone. When you lean into God's strength, boldness becomes steady rather than exhausting.

Today's encouragement is to draw strength from the Lord. You do not have to rely on your own power to move forward. As you remain rooted in Him, boldness will rise naturally and confidently.

Reflection

Where have you been relying on your own strength instead of God's?

Life Application

Pause today and intentionally place a responsibility or concern into God's hands, choosing to rely on His strength rather than your own.

Prayer

Father, help me be strong in You and not in myself. Teach me to rely on Your power and walk forward with boldness rooted in trust in You. Amen.

June 10

Boldness Sustained by Hope

Colossians 1:11 (NIV)
"Being strengthened with all power according to his glorious might so that you may have great endurance and patience."

Devotional

Boldness through Christ is not only about starting strong. It is about enduring with faith and patience. This verse reminds you that God strengthens you according to His power, not your own. That strength is designed to sustain you when bold obedience requires perseverance rather than immediate results.

Many people associate boldness with decisive moments, but Scripture highlights endurance as an essential part of courage. Patience does not mean passivity. It means remaining faithful and confident while waiting for God's purposes to unfold. Boldness is sustained when hope anchors your heart during seasons that test your resolve.

God's strength equips you to endure without becoming discouraged. It steadies you when progress feels slow and reminds you that His power is actively at work even when outcomes are not yet visible. As patience grows, boldness matures into quiet confidence.

Today's encouragement is to trust God for sustained strength. Allow His power to carry you through moments that require endurance. As you remain patient and hopeful, boldness will continue to rise within you.

Reflection

Where do you need endurance and patience in your walk with God right now?

Life Application

Choose to remain faithful today in one area that requires patience, trusting God to strengthen you as you wait.

Prayer

Father, thank You for strengthening me according to Your power. Help me endure with patience and hope as I walk forward in bold obedience. Amen.

June 11

Boldness That Holds Its Confidence

Hebrews 10:35 (NIV)

"So do not throw away your confidence; it will be richly rewarded."

Devotional

Boldness through Christ requires perseverance. Confidence can be challenged when outcomes take longer than expected or when obedience feels costly. This verse offers a steady reminder that confidence rooted in God is worth protecting. It is not wasted or misplaced.

Throwing away confidence often happens quietly. Doubt creeps in. Weariness sets in. Questions begin to cloud trust. Scripture calls you to hold onto confidence because God honors faith that remains steady even when results are delayed.

Confidence in Christ is not self-assurance. It is trust that God sees your obedience and values your faithfulness. Boldness grows as you refuse to abandon confidence during seasons that test your patience and resolve.

Today's encouragement is to guard your confidence. Do not release what God is building within you. As you continue walking in trust, boldness will remain strong and reward will follow in God's timing.

Reflection

What has tempted you to release confidence in recent seasons?

Life Application

Identify one area today where you need to intentionally hold onto confidence rather than retreating in doubt.

Prayer

Father, help me hold onto the confidence You have given me. Strengthen my trust in You and remind me that faithfulness is never wasted. Amen.

June 12

Boldness That Comes from Standing Firm

1 Corinthians 16:13 (NIV)
"Be on your guard; stand firm in the faith; be courageous; be strong."

Devotional

Boldness through Christ is not always about taking big leaps forward. Sometimes it is about standing firm where you are. This verse calls you to remain alert, rooted, and steady in your faith. Courage here is not impulsive. It is intentional and grounded in trust.

Standing firm requires awareness. You are reminded to be on guard, not out of fear, but out of wisdom. Faith is strengthened when you recognize what threatens to pull you away from truth and choose to remain anchored. Boldness grows as you refuse to drift or compromise under pressure.

Courage and strength are paired together in this verse for a reason. Courage without strength fades quickly, and strength without courage lacks direction. God invites you to hold both as you remain firm in your faith. This posture allows boldness to mature and endure.

Today's encouragement is to stand your ground. You do not have to move faster or prove anything. Remain rooted in faith, alert in spirit, and confident in God's presence. As you stand firm, boldness will continue to rise within you.

Reflection

Where is God asking you to stand firm rather than move ahead right now?

Life Application

Identify one area today where you need to remain rooted in faith and choose courage over hesitation.

Prayer

Father, help me stand firm in my faith. Strengthen my courage and help me remain steady and confident as I trust You. Amen.

June 13

Boldness That Refuses to Shrink Back

Habakkuk 2:4 (NLT)
"Look at the proud! They trust in themselves, and their lives are crooked. But the righteous will live by their faithfulness to God."

Devotional

Boldness through Christ is often expressed through faithfulness rather than visibility. This verse contrasts pride and instability with a steady life rooted in faith. The righteous are not described as loud or forceful, but as faithful. Boldness grows when you choose consistency over reaction.

Faithfulness requires resolve. It means continuing to trust God even when outcomes are delayed or opposition feels strong. While others may act out of fear or pride, God calls you to live anchored in trust. Boldness matures as you remain faithful without needing constant affirmation or immediate results.

Living by faithfulness does not mean ignoring challenges. It means refusing to let circumstances dictate your posture. Boldness is sustained when you trust God's process and remain committed to obedience even when it would be easier to retreat.

Today's encouragement is to remain faithful. Do not shrink back or grow weary. As you continue to live anchored in trust, boldness will remain steady and strong within you.

Reflection

Where do you need to choose faithfulness over fear right now?

Life Application

Commit today to one act of faithfulness, even if it feels unseen or unrecognized.

Prayer

Father, help me live by faithfulness and trust You fully. Strengthen my heart to remain steady and bold as I walk in obedience. Amen.

June 14

Courage That Stands Firm

Hebrews 10:39 (NLT)
"But we are not like those who turn away from God to their own destruction. We are the faithful ones, whose souls will be saved."

Devotional

Faith is revealed by what you refuse to abandon. This verse draws a clear distinction between retreat and resolve. Courage, in God's eyes, is not loud or impulsive. It is steady. It is the decision to remain faithful even when turning back would feel easier.

Standing firm does not mean the absence of fear or struggle. It means choosing perseverance over withdrawal. God calls His people faithful not because they never waver, but because they continue forward despite the pressure to quit.

This scripture reminds you that endurance is an act of trust. Each step you take in faith strengthens your soul and deepens your dependence on God. Courage grows when you commit to staying the course, confident that God honors faithfulness.

Reflection
Where are you being tempted to pull back instead of stand firm?

Life Application
When challenges arise today, choose perseverance over retreat and remind yourself that faithfulness leads to life.

Prayer
Lord, help me stand firm in my faith. Strengthen my courage so I remain faithful, trusting You with every step forward. Amen.

June 15

Steady Courage in the Face of Pressure

Proverbs 28:1 (NLT)
"The wicked run away when no one is chasing them, but the godly are as bold as lions."

Devotional

Boldness through Christ produces a steadiness that does not depend on circumstances. This verse contrasts two ways of living. Fear causes unnecessary retreat, while godliness produces quiet confidence. When your life is anchored in truth, you are not easily shaken or driven by pressure.

The boldness described here is not aggressive or loud. It is rooted in integrity and trust in God. When your conscience is clear and your heart is aligned with Him, you can move forward without fear of collapse or retreat. Courage grows when your foundation is secure.

Pressure often reveals what you trust. If your confidence is rooted in performance or approval, fear will follow. But when your confidence rests in God, boldness becomes a natural response. You are not running from what might happen. You are standing firm in who God is.

Today, allow this truth to strengthen you. Godly boldness does not rush or panic. It stands steady, confident that God is faithful and present.

Reflection

What helps you remain steady when pressure or fear tries to push you backward?

Life Application

Choose to respond with calm confidence today instead of reacting in fear.

Prayer

Father, anchor my heart in You so I may walk with steady courage. Help me trust You fully and live with boldness that comes from righteousness. Amen.

June 16

Courage That Flows From Trust

Psalm 27:14 (NLV)

"Wait for the Lord. Be strong and let your heart be brave. Yes, wait for the Lord."

Devotional

Boldness through Christ does not always look like immediate action. Sometimes it looks like the strength to wait. This verse calls for courage that is patient and rooted in trust. Waiting on the Lord is not passive. It requires resolve, discipline, and faith.

Waiting can feel uncomfortable, especially when answers are delayed or direction feels unclear. Yet God often strengthens your heart in seasons of waiting. Courage grows when you choose to trust God's timing instead of forcing your own solutions. Boldness is not rushing ahead. It is remaining faithful while you wait.

This verse also reminds you that strength and bravery are connected to hope. When you wait on the Lord, you are placing your confidence in His faithfulness. That kind of trust steadies your heart and keeps fear from taking over.

Today, allow waiting to become an act of courage. Trust that God is at work even when progress feels slow. Boldness flows when your heart remains anchored in Him.

Reflection

Where is God asking you to wait with courage rather than act out of fear?

Life Application

Choose to trust God's timing today, even if the next step feels unclear.

Prayer

Lord, strengthen my heart as I wait on You. Help me trust Your timing and walk forward with courage rooted in faith. Amen.

June 17

Courage That Is Anchored, Not Rushed

1 Peter 5:10 (NLT)

"In his kindness God called you to share in his eternal glory by means of Christ Jesus. So after you have suffered a little while, he will restore, support, and strengthen you, and he will place you on a firm foundation."

Devotional

Boldness through Christ is not formed in comfort alone. It is shaped through endurance and refined through trust. This verse acknowledges that hardship may come, but it also promises restoration and stability. God does not leave you weakened by what you walk through. He strengthens you because of it.

Courage grows when you understand that difficulty is not permanent. God's work in you continues beyond the season of struggle. Restoration is not rushed, but it is intentional. Each step you take in faith is met with God's sustaining power.

This verse also reminds you that boldness is anchored in God's character, not your circumstances. He restores, supports, and establishes you. When your foundation is secure, you do not need to fear the pressure of the moment or the weight of uncertainty.

Today, let this truth steady you. God is not finished with you. He is strengthening you and placing you firmly where you need to stand.

Reflection

How has God strengthened you through a season that once felt overwhelming?

Life Application

Reflect on a past challenge and acknowledge how God supported and restored you through it.

Prayer

Father, thank You for Your kindness and faithfulness. Strengthen me through every season and anchor my courage firmly in You. Amen.

June 18

Courage That Keeps Going

2 Chronicles 15:7 (NLT)
"But as for you, be strong and courageous, for your work will be rewarded."

Devotional

Boldness through Christ is often revealed in perseverance. This verse speaks directly to the strength required to keep going when progress feels slow or unseen. God's encouragement here is not abstract. It is practical and forward looking. Strength and courage are tied to continuing the work set before you.

There are seasons when obedience feels exhausting rather than exciting. In those moments, courage is not about dramatic faith moves. It is about staying committed. God sees faithfulness that others may overlook. He promises that continued obedience will not be wasted.

This verse also reminds you that courage is sustained by hope. Knowing that your labor has purpose allows you to move forward even when results are delayed. Boldness grows when you trust that God honors faithfulness in His timing.

Today, let this truth strengthen you. Do not give up. Remain courageous and steady. God is at work, and your faithfulness matters more than you realize.

Reflection

Where do you need renewed strength to keep going rather than pulling back?

Life Application

Choose to remain faithful today in one area where you have been tempted to grow weary.

Prayer

Father, strengthen my heart to remain courageous and faithful. Help me trust that You see my efforts and will reward obedience in Your time. Amen.

June 19

Courage That Trusts God's Nearness

Nahum 1:7 (NLT)
"The Lord is good, a strong refuge when trouble comes. He is close to those who trust in him."

Devotional

Boldness through Christ is not rooted in self-assurance. It grows from trusting God's nearness. This verse reminds you that courage does not come from avoiding trouble but from knowing where to turn when it arrives. God is not distant in difficult moments. He is a refuge and He is close.

Trust deepens when you understand that God's goodness does not disappear during hardship. He remains steady and present, offering strength when you feel vulnerable. Courage is often quiet confidence that God is with you even when circumstances feel uncertain.

This verse also reminds you that trust is relational. God draws near to those who place their confidence in Him. When you lean into His presence, fear loosens its grip and boldness takes root. You do not face challenges alone.

Today, allow this truth to anchor your heart. God is near, He is good, and He is your refuge. Courage grows when you rest in who He is rather than what you fear.

Reflection

How does knowing God is close change the way you face difficulty?

Life Application

When you feel pressure today, pause and remind yourself that God is your refuge and He is near.

Prayer

Father, thank You for being close and faithful. Help me trust You fully and walk forward with courage grounded in Your presence. Amen.

June 20

Courage That Is Built Over Time

Hebrews 3:14 (NLT)

"For if we are faithful to the end, trusting God just as firmly as when we first believed, we will share in all that belongs to Christ."

Devotional

Boldness through Christ is not something you borrow for a moment. It is built through consistency and endurance. This verse reminds you that courage is sustained when you continue trusting God with the same conviction you had at the beginning of your faith journey.

Over time, challenges can dull your confidence or cause you to question what you once believed with clarity. God calls you to remain steady. Faithfulness is not perfection. It is perseverance. Courage grows as you choose to keep trusting, even when the journey feels long.

This verse highlights the importance of holding firmly to your faith. Confidence does not come from new revelations alone. It comes from remaining rooted in truth you already know. Boldness matures when faith becomes steady rather than reactive.

Today, let this encourage you to stay the course. The courage you need for tomorrow is strengthened by faithfulness today. God honors those who continue trusting Him through every season.

Reflection

What helps you remain faithful when your confidence feels tested?

Life Application

Recommit today to trusting God with the same assurance you had when your faith was first ignited.

Prayer

Lord, help me remain faithful and steady in my trust. Strengthen my courage as I continue walking with You day by day. Amen.

June 21

Boldness That Comes From Belonging to Christ

Philippians 1:20 (NLT)
"For I fully expect and hope that I will never be ashamed, but that I will continue to be bold for Christ, as I have been in the past. And I trust that my life will bring honor to Christ, whether I live or die."

Devotional

Boldness through Christ is rooted in identity. This verse reflects a confidence that is not dependent on outcome, comfort, or approval. Paul's boldness flows from his belonging to Christ. His life is oriented toward honoring Christ regardless of circumstance.

This kind of boldness is not situational. It does not fade when life becomes uncertain or uncomfortable. When your confidence is anchored in Christ, you are free from the fear of embarrassment or failure. You no longer measure success by ease but by faithfulness.

Boldness expressed this way is purposeful. It shapes how you live, speak, and choose. You are not hiding your faith or diluting your convictions. You live openly aligned with Christ, trusting that your life reflects Him in both visible and quiet ways.

Today, allow this truth to steady you. Boldness is not about being fearless. It is about being unashamed. When Christ is your center, you can live confidently and fully for His glory.

Reflection

Where do you feel tempted to hold back your faith instead of living boldly for Christ?

Life Application

Choose one intentional way today to live openly aligned with Christ through your words or actions.

Prayer

Father, help me live boldly and unashamed for You. Anchor my confidence in who I am in Christ so my life brings You honor. Amen.

June 22

Boldness That Comes From Being Fully Convinced

Romans 14:5 (NLT)

"You may believe there is only one right way to serve the Lord, or you may believe another is better. But be fully convinced that whatever way you choose is best for you."

Devotional

Boldness through Christ includes the confidence to stand firm in conviction without needing universal agreement. This verse speaks to spiritual maturity. Being fully convinced does not mean being rigid or dismissive of others. It means living with clarity before God and taking responsibility for your own obedience.

Many people hesitate to move boldly because they are waiting for affirmation or approval. God calls you to live convinced, not confused. When your choices are rooted in prayer and alignment with Him, you can move forward without constantly questioning yourself.

Boldness grows when you understand that faith is lived personally before God. You are not called to copy another person's walk or compare your obedience to someone else's. Confidence comes when you trust God's guidance in your own life and walk it out faithfully.

Today, let this truth free you from hesitation. Boldness is not about proving your faith. It is about living it fully convinced that you are following God's leading with integrity.

Reflection

Where do you feel uncertain because you are seeking approval instead of trusting God's direction?

Life Application

Make one decision today with clarity and confidence, trusting that God is guiding you as you remain faithful.

Prayer

Lord, help me live fully convinced in my faith. Strengthen my confidence in You so I can walk boldly in obedience without fear or hesitation. Amen.

June 23

Boldness That Refuses to Hide

Matthew 5:14–16 (NLT)

"You are the light of the world - like a city on a hilltop that cannot be hidden. No one lights a lamp and then puts it under a basket. Instead, a lamp is placed on a stand, where it gives light to everyone in the house. In the same way, let your good deeds shine out for all to see, so that everyone will praise your heavenly Father."

Devotional

Boldness through Christ is never meant to stay hidden. Jesus makes it clear that when your life is shaped by Him, it will be visible. Light naturally shines. It does not need to announce itself or force attention. Boldness flows when you live authentically aligned with Christ rather than trying to blend in.

Many people silence their faith out of fear of standing out. Yet Jesus calls you to live openly, allowing your actions to reflect His presence in you. This is not about performance or recognition. It is about living truthfully, without shrinking back from who God has called you to be.

Boldness expressed this way brings glory to God, not to you. When your life reflects His goodness, others are drawn to Him. You are not responsible for how people respond. You are responsible for allowing your faith to be seen through obedience and integrity.

Today, consider where you may be hiding your light. Boldness through Christ invites you to live visibly faithful, trusting that God will use your life to point others to Him.

Reflection

Where might God be inviting you to stop hiding your faith and live more openly for Him?

Life Application

Choose one way today to let your faith be visible through your actions or words.

Prayer

Father, help me live boldly and openly for You. Give me confidence to let my life reflect Your light so that You are glorified through me. Amen.

June 24

Boldness That Flows From a Living Faith

Philemon 1:6 (NLT)
"And I am praying that you will put into action the generosity that comes from your faith as you understand and experience all the good things we have in Christ."

Devotional

Boldness through Christ is not only something you believe. It is something you live out. This verse connects faith directly to action. As you grow in your understanding of who you are in Christ, your faith naturally begins to express itself through generosity, obedience, and confidence.

Many people separate belief from behavior, but Scripture does not. When your faith is alive, it moves. Boldness shows up when you put truth into action rather than keeping it theoretical. Confidence in Christ becomes visible through how you love, serve, and respond to others.

This verse also reminds you that boldness grows as you experience the goodness of Christ personally. When you truly grasp what you have been given, fear loses its grip. You are no longer operating from lack or insecurity. You are living from fullness.

Today, let your faith move beyond words. Boldness through Christ is revealed when your life reflects what you believe and the generosity of spirit that flows from it.

Reflection

How is your faith currently being expressed through your actions?

Life Application

Look for one intentional way today to put your faith into action through generosity, service, or obedience.

Prayer

Lord, help my faith be active and alive. As I grow in understanding all You have given me, let my life reflect boldness rooted in Christ. Amen.

June 25

Boldness That Moves Without Apology

Acts 28:31 (NLT)
"He proclaimed the Kingdom of God and taught about the Lord Jesus Christ with all boldness and without hindrance."

Devotional

Boldness through Christ is not cautious or restrained by fear. This verse describes Paul preaching freely, confidently, and without apology. Even while under limitation, his faith was not restricted. His boldness was rooted in conviction, not circumstance.

This kind of boldness flows from clarity of purpose. When you are confident in what God has called you to do, you are less concerned with obstacles or approval. You move forward because obedience matters more than comfort. Boldness is not the absence of opposition. It is faithfulness in the midst of it.

The phrase "without hindrance" reminds us that external limits do not have to become internal barriers. God's work is not stopped by confinement, resistance, or uncertainty. Boldness through Christ allows you to live fully aligned with Him regardless of what surrounds you.

Today, reflect on how God may be calling you to move forward with greater confidence. Boldness is expressed when you live unapologetically faithful, trusting God to work through you.

Reflection

Where might God be inviting you to live or speak more boldly without fear of restraint?

Life Application

Take one step today that reflects confident obedience, even if it stretches you beyond your comfort zone.

Prayer

Lord, help me live boldly and faithfully for You. Remove any hesitation that keeps me from walking fully in obedience and confidence in Christ. Amen.

June 26

Boldness That Comes From Hope

2 Corinthians 3:12 (NLT)
"Since this new way gives us such confidence, we can be very bold."

Devotional

Boldness through Christ is born from hope, not pressure. This verse reminds you that confidence flows from what God has already done, not from what you are trying to prove. Because of the new life you have in Christ, boldness becomes a natural response rather than a forced one.

Hope reshapes how you live. When you trust what God has established, you no longer move hesitantly or second-guess your steps. Confidence grows because your foundation is secure. Boldness flows when you understand that your life is held by God's faithfulness, not your performance.

This verse also speaks to freedom. The new way Christ has made invites you to live openly, confidently, and without fear of failure. Boldness is not arrogance. It is assurance rooted in truth. When your hope is anchored in Christ, boldness follows.

Today, especially on a day that marks your life, let this truth settle deeply. You can live boldly because your confidence is grounded in Christ and the new life He has given you.

Reflection

How does your hope in Christ shape the way you move forward with confidence?

Life Application

Celebrate today by acknowledging one way God has grown your confidence through faith in Him.

Prayer

Father, thank You for the confidence I have through Christ. Help me live boldly, anchored in hope and trusting fully in the new life You have given me. Amen.

June 27

Boldness That Stands Without Wavering

Psalm 112:7 (NLT)
"They do not fear bad news; they confidently trust the Lord to care for them."

Devotional

Boldness through Christ produces a steady confidence that is not shaken by circumstances. This verse describes a life rooted in trust rather than fear. When your confidence is anchored in the Lord, unsettling news does not control your response or determine your peace.

Many people equate boldness with outward expression, but Scripture often presents boldness as inner stability. Confidence in God allows you to remain calm, grounded, and faithful even when situations feel uncertain. Trust becomes the foundation that keeps you from wavering.

This verse reminds you that boldness is not denial of reality. It is trust in God's care despite it. When your heart is fixed on Him, fear loses its authority. You are free to move forward without being governed by anxiety or worst-case thinking.

Today, let this truth strengthen your posture. Boldness through Christ allows you to stand steady, trusting that God is faithful to care for you in every season.

Reflection

What situation is challenging your trust in God's care right now?

Life Application

When uncertainty arises today, choose to respond with trust instead of fear, reminding yourself that God is caring for you.

Prayer

Father, help me trust You fully and stand confidently in Your care. Strengthen my heart so I may live boldly, anchored in faith rather than fear. Amen.

June 28

Boldness That Is Strengthened by Encouragement

2 Thessalonians 2:16–17 (NLT)
"May our Lord Jesus Christ himself and God our Father, who loved us and by his grace gave us eternal comfort and a wonderful hope, comfort you and strengthen you in every good thing you do and say."

Devotional

Boldness through Christ is strengthened when your heart is encouraged by truth. This verse reminds you that confidence does not come from striving harder, but from receiving comfort and hope that God freely gives. When you are strengthened by Him, boldness becomes steady and sustainable.

Encouragement is often overlooked as a source of boldness, yet it is essential. When God comforts you, He reinforces your confidence and renews your strength. Hope fuels obedience. Confidence grows when you remember that God is actively strengthening you in both word and action.

This verse also highlights that boldness touches how you live and how you speak. God empowers you to move forward faithfully in every good thing you do and say. Boldness through Christ is not limited to isolated moments. It shapes the rhythm of your daily life.

Today, receive the encouragement God offers. Allow His comfort and hope to strengthen you so you can continue living boldly and faithfully in every area of your life.

Reflection

How has God's encouragement strengthened your confidence in a difficult season?

Life Application

Pause today to receive God's comfort and allow it to strengthen your confidence and actions.

Prayer

Father, thank You for the comfort and hope You give so freely. Strengthen me in all I do and say and help me live boldly through the confidence You provide. Amen.

June 29

Boldness That Is Grounded in God's Faithfulness

1 Thessalonians 5:24 (NLT)
"God will make this happen, for he who calls you is faithful."

Devotional

Boldness through Christ grows when you trust God's faithfulness more than your own ability. This verse places the responsibility for fulfillment where it belongs. God is the one who calls, and God is the one who completes what He begins. Your confidence rests in His character, not your performance.

Many people hesitate because they feel unqualified or uncertain. This verse removes that burden. Boldness does not come from having everything figured out. It comes from trusting the One who is faithful to carry out His purpose in you.

Faithfulness means consistency, dependability, and follow-through. When God calls you, He remains committed to His work in your life. That assurance allows you to move forward without fear of failure or abandonment. Boldness grows when you believe that God will finish what He starts.

Today, let this truth steady your heart. You are not responsible for the outcome. You are responsible for obedience. God's faithfulness covers the rest.

Reflection

Where do you need to trust God's faithfulness instead of relying on your own strength?

Life Application

Take one step today in obedience, trusting that God will carry the responsibility for the outcome.

Prayer

Father, thank You for Your faithfulness. Help me live boldly, trusting that You will complete the work You have begun in me. Amen.

June 30

Boldness to Finish Strong

Acts 18:9–10 (NLT)

"One night the Lord spoke to Paul in a vision and told him, 'Don't be afraid! Speak out! Don't be silent! For I am with you, and no one will attack and harm you, for many people in this city belong to me.'"

Devotional

Boldness through Christ is not only about starting strong. It is about finishing faithfully. In this moment, Paul receives direct reassurance from the Lord. God does not minimize fear. He addresses it directly and then commands bold action. Speak. Do not be silent. Keep going.

This boldness is rooted in God's presence. The instruction is not based on Paul's ability or circumstances, but on God's promise to be with him. When God affirms His presence, fear loses its authority. Boldness becomes a response to trust rather than pressure.

God also reminds Paul that his obedience has purpose beyond what he can see. There are people connected to this assignment. Boldness through Christ often requires continuing when you cannot yet see the fruit. Confidence grows when you trust that God is already at work ahead of you.

As this month comes to a close, let this truth anchor you. Boldness is sustained when you remember who is with you and why you are called. Finish this month confident, faithful, and willing to speak and live openly for Christ.

Reflection

Where might God be inviting you to keep going instead of growing quiet or pulling back?

Life Application

Choose today to speak or act boldly in one area where you have been hesitant, trusting that God is with you.

Prayer

Father, thank You for Your presence and reassurance. Help me finish this season boldly, trusting that You are with me and working through my obedience. Amen.

July

Living in Freedom and Grace

July invites you into the fullness of life that comes from living free and grounded in grace. This month is about releasing what no longer has authority over you shame, guilt, regret, fear, and striving and learning how to walk daily in the freedom Christ has already secured. Freedom is not something you earn through effort. It is something you receive and steward through truth.

Grace is the atmosphere where freedom grows. When you understand grace, you stop living as though you must constantly prove yourself to God or others. You begin to rest in what Christ has already finished. This month will guide you in recognizing the difference between conviction and condemnation, obedience and performance, discipline and self-punishment. Living in freedom means you are no longer driven by who you were, but anchored in who God says you are.

As you move through these days, you will be invited to loosen your grip on the things that keep you bound and strengthen your trust in God's redemptive work. Freedom does not remove responsibility, but it does remove fear. Grace does not excuse growth, but it empowers it. This month will help you walk forward lighter, clearer, and more confident in the freedom Christ intended for you to live in every day.

July 1

Freedom Begins With Identity

1 Peter 2:16 (NLT)
"For you are free, yet you are God's slaves, so don't use your freedom as an excuse to do evil."

Devotional

Freedom in Christ begins with understanding who you belong to. This verse reminds you that biblical freedom is not independence from God, but alignment with Him. You are free, yet you live under the loving authority of God. That relationship is not restrictive. It is what makes freedom sustainable and safe.

Many people misunderstand freedom as the absence of boundaries. Scripture presents freedom differently. True freedom is the ability to live fully without being controlled by sin, fear, or old patterns. When you belong to God, you are no longer driven by impulses or expectations that once ruled your life. Grace gives you space to grow without shame, and freedom gives you strength to choose wisely.

This verse also clarifies that freedom is not permission to return to what once held you captive. Grace does not excuse harmful behavior. It empowers transformation. Living free means you are no longer defined by who you were, but guided by who God is shaping you to become.

Today, allow this truth to ground you. Your freedom is real, purposeful, and rooted in belonging to God. As you walk in grace, freedom becomes a daily posture rather than a distant goal.

Reflection

How does knowing you belong to God shape the way you understand freedom in your life?

Life Application

Identify one area where you can choose freedom through obedience rather than old habits or patterns.

Prayer

Father, thank You for the freedom You have given me through Christ. Help me live in that freedom with wisdom, grace, and alignment with Your will. Amen.

July 2

Transferred Into Freedom

Colossians 1:13 (NLT)

"For he has rescued us from the kingdom of darkness and transferred us into the Kingdom of his dear Son."

Devotional

Freedom in Christ is not a mindset shift alone. It is a spiritual relocation. This verse makes it clear that God did not simply improve your situation. He rescued you and transferred you. You no longer belong to what once governed your thoughts, habits, or fears. You live under a new authority and a new covering.

Many people struggle to walk in freedom because they still see themselves as tied to their past. This verse reminds you that your freedom was initiated by God, not earned through effort. Rescue implies intervention. Transfer implies permanence. What once defined you no longer has jurisdiction over your life.

Grace helps you understand that freedom is not fragile. You are not constantly at risk of being pulled back into darkness unless you make a mistake. God intentionally moved you into His Kingdom, where grace sustains growth and truth reshapes identity. Freedom grows as you learn to live from where you now stand.

Today, allow this truth to settle deeply. You are no longer living under old rule or old expectations. You have been transferred into freedom through Christ, and grace is the environment where that freedom continues to flourish.

Reflection

In what ways do you still think or act as though your past has authority over you?

Life Application

When old thoughts or patterns surface today, remind yourself that you no longer live under that authority.

Prayer

Lord, thank You for rescuing me and placing me into Your Kingdom. Help me live freely and confidently in the grace You have given me through Christ. Amen.

July 3

Freedom That Breaks Old Chains

Galatians 5:1 (NLT)

"So Christ has truly set us free. Now make sure that you stay free, and don't get tied up again in slavery to the law."

Devotional

Freedom in Christ is both a gift and a responsibility. This verse declares that Christ has already accomplished the work of setting you free. Your role is not to earn that freedom, but to guard it. Grace gives you freedom, and wisdom helps you remain in it.

Many believers struggle not because freedom is unavailable, but because old patterns still feel familiar. This verse acknowledges that it is possible to return mentally or spiritually to what once held you captive. Grace does not remove choice. It strengthens it. Staying free requires awareness and intentional trust in Christ rather than reliance on old systems of control or performance.

Freedom through Christ is not fragile, but it can be neglected. When you begin to measure yourself by rules, approval, or perfection, you quietly drift back toward bondage. Grace invites you to live anchored in truth rather than fear. Freedom grows as you learn to rest in what Christ has already finished.

Today, consider what staying free looks like for you. Freedom is not about striving harder. It is about trusting deeper and refusing to carry what Christ has already lifted from you.

Reflection

What old mindset or habit tries to pull you back into bondage rather than freedom?

Life Application

Notice when you begin operating from pressure or performance and intentionally return to grace and trust.

Prayer

Father, thank You for the freedom Christ has given me. Help me stay grounded in grace and resist returning to anything that no longer has authority over my life. Amen.

July 4

Freedom Secured by Grace

Ephesians 1:7 (NLT)

"He is so rich in kindness and grace that he purchased our freedom with the blood of his Son and forgave our sins."

Devotional

Freedom in Christ is not abstract or symbolic. It was purchased. This verse anchors your freedom in the grace of God and the finished work of Jesus. Your forgiveness and freedom were not granted casually. They were secured through sacrifice, love, and intention.

Grace reminds you that freedom is not something you negotiate with God. It is something He willingly gave. When you understand this, shame loses its grip. You no longer live as though you must earn your place or repay a debt that has already been settled. Grace declares that the cost has been paid in full.

Many people struggle to live free because they continue to punish themselves for what God has already forgiven. This verse invites you to rest in the truth that your freedom and forgiveness flow from God's kindness, not your consistency. Grace does not ignore sin, but it does remove condemnation.

Today, let this truth realign your heart. Your freedom is rooted in grace and sealed by Christ's sacrifice. You are forgiven, redeemed, and invited to live without carrying what no longer belongs to you.

Reflection

What does it look like for you to truly live forgiven rather than merely knowing you are forgiven?

Life Application

Release any lingering guilt today by reminding yourself that your freedom has already been purchased through Christ.

Prayer

Father, thank You for the grace that secured my freedom. Help me live forgiven, confident, and unburdened by what You have already redeemed. Amen.

July 5

Freedom to Let Go

Isaiah 43:18–19 (NLT)

"But forget all that. It is nothing compared to what I am going to do. For I am about to do something new. See, I have already begun. Do you not see it? I will make a pathway through the wilderness. I will create rivers in the dry wasteland."

Devotional

Freedom in Christ often begins with release. This passage invites you to stop rehearsing what has already passed and to lift your eyes toward what God is doing now. Grace gives you permission to let go of former seasons, former failures, and even former victories that no longer serve where God is leading you.

Many people remain bound not because God is not moving, but because they are still holding tightly to what He has already redeemed or completed. This scripture reminds you that God's work is active and forward moving. Freedom grows when you trust Him enough to release the familiar and step into the new.

Letting go is not denial of the past. It is discernment. God acknowledges what has been, but He does not allow it to define what will be. Grace empowers you to move forward without dragging old weight into a new season. Freedom comes when you recognize that God is already making a way, even if you have not fully seen it yet.

Today, allow this truth to encourage you. You do not have to cling to what God is asking you to release. Freedom is found when you trust that what lies ahead is shaped by His faithfulness and grace.

Reflection

What is God inviting you to release so that you can fully step into what He is doing now?

Life Application

Identify one thought, habit, or memory that no longer serves your growth and intentionally place it in God's hands today.

Prayer

Father, help me release what no longer belongs in this season. Give me eyes to see the new work You are doing and the freedom to walk forward with trust and grace. Amen.

July 6

Freedom to Live Unburdened

Psalm 55:22 (NLT)
"Give your burdens to the Lord, and he will take care of you. He will not permit the godly to slip and fall."

Devotional

Freedom in Christ is experienced most deeply when you stop carrying what was never meant to rest on your shoulders. This verse invites you to release the weight of worry, responsibility, and fear into God's care. Grace reminds you that you are not required to manage everything alone.

Many people live bound by invisible burdens. Expectations, regrets, unanswered questions, and pressure quietly shape how they move through life. This scripture reassures you that God is both willing and able to sustain you. Freedom grows when trust replaces self-reliance.

Letting go does not mean disengaging from life. It means trusting God with what overwhelms you. Grace teaches you that strength is not proven by how much you carry, but by how willing you are to release. Freedom comes when you allow God to support you rather than striving to hold everything together.

Today, consider what burden you have been holding unnecessarily. Christ invites you into a lighter way of living. Freedom is found when you trust God enough to place the weight of your concerns into His hands.

Reflection

What burden have you been carrying that God is inviting you to release?

Life Application

Take a moment today to intentionally give one concern to God and resist the urge to take it back.

Prayer

Father, thank You for inviting me to release my burdens to You. Help me trust Your care and live freely without carrying what You have promised to sustain. Amen.

July 7

Freedom From Condemnation

Romans 8:1 (NLT)
"So now there is no condemnation for those who belong to Christ Jesus."

Devotional

One of the greatest threats to freedom is condemnation. Even after forgiveness, many people continue to live under the weight of guilt, shame, or self-accusation. This verse speaks directly to that struggle. In Christ, condemnation no longer has authority over you.

Grace does not deny accountability, but it removes the sentence of guilt. Condemnation keeps you stuck in who you were. Grace anchors you in who you are becoming. When you understand this distinction, freedom begins to take root at a deeper level.

Living free means you stop rehearsing past mistakes as if they still define you. Condemnation drains confidence and silences growth. Grace restores your ability to move forward with clarity and peace. Freedom grows when you accept that Christ has already spoken the final word over your life.

Today, allow this truth to reset your posture. You belong to Christ. You are not condemned. Freedom is not something you must achieve. It is something you are invited to live out daily through grace.

Reflection

Where have you been holding onto condemnation even though God has already forgiven you?

Life Application

When self-criticism or guilt surfaces today, intentionally replace it with the truth that you are no longer condemned in Christ.

Prayer

Lord, thank You for removing condemnation from my life. Help me live freely, grounded in grace and confident in who I am through Christ. Amen.

July 8

Freedom That Cancels the Record

Colossians 2:14 (NLT)
"He canceled the record of the charges against us and took it away by nailing it to the cross."

Devotional

Freedom begins where accusation ends. This verse declares a finished work that cannot be undone. The record that once stood against you has been completely removed, not revised or reduced, but canceled through the sacrifice of Christ.

God does not merely overlook sin. He deals with it fully. By nailing the record to the cross, Jesus removed every charge that sought to define you by your past. Shame no longer has authority where forgiveness has already been granted.

This freedom changes how you move forward. You are no longer carrying what Christ has already taken away. The cross stands as proof that condemnation has been silenced and grace has taken its place.

Living in freedom means refusing to revisit what God has erased. When guilt tries to resurface, return to this truth. The record is canceled. You are forgiven, restored, and free.

Reflection
What past accusation do you need to release today?

Life Application
When guilt or shame arises, remind yourself that Christ has already canceled the record against you.

Prayer
Jesus, thank You for canceling every charge against me. Help me live in the freedom You secured and walk forward without shame or fear. Amen.

July 9

Freedom Defined by Christ

John 8:36 (NLT)
"So if the Son sets you free, you are truly free."

Devotional

Freedom in Christ is not a feeling or a temporary release from pressure. It is a settled reality established by Jesus Himself. This verse removes every question about the source and permanence of freedom. If Christ is the one who sets you free, that freedom is complete and unquestionable.

Many people measure freedom by circumstance or emotional state. Scripture defines it differently. Freedom is rooted in who Christ is and what He has done, not in how you feel on a given day. When Jesus declares you free, no past failure, accusation, or fear has the authority to contradict that truth.

Grace helps you live from this place of assurance. You do not have to constantly evaluate whether you are free enough or doing enough. Freedom is not something you maintain through effort. It is something you live out through trust and obedience.

Today, let this verse settle deeply. Your freedom is not conditional or partial. It is real, secure, and anchored in Christ. Living in freedom means believing what Jesus has already declared over your life.

Reflection

Where do you still measure freedom by circumstances instead of Christ's truth?

Life Application

When doubt or pressure arises today, remind yourself that Christ has already declared you truly free.

Prayer

Father, thank You for the freedom that comes through Christ alone. Help me live confidently in the truth that I am truly free because of Him. Amen.

July 10

Freedom to Walk Lightly

Matthew 11:28–29 (NLT)
"Then Jesus said, 'Come to me, all of you who are weary and carry heavy burdens, and I will give you rest. Take my yoke upon you. Let me teach you, because I am humble and gentle at heart, and you will find rest for your souls.'"

Devotional

Freedom in Christ is often felt most clearly as rest. Jesus does not invite you into another system of pressure or performance. He invites you to come as you are, weary and burdened, and receive rest for your soul. Grace creates space for your heart to breathe again.

Many people confuse freedom with doing more or striving harder. This passage reframes freedom as release. When you take on Christ's yoke, you are not adding weight. You are exchanging what exhausts you for what sustains you. His way is not harsh or demanding. It is gentle and life giving.

Walking lightly does not mean avoiding responsibility. It means learning a new posture. Grace teaches you how to move through life without carrying unnecessary heaviness. Freedom grows when you allow Christ to lead rather than trying to hold everything together yourself.

Today, listen to the invitation of Jesus. Freedom is not found in pushing through exhaustion. It is found in coming close to Him and learning how to walk in rest, trust, and grace.

Reflection

What burden have you been carrying that Jesus may be inviting you to release?

Life Application

Pause today and intentionally place one source of weariness into God's hands, choosing rest instead of striving.

Prayer

Lord, thank You for inviting me into rest. Teach me how to walk lightly, trusting You with what weighs me down and living freely through Your grace. Amen.

July 11

Freedom to Live Unrestricted

2 Corinthians 3:17 (NLT)
"For the Lord is the Spirit, and wherever the Spirit of the Lord is, there is freedom."

Devotional

Freedom is not found in the absence of limits, but in the presence of God's Spirit. This verse reminds you that true freedom flows from relationship, not circumstance. Where the Spirit of the Lord is active, restriction loses its power.

Living unrestricted does not mean living without responsibility or direction. It means being released from fear, shame, and bondage that once constrained you. The Spirit brings clarity, peace, and the ability to move forward without the weight of what once held you back.

God's Spirit creates space for growth. When He leads, freedom follows. You are no longer bound by old patterns or internal barriers. His presence invites you to live fully, guided by truth rather than limitation.

This scripture calls you to remain aware of where your freedom comes from. As you stay connected to God's Spirit, freedom becomes a way of life, shaping how you think, choose, and move forward each day.

Reflection
Where do you need to invite God's Spirit to bring greater freedom?

Life Application
Today, release one internal limitation and ask the Spirit to guide you forward in freedom.

Prayer
Lord, thank You for the freedom found in Your presence. Help me live unrestricted, led by Your Spirit and grounded in Your truth. Amen.

July 12

Freedom That Is Governed by Peace

Colossians 3:15 (NLT)
"And let the peace that comes from Christ rule in your hearts. For as members of one body you are called to live in peace. And always be thankful."

Devotional

Freedom in Christ is sustained when peace is allowed to lead. This verse reminds you that peace is not just a feeling to experience occasionally. It is meant to rule. When Christ's peace governs your heart, it becomes a steady guide for your decisions, responses, and relationships.

Many people lose their sense of freedom when they allow anxiety, pressure, or internal conflict to take control. Grace invites you into a different rhythm. When peace rules, you are no longer driven by urgency or fear. You are guided by trust and clarity. Freedom grows when you let peace set the pace of your life.

This verse also connects peace with gratitude. A thankful heart recognizes grace at work and resists the pull of dissatisfaction or comparison. Freedom flourishes when you remain grounded in what Christ has already provided rather than chasing what you think is missing.

Today, consider what is ruling your heart. Freedom through Christ deepens when peace is given authority. Grace allows you to slow down, listen, and live from a place of calm assurance rather than inner striving.

Reflection

What tends to rule your heart when you feel pressured or uncertain?

Life Application

Pause today and intentionally choose peace as your guide before making a decision or responding to a situation.

Prayer

Father, thank You for the peace that comes through Christ. Help me allow that peace to rule my heart so I can live freely, grounded in grace and trust. Amen.

July 13

Freedom That Flows From Forgiveness

Ephesians 4:32 (NLT)

"Instead, be kind to each other, tenderhearted, forgiving one another, just as God through Christ has forgiven you."

Devotional

Freedom in Christ is sustained through forgiveness. This verse reminds you that grace is not only something you receive, but something you are invited to extend. When forgiveness flows freely, it releases both the giver and the receiver from the weight of offense and resentment.

Many people remain bound not because God has withheld grace, but because unforgiveness has quietly taken root. Holding onto hurt often feels justified, yet it slowly restricts your freedom. Grace teaches you that forgiveness is not minimizing pain or excusing wrongdoing. It is choosing not to remain tethered to what wounded you.

This verse grounds forgiveness in Christ's example. You forgive not because the other person deserves it, but because you have been forgiven. Grace reshapes your response to others by reminding you how deeply God has extended mercy toward you. Freedom grows when forgiveness becomes a posture rather than a struggle.

Today, reflect on where forgiveness may still be needed. Living free means releasing what no longer has authority over your heart. Grace gives you the strength to forgive, not through force, but through trust in God's justice and healing.

Reflection

Is there anyone or any situation you may still be holding onto that God is inviting you to forgive?

Life Application

Ask God to show you one place where forgiveness could bring greater freedom to your heart and take a step toward release.

Prayer

Father, thank You for the forgiveness You have given me through Christ. Help me extend that same grace to others so I may live freely, unburdened by resentment or offense. Amen.

July 14

Freedom to Walk Without Fear

Psalm 34:4 (NLT)

"I prayed to the Lord, and he answered me. He freed me from all my fears."

Devotional

Freedom in Christ is deeply connected to freedom from fear. This verse captures a simple yet powerful exchange. Prayer becomes the place where fear loses its hold. When you bring what frightens you into God's presence, He responds not just with comfort, but with deliverance.

Fear often disguises itself as caution, logic, or self-protection. Over time, it can quietly restrict your decisions, limit your obedience, and shrink your confidence. Grace invites you to confront fear honestly rather than accommodate it. Freedom grows when fear is named and surrendered instead of managed.

This verse also reminds you that freedom from fear is relational. The psalmist prayed, and the Lord answered. God does not dismiss your fears or shame you for having them. He meets you in them. Grace assures you that fear does not disqualify you. It becomes the very place where God demonstrates His faithfulness.

Today, consider what fear has been influencing your thoughts or actions. Living in freedom means trusting God enough to bring fear into the light and allow Him to replace it with peace, confidence, and assurance.

Reflection

What fear has been quietly influencing your decisions or limiting your obedience?

Life Application

Take time today to pray specifically about one fear and trust God to meet you with freedom and peace.

Prayer

Father, thank You for hearing me when I call on You. Help me release every fear into Your hands and walk forward in the freedom You provide through grace. Amen.

July 15

Freedom to Be Led, Not Driven

Romans 8:14 (NLT)

"For all who are led by the Spirit of God are children of God."

Devotional

Freedom in Christ changes the way you move through life. Instead of being driven by pressure, fear, or expectation, you are invited to be led by the Spirit of God. This verse reminds you that your identity as God's child is closely connected to how you are guided. Freedom is not found in control, but in trust.

Many people live driven lives without realizing it. They feel compelled to prove themselves, meet every demand, or respond to every urgency. Grace introduces a different rhythm. When you are led by the Spirit, your steps are intentional rather than reactive. Freedom grows as you learn to listen and follow rather than rush and strive.

Being led by the Spirit does not mean life becomes effortless. It means your direction is anchored. You are no longer making decisions out of fear of falling behind or missing out. Instead, you move with confidence, knowing that God is actively guiding your path and shaping your growth.

Today, consider what has been driving you lately. Freedom in Christ invites you to slow down and allow the Spirit to lead. Grace assures you that being led is safer and more sustaining than being driven.

Reflection

Where do you notice pressure or urgency driving your decisions rather than the Spirit's leading?

Life Application

Pause before your next decision today and ask the Holy Spirit to guide you rather than relying on habit or pressure.

Prayer

Father, thank You for calling me Your child and guiding me by Your Spirit. Help me live freely by following Your leading and releasing the need to be driven by pressure or fear. Amen.

July 16

Freedom to Live Authentically

Psalm 139:23–24 (NLT)
"Search me, O God, and know my heart; test me and know my anxious thoughts. Point out anything in me that offends you, and lead me along the path of everlasting life."

Devotional

Freedom in Christ allows you to live honestly before God without fear of rejection. This verse is an invitation to openness, not exposure. Grace creates a safe place where you can bring your whole self before God, trusting that His guidance is rooted in love, not condemnation.

Many people avoid self-examination because they associate it with shame or criticism. Scripture presents it differently. When you invite God to search your heart, you are trusting Him to lead you toward freedom rather than punishment. Authenticity becomes possible when you believe God is for you, not against you.

This verse also highlights the connection between freedom and guidance. God does not reveal areas of growth to leave you stuck. He reveals them to lead you forward. Grace gives you the courage to face what needs healing, knowing that God's intention is restoration and life.

Today, consider what it means to live authentically before God. Freedom is not pretending everything is fine. It is trusting God enough to let Him guide you honestly and gently into deeper life with Him.

Reflection

What might God be inviting you to acknowledge or bring honestly before Him right now?

Life Application

Take a quiet moment today to invite God to search your heart and trust His guidance without fear.

Prayer

Father, thank You for loving me enough to guide me with truth and grace. Help me live authentically before You, trusting Your direction and walking freely in Your care. Amen.

July 17

Freedom That Walks in Truth

Psalm 119:45 (NLT)
"I will walk in freedom, for I have devoted myself to your commandments."

Devotional

Freedom in Christ is not random or reckless. It is rooted in truth. This verse connects freedom directly to devotion to God's ways. Scripture makes it clear that freedom grows when your life is aligned with truth rather than ruled by impulse or emotion.

Many people believe freedom means doing whatever feels right in the moment. The psalmist presents a different picture. True freedom is found in walking according to God's wisdom. Grace teaches you that obedience is not restrictive. It is protective. When your steps are guided by truth, you are freed from confusion, regret, and unnecessary consequences.

This verse also highlights intentionality. Freedom is not passive. It is a choice to walk differently, guided by God's Word. Grace empowers you to live with clarity and purpose rather than reacting to every feeling or circumstance. Freedom becomes a daily posture shaped by devotion and trust.

Today, consider what it means to walk in freedom rather than merely desire it. Living free is not about resisting God's guidance. It is about embracing it as the path that leads to peace, confidence, and lasting growth.

Reflection

How does your understanding of freedom change when it is connected to truth and obedience?

Life Application

Choose one area today where you will intentionally align your actions with God's truth rather than habit or impulse.

Prayer

Father, thank You for guiding me with truth. Help me walk in freedom as I devote my life to Your ways, trusting that Your guidance leads to life and peace. Amen.

July 18

Freedom That Chooses a New Way

Romans 6:18 (NLT)
"Now you are free from your slavery to sin, and you have become slaves to righteous living."

Devotional

Freedom in Christ is not simply release from what once bound you. It is an invitation into a new way of living. This verse reminds you that freedom always leads somewhere. When sin no longer has authority over you, righteousness becomes the new direction of your life.

Grace reframes the idea of obedience. Righteous living is not forced or restrictive. It is the natural result of being set free. When old chains are broken, new choices become possible. Freedom grows as you learn to walk in alignment with who God has made you to be rather than who you used to be.

This verse also challenges the belief that freedom means living without guidance. Scripture presents freedom as being rightly aligned. When you belong to Christ, your life is shaped by truth, purpose, and clarity. Grace empowers you to choose what leads to life rather than what leads back to bondage.

Today, consider how freedom is shaping your choices. Living free means you are no longer controlled by old patterns. You are free to choose what reflects the new life God is forming within you.

Reflection

How has freedom in Christ changed the choices you are making in this season?

Life Application

Identify one decision today where you can intentionally choose what aligns with the new life God is shaping in you.

Prayer

Father, thank You for freeing me from what once controlled my life. Help me walk confidently in the new way You have set before me, choosing righteousness through grace. Amen.

July 19

Freedom That Is Marked by Mercy

Micah 7:18 (NLT)
"Where is another God like you, who pardons the guilt of the remnant, overlooking the sins of his special people? You will not stay angry with your people forever, because you delight in showing unfailing love."

Devotional

Freedom in Christ is deeply connected to the mercy of God. This verse reveals God's heart not as distant or easily angered, but as one who delights in forgiveness. Grace is not something God offers reluctantly. It flows from His nature and His love for His people.

Many people struggle to live freely because they assume God remains frustrated or disappointed with them. This scripture dismantles that belief. God does not cling to anger. He releases guilt. Mercy clears the way for freedom by removing the weight of shame that keeps you stuck in the past.

Grace allows you to see God clearly. He is not counting failures or waiting for you to prove yourself. He delights in restoring you. Freedom grows when you believe that mercy is not temporary, but a defining feature of your relationship with God.

Today, let this truth soften your heart. Living in freedom means trusting that God's mercy is greater than your mistakes and stronger than your fear. Grace invites you to live unburdened, confident in His unfailing love.

Reflection

What does it look like for you to truly believe that God delights in showing you mercy?

Life Application

Release any lingering guilt today by reminding yourself of God's mercy and choosing to move forward freely.

Prayer

Father, thank You for Your mercy and unfailing love. Help me live freely, trusting that You pardon my guilt and invite me forward with grace. Amen.

July 20

Freedom That Is Rooted in Grace

2 Timothy 1:9 (NLT)
"For God saved us and called us to live a holy life. He did this, not because we deserved it, but because that was his plan from before the beginning of time - to show us his grace through Christ Jesus."

Devotional

Freedom in Christ begins with understanding that grace was never a response to your performance. This verse reminds you that God's decision to save and call you was intentional and established long before you could earn or disqualify yourself. Freedom grows when you stop trying to justify your worth and rest in God's purpose.

Many people struggle to live freely because they believe they must continually prove themselves to God. Grace dismantles that pressure. Your calling is not built on your effort, but on God's plan. When you understand this, striving gives way to peace, and freedom replaces fear.

This verse also connects freedom to purpose. Grace does not remove responsibility, but it removes shame. You are called to live a life shaped by holiness, not as a burden, but as a response to God's love. Freedom flourishes when obedience flows from gratitude rather than obligation.

Today, allow this truth to settle in your heart. You are not living under earned approval. You are living within God's gracious design. Freedom in Christ means you are secure, called, and sustained by grace.

Reflection

Where do you still feel pressure to earn what God has already given freely?

Life Application

When feelings of inadequacy arise today, remind yourself that God's grace and calling were established long before your efforts.

Prayer

Father, thank You for saving and calling me by Your grace. Help me live freely, grounded in Your purpose and released from the need to earn Your love. Amen.

July 21

Freedom to Draw Near

Psalm 130:4 (NLT)
"But you offer forgiveness, that we might learn to fear you."
Devotional

Freedom in Christ creates access rather than distance. This verse reveals a powerful truth. God's forgiveness does not push you away in shame. It draws you closer in reverence and trust. Grace removes fear of rejection and replaces it with a desire for relationship.

Many people assume forgiveness should lead to guilt or self-restraint. Scripture shows the opposite. Forgiveness opens the door for intimacy with God. When you know you are forgiven, you are no longer hiding or hesitating. Freedom grows as you approach God honestly rather than cautiously.

This verse also reframes what it means to fear the Lord. It is not terror or anxiety. It is awe and respect rooted in love. Grace teaches you that God's forgiveness is not casual, but it is generous. Freedom allows you to come near with humility and confidence at the same time.

Today, reflect on how forgiveness shapes your relationship with God. Living in freedom means you no longer keep your distance. Grace invites you to draw near, trusting that God's mercy welcomes you fully.

Reflection

How does knowing you are forgiven change the way you approach God?
Life Application

Spend intentional time today drawing near to God in prayer, trusting His forgiveness rather than holding back.
Prayer

Father, thank You for Your forgiveness that invites me closer to You. Help me live freely, approaching You with trust, reverence, and gratitude for Your grace. Amen.

July 22

Freedom from the Weight of Yesterday

Psalm 103:11–12 (NIV)

"For as high as the heavens are above the earth, so great is his love for those who fear him; as far as the east is from the west, so far has he removed our transgressions from us."

Devotional

Many people struggle to walk freely with God not because they are still sinning, but because they are still carrying what God has already removed. This scripture paints a picture of distance that cannot be measured. East and west never meet, and that is how completely God has separated you from your past.

Grace is not partial forgiveness. It is not probation. It is not God waiting to see if you will mess up again. Grace is full removal. When God forgives, He does not revisit the offense. He does not rehearse it. He does not hold it over your head. What He removes, He removes completely.

Yet often, we continue to live as though our past still has authority. We rehearse old failures, replay former mistakes, and allow shame to speak louder than truth. But grace calls you to a different posture. It invites you to stop identifying with what God has already released and start living from what He has restored.

Freedom begins when you agree with God more than you agree with your memory. Today is an invitation to loosen your grip on yesterday and stand firmly in the grace that is already yours.

Reflection

What past mistake or memory do you continue to carry that God has already forgiven?

Life Application

When shame or regret tries to resurface today, intentionally remind yourself that God has removed it completely and you are free to move forward.

Prayer

Father, thank You for removing my sins completely and loving me without condition. Help me stop carrying what You have already taken away and teach me to walk fully in the freedom of Your grace. Amen.

July 23

Unshaken by Love

Isaiah 54:10 (NLT)

"For the mountains may move and the hills disappear, but even then my faithful love for you will remain. My covenant of blessing will never be broken," says the Lord, who has mercy on you.

Devotional

Life has a way of shifting what once felt stable. Relationships change, plans unravel, and seasons move in unexpected directions. God acknowledges that reality in this verse. He does not promise that circumstances will never shake. He promises that His love will not.

God's faithful love is not tied to external stability. It is rooted in His character. Even when everything around you feels uncertain, His covenant remains intact. His mercy does not weaken under pressure, and His blessing is not revoked by transition or loss.

Freedom grows when you stop anchoring your security to things that can move and instead rest in what cannot. God's love is unshaken, unchanging, and unwavering. When you believe this, fear loses its grip and confidence begins to rise again.

Today, let God's faithful love steady your heart. You are held by a promise that cannot be broken, no matter what shifts around you.

Reflection

What areas of your life feel uncertain right now, and how does knowing God's love is unshaken bring peace?

Life Application

When circumstances feel unstable today, pause and remind yourself that God's faithful love remains constant.

Prayer

Lord, thank You that Your love does not change when life does. Help me rest in Your mercy and trust Your promises even when things around me feel uncertain. Amen.

July 24

Joy in Being Forgiven

Psalm 32:1 (NLT)

"Oh, what joy for those whose disobedience is forgiven, whose sin is put out of sight."

Devotional

There is a deep and freeing joy that comes from knowing you are forgiven. Not managed. Not tolerated. Forgiven. This verse reminds us that forgiveness is not meant to leave us in shame or quiet relief. It is meant to restore joy.

Many people carry the weight of past mistakes long after God has released them. They believe forgiveness removes the penalty but not the memory. Yet Scripture tells us that God puts our sin out of sight. When He forgives, He does not keep reminding. He restores relationship and invites you to live unburdened.

Grace allows you to stop rehearsing what God has already erased. It gives you permission to smile again, to breathe freely, and to walk forward without dragging guilt behind you. Forgiveness is not just a theological truth. It is a daily invitation to live lighter.

Today, allow joy to rise again. You are forgiven, and what God has put out of sight does not need to remain in yours.

Reflection

What past failure or mistake do you find yourself revisiting even though God has forgiven it?

Life Application

When guilt surfaces today, intentionally thank God for His forgiveness and choose joy instead of self-condemnation.

Prayer

Father, thank You for forgiving me completely and restoring joy to my heart. Help me release what You have already put out of sight and walk freely in Your grace. Amen.

July 25

Made Clean by Grace

Isaiah 1:18 (NLT)

"Though your sins are like scarlet, I will make them as white as snow. Though they are red like crimson, I will make them as white as wool."

Devotional

God does not minimize sin, but He never magnifies it more than His grace. This verse acknowledges the depth of brokenness while declaring the greater power of restoration. What once marked you does not have to define you. God specializes in transformation that goes deeper than appearance and reaches the heart.

Grace is not about pretending the past never happened. It is about allowing God to redeem it completely. He takes what feels stained, heavy, and permanent and makes it clean again. When God restores, He does not leave residue behind. He renews fully and intentionally.

Many people struggle to accept this level of grace because it feels too generous. They believe forgiveness must be earned or proven over time. Yet God's grace works instantly. The moment you turn toward Him, He responds with cleansing, not condemnation.

Today, let go of the labels you have placed on yourself. God calls you clean, restored, and renewed. Walk forward with confidence, knowing that grace has rewritten your story.

Reflection

What past mistake or memory do you struggle to believe God has fully cleansed?

Life Application

When feelings of guilt or shame arise today, speak God's promise aloud and remind yourself that you have been made clean by His grace.

Prayer

Lord, thank You for Your mercy that restores and renews completely. Help me trust Your grace and live confidently as someone You have made clean. Amen.

July 26

No Longer a Slave

Romans 8:15 (NLT)

"So you have not received a spirit that makes you fearful slaves. Instead, you received God's Spirit when he adopted you as his own children. Now we call him, 'Abba, Father.'"

Devotional

Freedom begins with understanding who you belong to. This verse makes a clear distinction between fear driven living and Spirit led identity. God did not save you so you could continue living bound by fear, shame, or insecurity. He adopted you into His family and gave you access to Him as Father.

Many people live like servants in a house where they are actually sons and daughters. They obey out of fear rather than love and hesitate instead of trusting. But adoption changes everything. It grants intimacy, security, and confidence. You are not tolerated in God's presence. You are welcomed.

Grace invites you to stop striving for approval and start living from acceptance. When you know you are adopted, fear loses its authority. You no longer have to prove yourself or hide your weakness. You can approach God freely, knowing He delights in you.

Today, let this truth settle deeply in your heart. You are no longer a slave to fear. You are a child of God, held securely in His love.

Reflection

In what ways do you still find yourself responding to God from fear instead of trust?

Life Application

When fear tries to influence your decisions today, pause and remind yourself that you are God's child, not a slave.

Prayer

Father, thank You for adopting me into Your family and freeing me from fear. Help me live with confidence rooted in Your love and trust You fully as my Father. Amen.

July 27

Living Under Grace

Romans 6:14 (NIV)
"For sin shall no longer be your master, because you are not under the law, but under grace."

Devotional

Grace changes who holds authority in your life. This verse does not suggest that sin becomes quieter or less tempting. It declares that sin loses its power to rule. When grace governs your life, old patterns no longer get the final say.

Many believers live forgiven but still feel controlled. They try to manage behavior through willpower instead of trusting the freedom grace provides. But grace is not passive. It actively reshapes how you think, choose, and respond. It gives you strength to live differently, not because you must, but because you can.

Living under grace means you are no longer driven by fear of failure or pressure to perform. Obedience becomes a response to love rather than an attempt to earn it. Grace empowers you to rise when you fall and keep moving forward without shame.

Today, remind yourself who is in charge. Grace leads your life now. You are no longer mastered by what once held you captive.

Reflection

Where do you still feel controlled by habits or thoughts that grace has already addressed?

Life Application

When temptation or discouragement appears today, consciously choose to rely on God's grace instead of self-effort.

Prayer

Lord, thank You for Your grace that frees me and leads me. Help me live confidently under Your grace and no longer submit to what once ruled me. Amen.

July 28

Made New in Christ

2 Corinthians 5:17 (NKJV)

"Therefore, if anyone is in Christ, he is a new creation; old things have passed away; behold, all things have become new."

Devotional

Newness in Christ is not symbolic language. It is a spiritual reality. This verse declares that when you belong to Christ, something fundamental has changed. Your identity is no longer anchored to who you were or what you have done. You are made new from the inside out.

Many people accept forgiveness but struggle to embrace transformation. They believe God has covered their past but still expect to live under its influence. Yet Scripture says old things have passed away. That includes former labels, patterns, and limitations that no longer have authority over you.

Grace invites you to stop introducing yourself by your history and start living from your renewal. Being made new does not mean you never struggle. It means struggle no longer defines you. Growth becomes possible because your foundation has changed.

Today, choose to live as someone who has been made new. Let your thoughts, choices, and confidence reflect the work God has already completed in you.

Reflection

What old mindset or identity do you need to release so you can fully embrace who you are in Christ?

Life Application

When old thoughts resurface today, intentionally replace them with the truth that you are a new creation in Christ.

Prayer

Lord, thank You for making me new in Christ. Help me release what has passed away and live confidently in the renewal You have given me. Amen.

July 29

Fruit That Comes from Growth

Hebrews 12:11 (NIV)

"No discipline seems pleasant at the time, but painful. Later on, however, it produces a harvest of righteousness and peace for those who have been trained by it."

Devotional

Growth often feels uncomfortable before it becomes fruitful. This verse speaks honestly about the process of becoming more mature in Christ. Discipline is rarely enjoyable in the moment, but it carries a purpose that reaches far beyond temporary discomfort.

God's work in your life is intentional. He is not trying to restrict you but to strengthen you. The stretching, refining, and pruning you experience are not signs of punishment. They are evidence that God is shaping you for greater peace and righteousness.

Freedom does not mean the absence of discipline. It means trusting God enough to submit to the process that produces lasting change. When you allow God to train you, He develops endurance, wisdom, and stability that cannot be gained any other way.

Today, resist the urge to rush past discomfort. Trust that God is using this season to produce something good and lasting in you.

Reflection

What area of your life feels uncomfortable right now but may be producing growth beneath the surface?

Life Application

When challenges arise today, ask God what He is teaching you instead of trying to escape the discomfort.

Prayer

Father, thank You for loving me enough to grow me. Help me trust the process and remain faithful as You shape my life for peace and righteousness. Amen.

July 30

Brought to Life by Mercy

Ephesians 2:4–5 (NLT)

"But God is so rich in mercy, and he loved us so much, that even though we were dead because of our sins, he gave us life when he raised Christ from the dead. It is only by God's grace that you have been saved."

Devotional

Grace is not a response to effort. It is an expression of God's mercy. This passage reminds us that salvation began with God, not with us. When we were unable to help ourselves, God moved toward us with love and compassion.

Being brought to life in Christ means more than forgiveness. It means renewal at the deepest level. God did not simply improve your condition. He transformed it. Where there was once spiritual emptiness, He placed life. Where there was distance, He created connection.

Freedom grows when you understand that grace is not fragile. It does not depend on your consistency or performance. It rests on God's mercy and love. This truth allows you to live boldly and confidently, knowing your standing with God is secure.

Today, remember where your life comes from. You are alive in Christ because of grace, and that grace continues to sustain you every day.

Reflection

How does knowing that God acted first in mercy change the way you see yourself and your faith journey?

Life Application

When you feel discouraged today, remind yourself that your life in Christ is rooted in God's mercy, not your effort.

Prayer

Father, thank You for Your mercy that brought me to life in Christ. Help me walk confidently in the grace that saved me and continues to sustain me. Amen.

July 31

Held by Unfailing Love

Lamentations 3:31–32 (NLT)

"For no one is abandoned by the Lord forever. Though he brings grief, he also shows compassion because of the greatness of his unfailing love."

Devotional

This month ends with reassurance. God's love does not walk away when seasons are heavy or when life feels uncertain. Scripture is clear that even when grief is present, abandonment is not. God remains near, steady, and compassionate.

Freedom and grace are not the absence of difficulty. They are the assurance that difficulty does not define the end of the story. God's unfailing love is greater than any moment of loss, disappointment, or delay. What feels heavy now is not permanent, and what feels painful is not proof of His absence.

Grace allows you to trust God in the middle, not just at the outcome. It reminds you that compassion flows from His character and not from your circumstances. Even when life feels quiet or slow, God is still working with care and intention.

As this month closes, rest in this truth. You are held by unfailing love. What God begins, He completes, and His compassion will meet you again in the next season.

Reflection

Where have you questioned God's presence during a difficult season, and how does this verse reshape that perspective?

Life Application

As you close this month, intentionally thank God for His compassion and trust Him with what lies ahead.

Prayer

Father, thank You for Your unfailing love and compassion that never abandon me. Help me rest in Your faithfulness as I step into the next season with trust and hope. Amen.

August

Walking in Your God-Given Purpose

August invites you to live with clarity, courage, and conviction about why you are here. Purpose is not something you rush to discover or chase through performance. It is something God reveals as you walk closely with Him. Your purpose unfolds through obedience, alignment, and trust, often in quiet, faithful steps rather than dramatic moments. This month reminds you that your life is intentional, your calling is personal, and your journey is guided by God's hand.

Walking in your God-given purpose requires discernment and surrender. It asks you to release comparison, impatience, and the pressure to arrive. Purpose is not limited to titles, platforms, or outcomes. It is expressed in how you love, how you serve, how you remain faithful when no one is watching, and how you respond when God redirects your path. Each step of obedience, no matter how small it feels, carries eternal significance.

As you journey through August, you will be invited to trust God with both the process and the timing of your purpose. You are not behind. You are not overlooked. You are being prepared. Purpose is revealed as you stay rooted in God's presence and willing to follow His lead. Each day offers an opportunity to walk confidently in who He created you to be, knowing that every step forward is moving you deeper into His design for your life.

August 1

Committed Steps

Proverbs 16:3 (NLT)
"Commit your actions to the Lord, and your plans will succeed."

Devotional

Purpose does not begin with perfect clarity. It begins with surrender. This verse reminds us that success, in God's economy, flows from commitment before direction. When you commit your actions to the Lord, you are placing your daily decisions, intentions, and efforts into His hands, trusting Him to shape the outcome according to His will.

Many people wait to feel confident about their purpose before they move forward. God invites you to take the opposite approach. Commit first. Walk faithfully. Allow Him to establish your steps along the way. Purpose unfolds as you consistently bring your plans, both big and small, before God and invite Him to lead rather than asking Him to bless what you have already decided.

As you begin this month, let commitment be your foundation. You do not need to have every answer. You need a willing heart and obedient steps. When your actions are surrendered to God, He brings alignment, clarity, and fruit in ways you could not manufacture on your own.

Reflection

What areas of your life or plans do you need to fully commit to God instead of trying to manage on your own?

Life Application

Before making decisions today, pause and intentionally commit your actions to the Lord in prayer.

Prayer

Father, I commit my actions, plans, and desires to You. Order my steps and establish my path according to Your will. Help me trust You as I walk forward in purpose. Amen.

August 2

Led with Wisdom

James 3:17 (NIV)
"But the wisdom that comes from heaven is first of all pure; then peace loving, considerate, submissive, full of mercy and good fruit, impartial and sincere."

Devotional

Walking in your God-given purpose requires more than ambition or talent. It requires wisdom from God. This verse reminds us that heavenly wisdom looks different from worldly success. It is not driven by urgency, ego, or comparison. God's wisdom leads with purity, peace, and integrity, shaping both your decisions and your character.

Many people confuse being busy with being purposeful. Wisdom slows you down long enough to ask the right questions and listen for God's direction. When you are led by God's wisdom, your steps produce peace rather than pressure and fruit rather than frustration. Purpose guided by wisdom is sustainable and rooted in God's truth, not human approval.

As you walk forward this month, invite God's wisdom into every decision. Purpose does not demand perfection, but it does require discernment. When you choose to be led by wisdom from above, your life begins to reflect God's order, peace, and intention more clearly.

Reflection

Where do you need God's wisdom to guide your decisions rather than relying on your own understanding?

Life Application

Before making choices today, ask God for wisdom and allow peace to be your confirmation.

Prayer

Lord, I ask for Your wisdom to guide my steps. Help me make decisions that honor You and align with Your purpose for my life. Teach me to move with peace, humility, and discernment. Amen.

August 3

Faithful in the Doing

Ecclesiastes 11:6 (NIV)

"Sow your seed in the morning, and at evening let your hands not be idle, for you do not know which will succeed, whether this or that, or whether both will do equally well."

Devotional

Purpose is often revealed through faithfulness in action rather than certainty in outcome. This verse reminds us that obedience is not dependent on knowing the results. God calls you to keep sowing, keep showing up, and keep doing the work He has placed in your hands, trusting Him with what will ultimately bear fruit.

Many people hesitate to move forward because they want guarantees. They want to know which effort will matter most or which decision will bring the greatest return. God invites you to a different posture. He asks you to remain diligent, consistent, and faithful, even when the outcome is unclear. Purpose grows in the soil of obedience, not prediction.

As you walk in your God-given purpose, resist the temptation to measure progress too quickly. Every seed sown in faith matters. God sees your consistency, your effort, and your willingness to serve. In His timing, He brings growth in ways you could not have planned or anticipated.

Reflection

Where might God be inviting you to keep sowing faithfully without needing immediate results?

Life Application

Commit to showing up fully today, trusting God with the outcome of your obedience.

Prayer

Father, help me remain faithful in the work You have given me. Teach me to trust You with the results and to walk confidently in obedience, knowing You are bringing growth in Your perfect timing. Amen.

August 4

Finishing What You Were Given

Acts 20:24 (NIV)

"However, I consider my life worth nothing to me; my only aim is to finish the race and complete the task the Lord Jesus has given me, the task of testifying to the good news of God's grace."

Devotional

Purpose is not proven by how loudly you start but by how faithfully you finish. In this verse, Paul reveals a deep understanding of calling. His focus is not on comfort, recognition, or ease. His aim is clear. He is committed to completing the task God entrusted to him, no matter the cost. Purpose becomes clearer when you decide that obedience matters more than outcomes.

Many people abandon their purpose when it becomes inconvenient or difficult. God never promised that walking in purpose would be easy, but He did promise it would be meaningful. Completing the task God has given you requires endurance, humility, and a willingness to stay aligned even when the journey stretches longer than expected.

As you walk forward this month, ask yourself what God has entrusted to you. Purpose is not about doing everything. It is about finishing what He assigned. When you stay focused on His call rather than distractions or fear, you grow stronger, more confident, and more anchored in the work He has placed in your hands.

Reflection

What task or calling has God placed on your heart that requires renewed commitment and endurance?

Life Application

Identify one responsibility God has given you and recommit to seeing it through with faith and consistency.

Prayer

Father, help me stay focused on the task You have given me. Strengthen my resolve to walk in obedience and finish with faithfulness. I trust You to sustain me as I pursue Your purpose for my life. Amen.

August 5

Taught by God

Psalm 25:4–5 (NLT)

"Show me the right path, O Lord; point out the road for me to follow. Lead me by your truth and teach me, for you are the God who saves me. All day long I put my hope in you."

Devotional

Purpose is not something you figure out alone. It is something you are taught as you walk with God. In this passage, the psalmist does not demand answers or rush the process. He humbly asks God to show him the path and to lead him in truth. This posture matters. When you invite God to teach you, you acknowledge that purpose is discovered through relationship, not control.

Many people want clarity without submission. They want direction without dependence. But walking in your God-given purpose requires a willingness to be led, corrected, and shaped by God's truth. Sometimes the path becomes clear only after you take the next obedient step. God teaches as you go, revealing direction in seasons, not all at once.

As you continue through this month, allow God to guide you daily. Purpose grows as you stay teachable and hopeful, trusting that God is actively leading you. When you put your hope in Him, even uncertain seasons become places of growth and preparation.

Reflection

In what areas of your life do you need to ask God to teach and lead you more intentionally?

Life Application

Begin your day by asking God to guide your steps and remain open to His direction throughout the day.

Prayer

Lord, show me the path You desire for me to walk. Teach me through Your truth and help me trust You as You lead me step by step into Your purpose. Amen.

August 6

Called to Walk Forward

Micah 6:8 (NIV)
"He has shown you, O mortal, what is good. And what does the Lord require of you? To act justly and to love mercy and to walk humbly with your God."

Devotional

Walking in your God-given purpose does not require complexity. This verse makes God's expectations clear and accessible. Purpose is lived out through justice, mercy, and humility. It is expressed in how you treat others, how you respond to challenges, and how you stay connected to God in your daily walk.

Many people assume purpose must look impressive or public to matter. God often reveals purpose through faithful, humble obedience in everyday moments. Acting justly means choosing integrity even when it is inconvenient. Loving mercy means extending grace when it would be easier to withhold it. Walking humbly keeps you dependent on God rather than relying on your own strength.

As you continue through this month, remember that purpose is not found in striving to be seen. It is found in faithfully walking with God. When you choose humility and obedience, you walk forward in alignment with the life God designed for you.

Reflection

How can you walk more humbly and intentionally with God in your daily life?

Life Application

Choose one action today that reflects justice, mercy, or humility as you walk with God.

Prayer

Father, help me walk humbly with You. Teach me to live out my purpose through obedience, compassion, and integrity. Guide my steps as I seek to honor You in every part of my life. Amen.

August 7

Shaped by Faithfulness

1 Thessalonians 5:24 (NIV)

"The one who calls you is faithful, and he will do it."

Devotional

Purpose is sustained not by your strength, but by God's faithfulness. This verse offers deep reassurance that what God has called you to, He is fully committed to completing. Purpose does not rest on your ability to carry everything perfectly. It rests on God's promise to finish what He has begun in you.

Many people feel overwhelmed by the weight of their calling because they believe they must carry it alone. God reminds you here that your role is obedience, not outcome. Faithfulness is not about striving harder. It is about trusting deeper. When God calls you, He also provides the strength, wisdom, and endurance needed to walk out that calling.

As you continue through this month, let this truth settle your heart. You do not have to force purpose into being. God is faithful to do the work He started. When you remain available and obedient, He shapes your life according to His design, step by step.

Reflection

Where do you need to trust God's faithfulness instead of relying on your own effort?

Life Application

Release pressure today by reminding yourself that God is responsible for completing what He has called you to do.

Prayer

Father, thank You for Your faithfulness. Help me trust You with my calling and rest in the assurance that You will complete the work You have begun in me. Amen.

August 8

Equipped to Walk

Ephesians 2:10 (NLT)

"For we are God's masterpiece. He has created us anew in Christ Jesus, so we can do the good things he planned for us long ago."

Devotional

Walking in your God-given purpose begins with understanding who you are. This verse reminds you that your life is not accidental. You were intentionally created by God, shaped with care, and designed for specific works prepared in advance. Purpose is not something you invent. It is something you step into as you live from your identity in Christ.

Many people struggle with purpose because they doubt their worth or readiness. God calls you His workmanship, His masterpiece. That truth shifts how you see yourself and how you approach what He has placed before you. When you believe that God created you with intention, you begin to walk with confidence rather than comparison or hesitation.

As you continue this month, let this truth anchor you. You are already equipped for the path God has set before you. Purpose unfolds as you trust His design and walk faithfully in what He has prepared, one step at a time.

Reflection

How does knowing you were created intentionally by God change the way you view your purpose?

Life Application

Remind yourself today that you are God's workmanship and approach your responsibilities with confidence and gratitude.

Prayer

Father, thank You for creating me with intention and purpose. Help me walk confidently in the good works You have prepared for me, trusting Your design for my life. Amen.

August 9

Ordered Steps

Proverbs 20:24 (NLT)
"The Lord directs our steps, so why try to understand everything along the way?"

Devotional
Purpose does not require you to understand every detail of the journey. This verse gently reminds you that God is the One directing your steps, even when the path feels unclear. Purpose unfolds through trust, not total comprehension. When you release the need to control or predict each outcome, you make room for God to lead with wisdom and intention.

Many people become stalled because they believe clarity must come before movement. God often works in the opposite direction. He invites you to take the next step in faith, trusting that He is already guiding the way. Purpose grows as you learn to walk with confidence in God's direction rather than relying solely on your understanding.

As you continue through this month, allow yourself to rest in God's leadership. You do not need to have every answer to walk faithfully. When you trust God to order your steps, you move forward with peace, humility, and assurance that He is actively guiding your path.

Reflection
Where are you trying to understand everything instead of trusting God to lead you step by step?

Life Application
Release the need for full clarity today and focus on faithfully taking the next step God places before you.

Prayer
Father, thank You for directing my steps. Help me trust You even when I do not understand the full path ahead. Teach me to walk in faith and confidence as You lead me into Your purpose. Amen.

August 10

Steady Faithfulness

Luke 16:10 (NIV)
"Whoever can be trusted with very little can also be trusted with much, and whoever is dishonest with very little will also be dishonest with much."

Devotional
Purpose is often revealed through faithfulness in small things. This verse reminds you that God values consistency and integrity long before expansion or visibility. Walking in your God-given purpose does not always begin with major opportunities. It often begins with obedience in ordinary responsibilities that shape your character and prepare you for greater impact.

Many people desire more influence, clarity, or responsibility without recognizing the importance of stewardship where they are. God develops trust through faithfulness. When you handle small assignments with care, excellence, and integrity, you demonstrate readiness for what comes next. Purpose grows quietly through disciplined obedience.

As you continue this month, examine how you steward what God has already placed in your hands. Purpose is not rushed. It is built through trust. When you remain faithful in the little things, God faithfully expands your capacity and aligns you with His greater plans.

Reflection
What small responsibilities might God be using to prepare you for greater purpose?

Life Application
Approach today's tasks with faithfulness and integrity, trusting God with future growth.

Prayer
Father, help me be faithful in what You have entrusted to me. Teach me to honor You in small things and trust You as You prepare me for greater purpose. Amen.

August 11

Purpose Anchored in Hope

Romans 12:12 (NLT)
"Rejoice in our confident hope. Be patient in trouble, and keep on praying."

Devotional
Purpose is sustained by hope, especially when the path feels demanding. This verse reminds you that hope is not passive optimism but confident trust in God's faithfulness. Rejoicing in hope does not mean ignoring difficulty. It means choosing joy because you believe God is at work even when circumstances are challenging.

Walking in your God-given purpose requires patience during seasons of trouble. Purpose does not move in straight lines or on predictable timelines. Prayer keeps you connected to God's heart while patience strengthens your endurance. Together, they anchor you when progress feels slow or uncertain.

As you continue through this month, allow hope to steady your steps. Purpose grows when you remain prayerful, patient, and confident that God is leading you forward. Even in challenging moments, hope reminds you that your obedience is not wasted and your journey is not without meaning.

Reflection
Where do you need to lean into hope rather than focusing on frustration or delay?

Life Application
Set aside time today to pray intentionally, choosing hope and patience as you walk forward in purpose.

Prayer
Father, thank You for the hope You place within me. Help me remain patient in difficulty and faithful in prayer as I continue walking in the purpose You have given me. Amen.

August 12

Purpose Refined Through Obedience

John 14:21 (NIV)
"Whoever has my commands and keeps them is the one who loves me. The one who loves me will be loved by my Father, and I too will love them and show myself to them."

Devotional

Purpose becomes clearer through obedience. This verse reminds us that walking closely with Jesus is not rooted in knowledge alone, but in living out what He has instructed. Obedience positions your heart to recognize God's presence and direction more clearly. When you choose to follow God's commands, you invite deeper relationship and greater clarity into your life.

Many people desire revelation without obedience. They want direction without discipline. Jesus connects love, obedience, and revelation in this passage. As you walk in obedience, God reveals Himself more fully, shaping your understanding of purpose and strengthening your faith. Purpose unfolds as you align your life with His will.

As you continue through this month, allow obedience to guide your steps. Purpose is not something you force or rush. It is refined as you faithfully follow God's leading. When you choose obedience, you make room for God to reveal what comes next.

Reflection

Where might God be inviting you to respond with greater obedience in your daily life?

Life Application

Identify one area where God is prompting obedience and take a clear step forward today.

Prayer

Father, help me walk in obedience and trust Your guidance. Reveal Yourself to me as I follow You faithfully and continue walking in the purpose You have prepared for me. Amen.

August 13

Choosing the Path

Proverbs 4:26 (NLT)

"Mark out a straight path for your feet; stay on the safe path."

Devotional

Walking in your God-given purpose requires intentional choices. This verse reminds you that direction is not accidental. You are invited to be mindful of where you place your steps and how you move forward. Purpose is not only about knowing where God is leading you. It is also about choosing paths that align with His wisdom and truth.

Many people drift rather than decide. They allow circumstances, emotions, or outside voices to shape their direction. God calls you to mark your path deliberately. Staying on the safe path does not mean avoiding growth or challenge. It means choosing alignment over impulse and obedience over distraction. Purpose becomes clearer when your steps are intentional and grounded in God's guidance.

As you continue through this month, take time to evaluate the paths before you. Not every opportunity is an assignment, and not every open door leads to purpose. When you seek God's direction and choose your steps wisely, you walk forward with clarity, confidence, and peace.

Reflection

What paths or decisions require more intentional prayer and discernment right now?

Life Application

Pause before making decisions today and ask God to help you choose the path that aligns with His purpose for your life.

Prayer

Father, help me choose my steps with wisdom and intention. Guide me along the path You have set before me and keep me aligned with Your purpose. Amen.

August 14

Walking Forward in Trust

Psalm 37:23 (NLT)
"The Lord directs the steps of the godly. He delights in every detail of their lives."

Devotional

Purpose is not only about where you are going but about trusting God with how you get there. This verse reminds you that God is actively involved in directing your steps. He is not distant or disengaged. He delights in the details of your life, including the choices, transitions, and decisions that shape your journey.

Many people hesitate to move forward because they fear making the wrong choice. God offers reassurance that when you seek Him, He guides your steps with care and intention. Purpose is not fragile. It is supported by God's delight in leading you. When you trust Him, even imperfect steps become part of His greater plan.

As you continue through this month, allow yourself to move forward with confidence. Trust that God sees the whole picture and is guiding you with wisdom. When you release fear and lean into trust, your walk becomes steadier and your purpose clearer.

Reflection

Where do you need to trust God more fully with the direction of your steps?

Life Application

Before making decisions today, pause and remind yourself that God delights in guiding your life.

Prayer

Father, thank You for directing my steps and caring about every detail of my life. Help me walk forward in trust, confident that You are leading me according to Your purpose. Amen.

August 15

Strength to Stay the Course

2 Chronicles 15:7 (NIV)

"But as for you, be strong and do not give up, for your work will be rewarded."

Devotional

Walking in your God-given purpose requires endurance. There will be moments when progress feels slow, recognition is absent, and the work feels heavier than expected. This verse speaks directly to those moments. God's instruction is simple but powerful. Be strong. Do not give up. Your faithfulness is not overlooked.

Purpose is often tested in the middle, not at the beginning or the end. It is easy to start with passion and dream about completion, but strength is required to remain steady in between. God reminds you here that your work matters. Even when the results are not immediate, He sees your consistency, your obedience, and your willingness to keep going.

As you walk forward in purpose, let this truth anchor you. Strength is not about forcing progress. It is about trusting God enough to continue when the road feels long. Your work in the Lord carries reward, meaning, and impact beyond what you can currently see.

Reflection

Where do you feel tempted to grow weary or give up instead of staying strong?

Life Application

Encourage yourself today by remembering that God sees your effort and promises reward for faithfulness.

Prayer

Father, strengthen my resolve to remain faithful to the path You have set before me. Help me trust that my obedience has purpose and that You honor the work done in Your name. Amen.

August 16

Equipped on Purpose

Romans 12:6 (NIV)

"We have different gifts, according to the grace given to each of us."

Devotional

Purpose is not generic. It is personal, intentional, and shaped by the grace God has placed on your life. Romans 12:6 reminds us that our gifts are not accidental or random. They are given by God Himself, measured and assigned according to His wisdom and plan. You do not need what someone else has to fulfill what God has called you to do.

Many people delay walking fully in their purpose because they are waiting to feel more equipped, more confident, or more qualified. But this scripture shifts the perspective. You are already equipped with what you need for your assignment in this season. Grace did not just save you. Grace empowered you.

When you accept that your gifts come from God, comparison loses its grip. You stop striving to imitate someone else's calling and begin stewarding your own. Purpose flourishes when you honor what God has placed in your hands and trust Him to grow it in His timing.

Reflection

What gifts has God given you that you may be underestimating or overlooking?

Life Application

Identify one gift God has entrusted to you and intentionally use it today, even in a small way.

Prayer

Father, thank You for the grace You have entrusted to me. Help me recognize and steward the gifts You have given, so I walk boldly and faithfully in the purpose You designed for me. Amen.

August 17

Created for His Glory

Isaiah 43:7 (NLT)

"Bring all who claim me as their God, for I have made them for my glory. It was I who created them."

Devotional

Purpose is not something you invent. It is something you discover. In this verse, God makes it unmistakably clear that your life has intention behind it. You were created by Him, claimed by Him, and designed to reflect His glory. Your existence is not random, and your assignment is not accidental.

Being created for God's glory does not mean living a loud or public life. It means living a faithful one. It means that your decisions, your obedience, your character, and your willingness to follow God matter more than recognition or applause. Your purpose is fulfilled not by striving to be seen, but by faithfully becoming who God formed you to be.

Many people struggle with purpose because they are looking outward instead of upward. They measure their lives by comparison, productivity, or outcomes. God measures purpose by alignment. When your life is aligned with Him, your work, your influence, and your impact naturally flow from that place. You do not have to chase purpose when you are rooted in the One who created you.

Today, let this truth anchor you. You were created on purpose, for a purpose, and that purpose brings glory to God. When you walk in obedience and humility, your life reflects Him in ways you may never fully see, but He always does.

Reflection

Where might you be striving for purpose instead of resting in the truth that you were created intentionally by God?

Life Application

Today, pause before making decisions and ask yourself whether your actions align with honoring God and reflecting His glory.

Prayer

God, thank You for creating me with purpose and intention. Shape my life so it reflects Your glory in every choice, action, and attitude. Amen.

August 18

Faithful With What He Gave You

John 17:4 (NLT)
"I brought glory to you here on earth by completing the work you gave me to do."

Devotional

These words are spoken by Jesus in prayer, near the end of His earthly ministry. They reveal something powerful about purpose. Jesus did not measure His life by how much He accomplished compared to others, but by whether He completed what the Father entrusted to Him. Purpose is not about doing everything. It is about doing what God assigned you.

Many people feel pressure to carry responsibilities God never gave them. They exhaust themselves trying to prove worth, earn validation, or keep up with expectations that were never heaven-sent. Jesus shows us a different model. He lived with clarity. He stayed focused on His assignment. And because of that, He could say with confidence that His life brought glory to God.

Completing the work God gives you does not mean finishing every task perfectly. It means walking in obedience, even when the work feels slow, unseen, or misunderstood. Faithfulness matters more than visibility. When you remain aligned with God's direction, your life bears fruit that lasts, even when others do not notice.

Today, this verse invites you to release comparison and distraction. You are not called to finish someone else's work. You are called to be faithful with what God placed in your hands. When you honor that assignment, your life brings Him glory, just as Jesus modeled.

Reflection

What responsibilities or expectations might you be carrying that God did not assign to you?

Life Application

Take a moment today to ask God to clarify what He has truly entrusted to you and where He may be inviting you to release unnecessary pressure.

Prayer

Father, thank You for the work You have placed in my care. Keep my focus on Your assignment, free from comparison or distraction, so my life faithfully brings You glory. Amen.

August 19

Walk Worthy of the Calling

1 Thessalonians 2:12 (NKJV)
"that you would walk worthy of God who calls you into His own kingdom and glory."

Devotional

Calling is not something you chase. It is something you walk in. This verse reminds us that God does not simply give direction. He invites relationship. He calls you into His kingdom and into His glory, not just into productivity or achievement. Your calling flows from who He is and who you are becoming in Him.

Walking worthy does not mean striving to be good enough. It means living with awareness. Awareness that your life carries weight. Awareness that your decisions matter. Awareness that God has entrusted you with influence, even in spaces that feel ordinary or unnoticed. When you understand that God Himself has called you, you stop treating your days casually.

Many people feel overwhelmed by the idea of purpose because they think it must be dramatic or public to be meaningful. Scripture paints a different picture. Purpose is revealed in how you walk. How you love. How you respond. How you stay faithful when no one is applauding. A worthy walk is not loud. It is consistent.

Today, God is not asking you to figure out everything at once. He is inviting you to walk with intention. To align your life with the calling already placed on you. When you walk worthy of God, your life becomes a reflection of His kingdom wherever you go.

Reflection

What does it look like for you to walk with greater intention in this season of your life?

Life Application

Choose one area today where you will act with purpose and awareness rather than habit or pressure.

Prayer

Father, thank You for calling me into Your kingdom and glory. Help me walk with intention, humility, and faithfulness, honoring the life You have entrusted to me. Amen

August 20

Carry Out What He Gave You

Colossians 4:17 (NLT)
"And say to Archippus, 'Be sure to carry out the ministry the Lord gave you.'"

Devotional

This verse is brief, but it carries weight. Paul's instruction to Archippus is both personal and direct. It reminds us that purpose is not abstract. God gives specific assignments to specific people. Your calling is not accidental, and it is not interchangeable with someone else's.

There is a tendency to second-guess what God has already made clear. Doubt creeps in. Comparison distracts. Weariness settles. Yet this verse cuts through all of that with a simple charge: carry out what the Lord gave you. Not what others expect. Not what looks impressive. Not what feels safest. What God gave you.

Carrying out your assignment does not mean the path will always feel clear or easy. It means you stay committed even when progress feels slow or affirmation feels scarce. Faithfulness is often quiet. It shows up in consistency, obedience, and perseverance long before it shows up in results.

Today, let this verse bring both clarity and encouragement. God has entrusted you with something meaningful. You are not late. You are not behind. You are being reminded to stay faithful to what He placed in your hands. When you carry out what God gave you, your life aligns with purpose in a way nothing else can.

Reflection

What assignment or responsibility do you sense God has given you that requires renewed focus or commitment?

Life Application

Identify one practical step you can take today to move forward in the work God has entrusted to you, even if it feels small.

Prayer

Lord, thank You for trusting me with the work You have given me. Help me remain faithful, focused, and obedient as I carry out my assignment with confidence and humility. Amen.

August 21

Use What He Placed in You

1 Peter 4:10 (NLT)
"God has given each of you a gift from his great variety of spiritual gifts. Use them well to serve one another."

Devotional

God's design for your life includes intention and generosity. This verse reminds us that every gift we carry was given on purpose and with purpose. Nothing about you is random. Your abilities, insights, passions, and experiences were entrusted to you by God, not just for your benefit, but for the blessing of others.

Many people underestimate their gifts because they compare them to someone else's strengths. Others hide their gifts out of fear, insecurity, or feeling unqualified. Yet Scripture is clear. You have been given something valuable, and you are responsible for how you steward it. Purpose is not only discovered in what you do, but in how faithfully you use what God has already placed within you.

Using your gifts well requires humility and courage. Humility to recognize that the gift came from God. Courage to step forward and serve even when you feel uncertain. When you offer your gifts in love, God multiplies their impact far beyond what you could accomplish on your own.

Today is an invitation to stop holding back. You do not need to wait for perfection, permission, or applause. God has already equipped you. As you use what He placed in you, you walk confidently in your God-given purpose and become a living expression of His grace.

Reflection

What gift or ability has God given you that you may be underusing or overlooking?

Life Application

Intentionally use one of your gifts today to serve or encourage someone else, even in a simple way.

Prayer

Father, thank You for the gifts You have placed within me. Help me steward them well and use them with confidence and love to serve others and honor You. Amen.

August 22

Appointed for This Moment

Acts 17:26 (NKJV)
"And He has made from one blood every nation of men to dwell on all the face of the earth, and has determined their preappointed times and the boundaries of their dwellings."

Devotional

This verse quietly dismantles the lie that you are out of place or behind. Scripture tells us that God Himself determined the times and boundaries of our lives. That means your season, your setting, and your circumstances were not random. You are not here by accident. You were appointed for this moment.

It is easy to look around and question timing. You may wonder why you were born when you were, why you are facing certain challenges, or why your life has unfolded the way it has. Acts reminds us that God's sovereignty extends even to the details we do not understand. He placed you where you are for a reason that aligns with His greater purpose.

Walking in your God-given purpose requires trusting God's placement, not just His direction. Purpose is not only about where you are going. It is also about honoring where you are now. When you accept that God intentionally positioned you in this season, you stop resisting your reality and begin partnering with Him within it.

Today, let this truth settle your heart. You do not need a different timeline or a different starting point to live purposefully. God has already accounted for this season. Your obedience right where you are is what moves purpose forward.

Reflection

In what ways have you questioned God's timing or placement in your life?

Life Application

Practice gratitude today for the season you are in, trusting that God has purpose even in what feels uncertain.

Prayer

Father, thank You for placing me where I am in this season. Help me trust Your timing and walk faithfully within the boundaries You have set, knowing You are at work. Amen.

August 23

What God Has Called Will Remain

Romans 11:29 (NKJV)
"For the gifts and the calling of God are irrevocable."

Devotional

This verse brings relief to weary hearts and confidence to uncertain ones. God does not change His mind about what He has placed inside you. His calling is not fragile, conditional, or subject to expiration. What He has spoken over your life remains, even when seasons shift or progress feels slow.

Many people wrestle with the fear that they have missed their moment. Mistakes, delays, or detours can cause you to question whether your calling is still valid. Scripture answers that fear directly. God's gifts and calling are irrevocable. They are not withdrawn because of failure, age, timing, or comparison. When God calls, He commits.

This truth does not remove responsibility. Instead, it invites confidence. Knowing that God's calling remains gives you permission to reengage with purpose rather than retreat in shame or doubt. It allows you to return to obedience without feeling like you have to start over or earn your place again.

Today, let this verse settle any lingering insecurity. God has not changed His mind about you. The calling He placed on your life still stands. As you walk forward in obedience, you do so grounded in the assurance that what God began, He still intends to fulfill.

Reflection

Have you ever questioned whether your calling was still valid because of past mistakes or delays?

Life Application

Revisit something God once placed on your heart and ask Him how He wants you to reengage with it in this season.

Prayer

Father, thank You that Your calling over my life does not change. Help me walk forward with confidence, trusting that what You have spoken still stands. Amen.

August 24

Useful in the Master's Hands

2 Timothy 2:20–21 (NKJV)
"But in a great house there are not only vessels of gold and silver, but also of wood and clay, some for honor and some for dishonor. Therefore, if anyone cleanses himself from the latter, he will be a vessel for honor, sanctified and useful for the Master, prepared for every good work."

Devotional

Purpose is not only about calling. It is also about preparation. In this passage, Paul reminds us that usefulness in God's hands flows from a willing and surrendered life. God desires vessels that are ready, clean, and available for the work He intends to do through them.

This scripture shifts the focus from comparison to condition. The question is not whether you are gifted, qualified, or visible. The question is whether you are willing to be shaped. Cleansing is not about perfection. It is about alignment. It is the daily decision to let go of what contaminates your focus, motives, and obedience so that God can use you fully.

Being prepared for good work means allowing God to refine your character alongside your calling. Sometimes the preparation feels uncomfortable. It may involve pruning habits, reshaping priorities, or addressing areas you would rather ignore. Yet this process is what makes you useful in the Master's hands.

Today's invitation is one of readiness. God is not looking for flawless vessels. He is looking for surrendered ones. As you allow Him to shape you, you become prepared for the work He has already planned for your life.

Reflection

What areas of your life might God be inviting you to surrender or refine so you can be more useful in His hands?

Life Application

Ask God to reveal one area where He is preparing you for greater purpose and respond with obedience rather than resistance.

Prayer

Lord, prepare my heart and life for the work You desire to do through me. Shape me, refine me, and make me useful in Your hands. I want to be ready for every good work You have planned. Amen.

August 25

Chosen and Appointed

John 15:16 (NLT)
"You didn't choose me. I chose you. I appointed you to go and produce lasting fruit, so that the Father will give you whatever you ask for, using my name."

Devotional

Purpose begins with being chosen. Jesus makes it clear that your calling did not originate from your initiative, talent, or ambition. It began with Him. Long before you recognized your assignment, God had already selected you and appointed you to live a life that bears lasting fruit.

This truth removes pressure and restores confidence. You are not trying to prove your worth or earn your place. You are responding to a divine invitation. When God appoints, He also equips. The fruit He desires from your life is not temporary success or surface-level achievement, but impact that lasts beyond seasons, roles, and recognition.

Being chosen also carries responsibility. Jesus did not choose you to remain stagnant. He appointed you to go, to move forward, and to live intentionally. Purpose is active. It grows as you step out in obedience, trusting that God will meet you with provision, wisdom, and strength along the way.

Today, let this verse ground you. You are not walking blindly or alone. You are chosen, appointed, and empowered by God Himself. As you remain connected to Him, your life will produce fruit that reflects His heart and fulfills His purpose.

Reflection

How does knowing that God chose and appointed you change the way you view your purpose?

Life Application

Take one intentional step today toward something God has placed on your heart, trusting that He has already appointed you for it.

Prayer

Father, thank You for choosing me and appointing me for purpose. Help me walk with confidence and obedience, producing fruit that honors You and lasts beyond this season. Amen.

August 26

Pressing Forward With Purpose

Philippians 3:14 (NKJV)
"I press toward the goal for the prize of the upward call of God in Christ Jesus."

Devotional

Purpose is not passive. Paul's words remind us that living out God's calling requires intention, focus, and perseverance. To press forward means you have already decided that going back is not an option. You are moving ahead because something greater is calling you upward.

There are seasons when progress feels slow or resistance feels heavy. Distractions, disappointments, and delays can tempt you to lose focus or settle for comfort. Yet this verse anchors your heart in a higher perspective. The goal is not simply success or completion. The goal is alignment with God's upward call on your life.

Pressing forward does not mean ignoring the past. It means refusing to let it define your future. Paul understood that clarity of purpose fuels endurance. When you know what you are running toward, you stop wasting energy on what is behind you or around you. Your strength is reserved for what lies ahead.

Today, let this scripture renew your determination. God's call on your life is worth pursuing with discipline and hope. Keep pressing forward. The prize is not just what you accomplish, but who you become as you follow Him faithfully.

Reflection

What has been competing for your focus as you try to move forward in your purpose?

Life Application

Choose one distraction to release today so you can press forward with greater clarity and intention.

Prayer

Lord, help me stay focused on the upward call You have placed on my life. Give me strength to press forward with purpose, discipline, and trust as I pursue what You have set before me. Amen

August 27

Finish What God Started

2 Timothy 4:7 (NKJV)

"I have fought the good fight, I have finished the race, I have kept the faith."

Devotional

These words come from Paul at the end of his life, not from a place of regret but from confidence. He is not boasting about perfection. He is testifying to faithfulness. Paul understood that purpose is not proven by how loudly you begin, but by how faithfully you endure and how honestly you finish.

Finishing well requires resilience. Along the way, there will be opposition, discouragement, and moments where quitting feels easier than continuing. Yet Paul reminds us that the race is worth running because it is anchored in faith. He did not allow hardship to redefine his calling. He stayed committed even when obedience came at a cost.

This verse reframes success. It is not about speed or applause. It is about perseverance. Fighting the good fight means choosing faith when doubt whispers. Finishing the race means staying obedient when the journey feels long. Keeping the faith means trusting God even when the outcome is uncertain.

Today, let this scripture strengthen your resolve. God is still at work in you, and your story is still unfolding. Stay faithful. Keep running. Finish what God started, knowing that endurance honors Him just as much as obedience does.

Reflection

Where in your life do you need renewed strength to keep going rather than giving up?

Life Application

Encourage yourself today by reflecting on how far God has already brought you and recommit to finishing the race with faith.

Prayer

Father, give me strength to endure and faith to remain steadfast. Help me fight the good fight, finish the race You have set before me, and keep my trust anchored in You. Amen.

August 28

Steady in the Calling

1 Corinthians 15:58 (NLT)
"So, my dear brothers and sisters, be strong and immovable. Always work enthusiastically for the Lord, for you know that nothing you do for the Lord is ever useless."

Devotional

Purpose is sustained through steadiness. This verse does not call you to constant motion or visible success, but to faithfulness that does not waver. Being strong and immovable speaks to a life rooted in conviction rather than emotion. It is the kind of strength that holds firm when progress feels slow or affirmation is absent.

God's work in your life is never wasted, even when it feels unseen. Purpose is often built quietly through consistency, obedience, and perseverance. Every step of faith, every act of obedience, and every moment you choose faith over fear matters more than you realize. Nothing offered to God with sincerity is ever lost.

Working enthusiastically for the Lord does not mean pushing past exhaustion or ignoring rest. It means serving with a heart that remains committed even when circumstances shift. Enthusiasm rooted in purpose is not driven by pressure, but by trust that God is using your faithfulness in ways you may never fully see.

Today, let this scripture remind you that your calling is worth steady commitment. You do not need to rush, compare, or prove yourself. Stay rooted. Stay faithful. God is honoring your obedience, and your work in Him is producing fruit that lasts.

Reflection

Where might God be inviting you to remain steady and faithful rather than seeking immediate results?

Life Application

Choose one responsibility or assignment today and approach it with renewed faith, trusting that God sees and values your obedience.

Prayer

Father, help me remain strong and immovable in the calling You have placed on my life. Remind me that nothing done for You is ever wasted and give me faith to stay committed with joy and confidence. Amen.

August 29

Confirm the Calling

2 Peter 1:10 (NLT)
"So, dear brothers and sisters, work hard to prove that you really are among those God has called and chosen. Do these things, and you will never fall away."

Devotional

Calling is not something you announce. It is something you confirm through how you live. This verse does not suggest that you earn God's calling, but that you live in a way that reflects it. Your daily obedience, character, and commitment give evidence to what God has already spoken over your life.

To confirm your calling means aligning your actions with your identity in Christ. It is choosing consistency over convenience and faithfulness over comfort. Purpose is revealed not only in moments of clarity, but in the discipline to keep walking when the path feels ordinary or demanding.

This scripture also speaks to stability. When you live in alignment with God's calling, you are less likely to drift or fall away. Your foundation becomes firm because it is rooted in truth rather than emotion. Purpose strengthens your faith and anchors your decisions, especially during seasons of uncertainty.

Today, let this verse challenge and encourage you. God has called and chosen you. Your role is not to question that calling, but to live in a way that confirms it. As you walk faithfully, your life becomes a testimony of His purpose at work within you.

Reflection

What habits or choices in your life help confirm the calling God has placed on you?

Life Application

Identify one area where you can bring your actions into greater alignment with the calling God has given you.

Prayer

Father, thank You for calling and choosing me. Help me live with integrity and faithfulness so that my life reflects the purpose You have placed within me. Amen.

August 30

Rooted and Built Up

Colossians 2:6–7 (NLT)

"And now, just as you accepted Christ Jesus as your Lord, you must continue to follow him. Let your roots grow down into him, and let your lives be built on him. Then your faith will grow strong in the truth you were taught, and you will overflow with thankfulness."

Devotional

Purpose is sustained by depth, not speed. This passage reminds us that walking in your God-given purpose requires staying rooted in Christ. Growth does not happen by constantly moving on to the next thing, but by allowing your roots to grow deep where God has planted you.

Being built up in Christ speaks to stability. When your life is anchored in Him, you are not easily shaken by pressure, comparison, or shifting circumstances. Purpose flourishes when your foundation is secure. Faith grows stronger not through striving, but through consistent trust and obedience.

This verse also points to gratitude as a sign of maturity. When you are rooted in Christ, thankfulness becomes a natural response. You recognize that your strength, direction, and growth all come from Him. Gratitude keeps your heart aligned and your perspective grounded as you walk forward.

Today, let this scripture call you back to the basics. Stay rooted. Stay built on Christ. As you do, your life will continue to grow in strength, clarity, and purpose, producing fruit that lasts.

Reflection

What practices help keep you rooted in Christ when life feels busy or uncertain?

Life Application

Choose one intentional habit today that helps deepen your relationship with Christ and strengthens your spiritual foundation.

Prayer

Lord, help me stay rooted in You and build my life on Your truth. Strengthen my faith, steady my steps, and keep my heart aligned with Your purpose for my life. Amen.

August 31

Stand Firm and Finish Strong

1 Corinthians 16:13 (NLT)

"Be on guard. Stand firm in the faith. Be courageous. Be strong."

Devotional

This verse reads like a closing charge, and it is fitting for the final day of the month. Purpose is not only about discovering what God has called you to do. It is also about standing firm in that calling when challenges arise. As August ends, this scripture reminds you that walking in your God-given purpose requires spiritual awareness, courage, and strength.

Standing firm in the faith means refusing to waver when doubts surface or circumstances shift. It means anchoring yourself in truth rather than emotion. God's call on your life does not change because of opposition, delay, or uncertainty. When you stand firm, you affirm that your trust is rooted in God, not in outcomes.

Courage and strength are not traits you generate on your own. They are qualities God supplies as you lean into Him. Being courageous does not mean you never feel fear. It means you choose obedience even when fear is present. Strength grows as you continue showing up, trusting that God is working through your faithfulness.

Today is an invitation to finish this month with resolve. Guard what God has entrusted to you. Stand firm in the calling He has placed on your life. Move forward with courage and strength, knowing that the One who called you will continue to guide you into what comes next.

Reflection

Where do you need to stand more firmly in your faith as you continue walking in your purpose?

Life Application

As you move into the next month, identify one area where you will intentionally stand firm, choosing faith and courage over hesitation.

Prayer

Father, thank You for strengthening me as I walk in the purpose You have given me. Help me stand firm in faith, live with courage, and move forward with confidence as You lead me into the next season. Amen.

September

Pressing On with Perseverance

September invites you into the sacred work of endurance. By this point in the year, the initial excitement of new beginnings has settled, and the reality of sustained faith, discipline, and trust has taken center stage. This month is not about speed or visibility. It is about remaining steadfast when progress feels slow and the journey requires resilience rather than inspiration.

Perseverance is formed in the quiet middle spaces, where obedience is no longer fueled by novelty but by conviction. This month will remind you that God often does His deepest work not in moments of breakthrough, but in seasons of pressing forward one faithful step at a time. Endurance strengthens your spiritual muscles and refines your character, teaching you to rely on God's presence rather than external validation.

As you move through September, you will be encouraged to keep going with hope and purpose, even when the road feels long. Perseverance is not passive. It is an active choice to trust God, to continue believing His promises, and to remain anchored in faith. This month calls you to press on with confidence, knowing that what God is developing in you now is preparing you for what lies ahead.

September 1

What You Need Now

Hebrews 10:36 (NLT)

"Patient endurance is what you need now, so that you will continue to do God's will. Then you will receive all that he has promised."

Devotional

There are seasons when clarity is not what you need most. Strength is. This verse speaks directly to that moment. Patient endurance is not presented as optional or secondary. It is named as the very thing you need now. Not later, not once circumstances change, but right where you are.

Endurance keeps you aligned with God's will when emotions fluctuate and outcomes feel uncertain. It is the quiet decision to keep walking even when the reward feels distant. God is not asking you to rush or strive. He is inviting you to remain steady, anchored, and obedient while He works behind the scenes.

This scripture also reminds you that promise follows perseverance. Endurance is not meaningless waiting. It is purposeful faithfulness. Every act of obedience, every moment you choose trust over discouragement, is moving you closer to what God has already promised. Nothing is wasted in seasons that require patience.

As September begins, let this truth set the tone. You are not behind. You are not forgotten. You are being strengthened. What you need now is endurance, and God is faithful to supply it as you continue doing His will.

Reflection

Where in your life is God asking you to practice patient endurance rather than seek immediate results?

Life Application

Identify one area where you feel tempted to give up or rush ahead, and choose today to remain faithful and steady instead.

Prayer

Father, thank You for giving me strength to endure. Help me remain obedient and steady as I continue walking in Your will. Teach me to trust that Your promises are unfolding in Your perfect timing. Amen.

September 2

Renewed From the Inside

2 Corinthians 4:16 (NLT)
"That is why we never give up. Though our bodies are dying, our spirits are being renewed every day."

Devotional

Perseverance does not mean pretending you are unaffected by life's weight. This verse acknowledges reality while pointing to hope. There are days when you feel tired, stretched, or worn down by responsibilities and expectations. God does not deny that experience. Instead, He offers renewal that begins on the inside.

Spiritual renewal is a daily gift. It is not dependent on circumstances improving or challenges disappearing. Even when the outward parts of life feel heavy, God is quietly strengthening your spirit. This kind of renewal allows you to keep going without becoming hardened or discouraged.

This scripture also reframes what progress looks like. You may not always see visible change right away, but something meaningful is happening beneath the surface. Each day you choose faith, your spirit is being renewed with endurance, clarity, and hope. God is sustaining you in ways you may not immediately recognize.

Today, let this truth steady you. You do not have to rely on your own strength to persevere. God is renewing you day by day, giving you what you need to continue forward with faith and confidence.

Reflection

Where have you felt weary lately, and how might God be renewing your spirit even in that place?

Life Application

Pause today to acknowledge God's quiet renewal at work in you, even if your circumstances have not changed yet.

Prayer

Lord, thank You for renewing my spirit day by day. When I feel tired or discouraged, remind me that You are strengthening me from the inside out. Help me keep going with faith and trust in You. Amen.

September 3

Formed Through Discipline

Psalm 119:75 (NLT)

"I know, Lord, that your regulations are fair; you disciplined me because I needed it."

Devotional

Perseverance is often shaped through correction rather than comfort. This verse reflects a mature faith that recognizes God's discipline not as punishment, but as care. Discipline is evidence of God's involvement in your growth. It shows that He is invested in who you are becoming, not just in what you accomplish.

God's discipline brings clarity. It exposes patterns that need adjusting and redirects you toward what is life-giving. While discipline may feel uncomfortable in the moment, it serves a purpose that extends beyond immediate understanding. It refines your character and strengthens your ability to endure future challenges with wisdom and humility.

This scripture also reveals trust. The psalmist acknowledges that God's guidance is fair and necessary. That kind of trust grows over time as you witness how God's correction leads to greater peace, alignment, and spiritual maturity. Discipline becomes a tool God uses to steady your steps and deepen your dependence on Him.

Today, consider how God may be shaping you through discipline. Rather than resisting it, allow it to form you. What God is refining now is preparing you for greater faithfulness ahead.

Reflection

How have you seen God's discipline help shape your character or redirect your path in the past?

Life Application

When you encounter correction today, pause and ask God what He may be teaching you through it rather than reacting defensively.

Prayer

Father, thank You for caring enough to discipline me when I need it. Help me trust Your guidance and allow Your correction to shape my character and strengthen my faith. Amen.

September 4

Approved Through Endurance

James 1:12 (NKJV)

"Blessed is the man who endures temptation; for when he has been approved, he will receive the crown of life which the Lord has promised to those who love Him."

Devotional

Endurance reveals what is genuine. This verse reminds us that perseverance is not merely about surviving difficulty, but about remaining faithful when pressure tests the heart. Temptation and trial often expose what we rely on most. Enduring them shapes integrity and deepens trust in God.

Being approved does not happen in a moment. It is formed through repeated choices to honor God when the easier option is to compromise or quit. Endurance trains your spirit to hold steady, refining your character and strengthening your resolve. What God approves, He also sustains.

This promise of a crown of life speaks to eternal perspective. God sees beyond the immediate struggle and honors faithfulness that may go unnoticed by others. Your perseverance matters to Him. Every time you choose obedience, you are building a testimony of love and trust in God.

Today, let endurance reframe your challenges. What feels heavy now is shaping something lasting within you. God is using this season to approve, refine, and prepare you for what lies ahead.

Reflection

Where are you being tested to endure with faith and integrity right now?

Life Application

When temptation or pressure arises today, pause and choose the response that aligns with your love for God and His promises.

Prayer

Lord, strengthen me to endure with faith and integrity. Help me trust that You are using every challenge to refine me and prepare me for the life You have promised. Amen.

September 5

Enduring as a Child of God

Hebrews 12:7 (NLT)

"As you endure this divine discipline, remember that God is treating you as his own children. Whoever heard of a child who is never disciplined by its father?"

Devotional

Endurance takes on new meaning when you remember who you belong to. This verse reframes discipline as evidence of relationship rather than rejection. God's correction is not a sign that He is displeased with you. It is proof that you are His, and that He cares deeply about your growth and direction.

Divine discipline is rooted in love. It is intentional and purposeful, designed to shape your character and strengthen your faith. While discipline may feel uncomfortable or inconvenient, it serves a greater purpose. God is guiding you toward maturity, helping you develop endurance that can sustain you through future challenges.

This scripture also invites you to trust God's heart. A loving parent disciplines to protect, prepare, and teach. In the same way, God uses discipline to draw you closer to Him, refine your responses, and deepen your dependence on His wisdom. Endurance grows when you trust that God knows what you need, even when you do not fully understand the process.

Today, allow this truth to bring peace. You are not enduring alone or without purpose. God is walking with you, shaping you as His child, and strengthening you for the path ahead.

Reflection

How does viewing discipline as a sign of God's love change the way you respond to challenges?

Life Application

When you encounter correction or difficulty today, pause and remind yourself that God is guiding you with care and intention.

Prayer

Father, thank You for loving me enough to guide and discipline me. Help me trust Your heart and endure with faith, knowing You are shaping me as Your child. Amen.

September 6

Steady When It Is Hard

Isaiah 40:31 (NIV)
"But those who hope in the Lord will renew their strength. They will soar on wings like eagles; they will run and not grow weary, they will walk and not be faint."

Devotional

There are seasons when perseverance looks less like soaring and more like simply continuing to walk. This verse speaks to both. It acknowledges movement at different speeds and reminds you that strength is not self-generated. It is renewed through hope and trust in the Lord.

Waiting on God does not mean inactivity. It means choosing trust when progress feels slow and answers are delayed. Strength is renewed not when circumstances change, but when your reliance shifts. As you place your hope in God, He supplies what you need for the pace required in this season.

Notice the progression in this verse. There are moments of soaring, moments of running, and moments of walking. All are valid. All are faithful. Perseverance does not demand constant momentum. It asks for consistency. God is not disappointed by your pace. He is attentive to your posture of trust.

Today, allow yourself to move at the speed God is sustaining. You do not have to force strength or manufacture endurance. As you wait on Him, He will renew you for every step ahead.

Reflection

Where have you been pushing yourself instead of waiting on God for renewed strength?
What pace has God been inviting you to walk in during this season?

Life Application

Today, pause before making a decision or taking action and intentionally place your trust in God's timing and strength rather than your own urgency.

Prayer

Lord, help me wait on You with trust and patience. Renew my strength when I feel weary and steady my steps when the journey feels long. Teach me to move at the pace You are sustaining and to rely fully on You each day. Amen.

September 7

Staying the Course

Luke 9:62 (NLT)
"But Jesus told him, 'Anyone who puts a hand to the plow and then looks back is not fit for the Kingdom of God.'"

Devotional

Commitment is revealed in direction, not intention. Jesus' words in this verse are direct and uncompromising because discipleship requires focus. Staying the course means choosing forward movement even when the past tries to call you back.

Looking back often feels harmless. Memories, regrets, or former comforts can quietly pull your attention away from what God is doing now. But this scripture reminds you that divided focus weakens progress. The work God has placed before you requires your full attention and wholehearted devotion.

Staying the course does not mean denying where you have been. It means refusing to let it define where you are going. God calls you to keep your hands steady, your eyes forward, and your trust anchored in Him. The Kingdom work unfolding in your life deserves your full commitment.

Endurance is not about perfection. It is about resolve. When you choose not to look back, you create space for God to lead you fully into what lies ahead.

Reflection
What distractions or past attachments are tempting you to look back?

Life Application
Today, intentionally refocus on what God has called you to do and take one step forward without hesitation.

Prayer
Jesus, help me stay focused on the path You have set before me. Strengthen my resolve so I do not look back but move forward with trust and obedience. Amen.

September 8

Watching While You Wait

Micah 7:7 (NLT)
"As for me, I look to the Lord for help. I wait confidently for God to save me, and my God will certainly hear me."

Devotional

Perseverance is not passive waiting. It is active trust. This verse captures a posture that many believers must learn over time. Micah does not deny difficulty or pretend that answers are immediate. He makes a deliberate choice to look to the Lord and wait with confidence.

Waiting becomes heavy when it feels uncertain. But confidence shifts the experience. When you wait believing that God hears you, waiting transforms from frustration into expectation. Perseverance grows when you trust not only that God will respond, but that He is attentive even in the silence.

This scripture also reminds you where to place your focus. Looking to the Lord is a decision. It means resisting the urge to fix everything yourself or to measure progress by visible change alone. God works in ways you cannot always see, but His hearing is constant and His response is sure.

Today, perseverance may look like continued trust without immediate evidence. That is not weakness. It is faith refined. As you wait, keep your eyes on God, confident that He is present, attentive, and faithful to act in His time.

Reflection

Where have you been waiting without confidence instead of waiting with trust?
What would change if you believed fully that God hears you right now?

Life Application

Choose one situation you have been waiting on and intentionally shift your posture from frustration to confidence, reminding yourself that God hears and responds in His time.

Prayer

God, help me wait with confidence and not with doubt. Teach me to look to You for help and trust that You hear me even when answers feel delayed. Strengthen my faith as I persevere and rest in Your faithfulness. Amen.

September 9

Strength That Lasts

Colossians 1:11 (NLT)

"We also pray that you will be strengthened with all his glorious power so you will have all the endurance and patience you need. May you be filled with joy."

Devotional

Perseverance requires a specific kind of strength. This verse makes it clear that endurance and patience are not products of willpower alone. They flow from God's power working within you. When strength is self-generated, it eventually runs out. When strength is God-given, it sustains.

Notice what this strength is for. It is not primarily for achievement or visibility. It is for endurance and patience. These qualities allow you to remain steady over time, especially when circumstances do not change quickly. God knows exactly what this season demands, and He supplies strength accordingly.

There is also joy woven into this prayer. Joy does not wait until endurance is no longer necessary. It exists alongside it. As God strengthens you, He also guards your heart from bitterness and despair. Perseverance rooted in God's power does not harden you. It matures you.

Today, you do not need to borrow strength from tomorrow. God is giving you what you need for this moment. Allow Him to strengthen you from the inside so that endurance becomes sustainable, patient, and marked by quiet joy.

Reflection

Where have you been relying on your own strength instead of God's? What would it look like to receive endurance as a gift rather than a burden?

Life Application

Today, pause when you feel tired or pressured and intentionally ask God to strengthen you rather than pushing through on your own.

Prayer

Father, strengthen me with Your power so I can endure with patience and grace. Help me rely on You rather than my own strength and fill me with joy as I continue forward. I trust You to sustain me through every season. Amen.

September 10

Courage to Continue

Haggai 2:4 (NLT)
"But now the Lord says: Be strong, Zerubbabel. Be strong, Jeshua son of Jehozadak, the high priest. Be strong, all you people still left in the land. And now get to work, for I am with you, says the Lord of Heaven's Armies."

Devotional

Courage is often needed most in the middle of the work. This verse was spoken to people who were tired, discouraged, and questioning whether their efforts still mattered. God's response was not to remove the task, but to remind them of His presence.

Strength is repeated here because weariness makes courage fragile. God knows when His people need reassurance. The call to continue is not rooted in personal ability, but in divine companionship. "I am with you" is the foundation for perseverance.

This scripture affirms that progress sometimes requires renewed resolve rather than new direction. God does not always change the assignment. He strengthens the people carrying it. Courage grows when you remember that you are not working alone.

When fatigue threatens your faith, return to this truth. God remains present, engaged, and committed to what He has asked you to build. Continuing is an act of trust grounded in His faithfulness.

Reflection
Where do you feel weary but still called to continue?

Life Application
Choose one task today to approach with renewed courage, trusting that God is with you in the work.

Prayer
Lord, strengthen me when I feel tired or discouraged. Help me continue the work You have given me with confidence, knowing You are with me every step of the way. Amen.

September 11

Keep Your Eyes Ahead

Proverbs 4:25–27 (NLT)
"Look straight ahead, and fix your eyes on what lies before you. Mark out a straight path for your feet; stay on the safe path. Don't get sidetracked; keep your feet from following evil."

Devotional

Perseverance is protected by focus. This passage is practical and firm, reminding you that endurance is not only about spiritual strength but about intentional direction. Where you fix your eyes determines how steadily you walk.

Distraction is one of the quietest threats to perseverance. It does not always come in obvious forms. Sometimes it appears as comparison, overthinking, regret, or unnecessary detours. Scripture calls you back to simplicity. Look ahead. Stay the course. Do not allow side paths to drain your energy or weaken your resolve.

Marking a straight path requires awareness. It means recognizing what pulls you off course and choosing alignment again and again. Perseverance is sustained when your steps are deliberate and your focus is clear. God does not ask you to see the entire road. He asks you to keep moving in the direction He has set.

Today, this verse invites you to tighten your focus. Not everything deserves your attention. Staying the course sometimes means saying no to distractions so you can say yes to consistency, obedience, and peace.

Reflection

What distractions have been pulling your focus away from steady progress?
Where might God be asking you to simplify your path?

Life Application

Identify one distraction that has been sidetracking your attention and make a conscious decision today to redirect your focus forward.

Prayer

Lord, help me keep my eyes fixed on the path You have set before me. Guard my heart from distractions that weaken my endurance. Teach me to walk steadily, wisely, and faithfully as I continue forward. Amen.

September 12

Quiet Trust

Psalm 62:5 (NLT)

"Let all that I am wait quietly before God, for my hope is in him."

Devotional

Perseverance does not always announce itself loudly. Sometimes it looks like quiet trust. This verse invites you into a posture that resists panic, striving, and unnecessary noise. Waiting quietly before God is an act of maturity, not passivity.

Quiet trust requires restraint. It means you do not rush to explain yourself, force outcomes, or fill silence with activity. Instead, you anchor your hope in God and allow Him to work in ways that may not be immediately visible. This kind of perseverance steadies the heart and guards against burnout.

Notice where hope is placed. It is not in progress, answers, or timelines. It is in God Himself. When your hope rests there, waiting becomes sustainable. You are not enduring blindly. You are trusting intentionally.

Today, perseverance may mean resisting the urge to react and choosing stillness instead. God honors a heart that waits quietly, confident that He is present and faithful to fulfill what He has promised.

Reflection

Where have you been tempted to rush instead of wait quietly?
What does it look like to place your hope fully in God rather than outcomes?

Life Application

Create space today for intentional stillness with God, even if only for a few moments, and practice waiting without rushing or forcing clarity.

Prayer

God, help me wait quietly before You with trust and confidence. Teach me to place my hope fully in You and not in outcomes or timing. Calm my spirit and strengthen my faith as I continue to persevere. Amen.

September 13

Better Than the Beginning

Ecclesiastes 7:8 (NLT)
"Finishing is better than starting. Patience is better than pride."

Devotional

Perseverance is proven at the finish, not the start. This verse offers a quiet but powerful reminder that endurance carries more weight than enthusiasm. Beginnings are often fueled by excitement, but finishing requires patience, humility, and sustained commitment.

There is a temptation to value how something starts rather than how it is completed. God places greater emphasis on follow-through. Patience keeps you grounded when progress feels slow, while pride can push you to rush, quit, or seek shortcuts. Perseverance chooses steadiness over appearance.

This scripture also reframes success. Completion does not mean perfection. It means faithfulness. It means staying engaged even when the process stretches longer than expected. God honors the heart that remains committed through the middle and presses on toward the end.

Today, perseverance may look like continuing something you once felt excited about but now must finish with discipline. Trust that God sees your patience and values your willingness to remain faithful until the work is complete.

Reflection

What have you been tempted to abandon because the excitement has faded?
How might patience help you finish well in this season?

Life Application

Identify one commitment you have been tempted to rush or quit and choose today to continue with patience and humility.

Prayer

Lord, help me value finishing over starting and patience over pride. Strengthen my resolve to stay faithful through every stage of the journey. Teach me to endure with humility and trust as I continue walking with You. Amen.

September 14

Still Before God

Psalm 37:7 (NIV)
"Be still before the Lord and wait patiently for him; do not fret when people succeed in their ways, when they carry out their wicked schemes."

Devotional

Perseverance often requires stillness before it requires action. This verse speaks to the discipline of remaining calm and anchored when circumstances tempt you toward comparison, frustration, or anxiety. Waiting patiently before the Lord is not weakness. It is strength under control.

Stillness confronts the urge to react. When others seem to move ahead or succeed quickly, it can stir restlessness and doubt. God calls you away from fretting and into trust. Perseverance grows when you stop measuring your progress against someone else's path and remain grounded in God's timing.

Waiting patiently does not mean disengaging from responsibility. It means refusing to let impatience govern your spirit. God works with precision, not haste. Stillness creates space for clarity, discernment, and peace, even when outcomes remain unresolved.

Today, perseverance may look like resisting comparison and choosing calm confidence instead. God is attentive to your faithfulness. As you remain still before Him, He continues working on your behalf in ways you cannot yet see.

Reflection

Where have you been tempted to compare your progress to others? How might stillness before God help you persevere with peace?

Life Application

When feelings of frustration or comparison arise today, pause and intentionally choose stillness, reminding yourself that God's timing is trustworthy.

Prayer

Lord, teach me to be still before You and wait with patience. Guard my heart from comparison and frustration and help me trust Your timing as I continue to persevere. I place my confidence in You alone. Amen.

September 15

Not Shaken

2 Thessalonians 3:13 (CSB)

"But as for you, brothers and sisters, do not grow weary in doing good."

Devotional

Perseverance is often quiet and unseen. This verse speaks to the steady continuation of good even when fatigue sets in or recognition is absent. It acknowledges weariness without granting it authority. Doing good overtime requires resolve rooted in purpose, not in immediate results.

Growing weary does not mean you are weak. It means you have been consistent. The encouragement here is not to stop, but to remain anchored. God sees what others may overlook. Faithfulness carried out day after day builds spiritual strength and deepens character.

This scripture also reinforces stability. When your commitment is grounded in obedience rather than applause, your perseverance becomes less vulnerable to discouragement. You continue not because it feels easy, but because it matters. God values endurance that remains intact even when circumstances challenge your resolve.

Today, perseverance may mean continuing to do good without visible return. That steadiness matters. God is not shaken by delays, and neither are those who remain rooted in Him.

Reflection

Where have you begun to feel weary in doing good?
What helps you remain steady when encouragement feels limited?

Life Application

Choose one act of good today and complete it with intention, trusting that God sees and honors your faithfulness.

Prayer

God, strengthen me when weariness sets in. Help me remain faithful in doing good and steady in my obedience, even when results are not immediate. I trust You to sustain me as I persevere. Amen.

September 16

Steady in the Middle

Hebrews 10:23 (ESV)
"Let us hold fast the confession of our hope without wavering, for he who promised is faithful."

Devotional

The middle of the journey is often where perseverance is tested most. The beginning carried clarity and momentum. The ending holds promise. The middle asks you to stay anchored without the benefit of either. This verse speaks directly to that space, calling you to hold fast without wavering.

Holding fast is an intentional act. It means you do not loosen your grip on hope simply because progress feels slow or uncertain. Perseverance is strengthened when hope is treated as a conviction, not a feeling. You remain steady not because everything is resolved, but because God is faithful.

This scripture shifts the focus away from your consistency and places it on God's character. Faithfulness is not something you manufacture. It is something you trust. When doubts arise or confidence dips, this verse calls you back to the foundation. God keeps His promises, even when fulfillment takes time.

Today, perseverance may look like refusing to abandon hope in the middle. You are not required to see the outcome yet. You are only asked to remain anchored. The same God who promised is the God who will complete what He began.

Reflection

Where have you felt tempted to waver in your hope?
What does it look like to hold fast even when the middle feels uncertain?

Life Application

When doubts arise today, intentionally remind yourself of God's faithfulness and choose to hold steady rather than pull back.

Prayer

God, help me hold fast to hope without wavering. When the journey feels uncertain, remind me that You are faithful to every promise You have made. Strengthen my heart to persevere with trust and confidence in You. Amen.

September 17

Guarded Endurance

Proverbs 4:23 (NKJV)
"Keep your heart with all diligence, for out of it spring the issues of life."

Devotional

Perseverance is sustained by what you protect internally. This verse makes it clear that endurance is not only about what you do, but about what you guard. When the heart becomes depleted, distracted, or discouraged, perseverance weakens from the inside out.

Guarding your heart requires diligence. It means being intentional about what you allow to influence your thoughts, emotions, and expectations. Negative cycles, unresolved disappointment, and constant pressure can quietly erode endurance if left unchecked. God calls you to protect the source from which your life flows.

This scripture also highlights responsibility. While God supplies strength, you are called to steward your inner life. Perseverance grows when your heart remains aligned with truth rather than overwhelmed by circumstances. What you nurture internally will shape how you continue externally.

Today, perseverance may look like setting boundaries around your thoughts, conversations, or inputs. Guarding your heart is not withdrawal. It is wisdom. As you protect what God is shaping within you, endurance becomes steadier and more sustainable.

Reflection

What has been influencing your heart most lately?
Where might God be inviting you to guard your heart more carefully?

Life Application

Pay attention today to what affects your inner peace and intentionally choose what strengthens rather than drains your endurance.

Prayer

Lord, help me guard my heart with wisdom and diligence. Show me what needs protecting and what needs releasing. Strengthen my inner life so that I can continue forward with perseverance and peace. Amen.

September 18

Strengthened to Stand

Ephesians 6:13 (NIV)
"Therefore put on the full armor of God, so that when the day of evil comes, you may be able to stand your ground, and after you have done everything, to stand."

Devotional

Perseverance is not always about moving forward. Sometimes it is about standing firm. This verse speaks to seasons when endurance means holding your ground rather than advancing at full speed. Standing requires strength, resolve, and preparation.

The armor of God is not given for comfort. It is given for resistance. When pressure intensifies and challenges persist, perseverance shifts from action to stability. Standing firm keeps you anchored when circumstances try to push you backward or wear you down.

This scripture also acknowledges effort. After you have done everything, you are still called to stand. Perseverance does not guarantee immediate relief. It guarantees resilience. God equips you to remain steady even when the situation remains unresolved.

Today, perseverance may look like refusing to retreat in your faith or convictions. You do not need to force progress. You need to remain grounded. God has already given you what you need to stand, and His strength sustains you as you do.

Reflection

Where have you been tempted to give ground rather than stand firm? What does standing look like for you in this season?

Life Application

Identify one area where you need to stand your ground and intentionally rely on God's strength rather than your own resolve.

Prayer

God, strengthen me to stand firm when pressure rises. Help me rely on the strength You provide and remain grounded in faith even when progress feels slow. I trust You to sustain me as I persevere. Amen.

September 19

Held Through It All

Psalm 66:9 (CSB)

"He keeps us alive and does not allow our feet to slip."

Devotional

Perseverance is often sustained in ways you do not immediately notice. This verse highlights God's quiet faithfulness. While you focus on moving forward, God is focused on keeping you steady. You may not always feel strong, but you are being held.

There are seasons when progress feels fragile. You take careful steps, aware that fatigue or uncertainty could cause you to stumble. God's promise here is not that the path will be effortless, but that He will not allow your feet to slip. His protection operates beneath the surface, supporting you when your strength feels limited.

This scripture reframes endurance. Perseverance is not only about your ability to keep going. It is about God's commitment to keep you standing. Even when the road is uneven, His presence stabilizes you. What feels like survival is often sustained by grace you did not ask for but deeply need.

Today, take comfort in knowing that you are being held. Your perseverance is not resting solely on your resolve. God is actively preserving you, step by step, through every season you walk through.

Reflection

Where have you felt unsure or unsteady lately?
How does knowing God is holding you change how you view this season?

Life Application

When you feel uncertain today, pause and remind yourself that God is keeping you steady, even when the path feels uneven.

Prayer

God, thank You for holding me steady when I feel unsure. Thank You for keeping my feet from slipping and sustaining me when my strength feels small. Help me trust Your quiet faithfulness as I continue to persevere. Amen.

September 20

Unmoved

Psalm 125:1 (CSB)
"Those who trust in the Lord are like Mount Zion. It cannot be shaken; it remains forever."

Devotional

Perseverance is rooted in stability, not speed. This verse offers a powerful image of what trust in God produces. Mount Zion does not rush or strain to remain in place. It stands firm. In the same way, trust anchors you when circumstances attempt to unsettle your confidence or disrupt your peace.

Being unmoved does not mean untouched by difficulty. It means not being displaced by it. When trust is firmly placed in the Lord, endurance becomes less reactive. You are not swayed by every challenge or discouraged by every delay. Perseverance grows when your foundation remains secure.

This scripture reminds you that stability comes from where you place your trust. When trust is divided or conditional, shaking follows. When trust is centered on God, endurance becomes lasting. You remain steady not because life is predictable, but because God is faithful.

Today, perseverance may look like choosing trust again even after being tested. God is strengthening your foundation. As you remain anchored in Him, you will not be easily shaken by what surrounds you.

Reflection

What has been testing your sense of stability lately?
Where might God be inviting you to deepen your trust?

Life Application

When you feel unsettled today, intentionally place your trust in God rather than in outcomes or circumstances, reminding yourself that He is your firm foundation.

Prayer

Lord, help me remain anchored in You. When challenges arise, strengthen my trust so I am not shaken. Thank You for being my steady foundation and for sustaining me as I continue to persevere. Amen.

September 21

Sustained by Mercy

Psalm 94:18 (NIV)
"When I said, 'My foot is slipping,' your unfailing love, Lord, supported me."

Devotional

Perseverance is often strengthened in moments when you realize you cannot hold yourself up alone. This verse captures a vulnerable confession followed immediately by divine support. The psalmist does not deny instability. He names it. And God meets it with unfailing love.

There are times when endurance feels fragile. You sense yourself slipping emotionally, spiritually, or mentally. This scripture reminds you that awareness of weakness is not failure. It is an opening for God's support to become evident. His love does not wait for you to regain balance. It steps in when you cannot.

God's unfailing love is not reactive. It is sustaining. Even when you feel unsure or off balance, His support is already present, holding you steady beneath the surface. Perseverance grows when you trust that God is supporting you even before you feel secure again.

Today, endurance may look like admitting where you feel unsteady and allowing God to support you there. You are not required to hold yourself together. God's love is actively keeping you from falling.

Reflection

Where have you felt unsteady or close to slipping lately?
How does knowing God supports you change how you view this moment?

Life Application

When you feel overwhelmed today, pause and acknowledge your need for God's support instead of trying to push through on your own.

Prayer

Lord, thank You for supporting me when I feel unsteady. When my strength feels limited, remind me that Your unfailing love is holding me. Help me persevere with trust, knowing You are sustaining me every step of the way. Amen.

September 22

Strength in Waiting

Isaiah 30:18 (ESV)
"Therefore the Lord waits to be gracious to you, and therefore he exalts himself to show mercy to you. For the Lord is a God of justice; blessed are all those who wait for him."

Devotional

Perseverance is often misunderstood as relentless action. This verse reframes endurance as a shared posture between you and God. While you are waiting, God is also waiting, not in delay, but in intention. He waits to be gracious. He waits to show mercy.

Waiting can feel like inactivity when you want movement or resolution. Yet Scripture reveals that waiting is not empty space. It is the environment where grace and mercy are prepared to meet you. Perseverance deepens when you trust that God's timing is purposeful, not passive.

This verse also affirms God's character. He is a God of justice, which means nothing is mishandled, overlooked, or mistimed. Waiting becomes an act of trust rooted in who God is, not in how quickly circumstances change. Blessing is attached not to rushing ahead, but to remaining aligned.

Today, perseverance may look like honoring the wait rather than resisting it. God is not withholding goodness. He is positioning you to receive it fully. Strength grows when you trust that waiting is part of how God works.

Reflection

Where have you struggled most with waiting?
How does knowing God waits with intention change your perspective?

Life Application

When impatience arises today, intentionally pause and remind yourself that God's timing is purposeful and anchored in grace and mercy.

Prayer

God, help me trust You in the waiting. Teach me to see this season as purposeful and grounded in Your grace. Strengthen my heart to persevere with patience, knowing You are working with justice and mercy on my behalf. Amen.

September 23

Held in the Waiting

Nahum 1:7 (NIV)
"The Lord is good, a refuge in times of trouble. He cares for those who trust in him."

Devotional

Perseverance is sustained by knowing where to take refuge. This verse reminds you that endurance is not about standing exposed to difficulty. It is about remaining close to God when trouble presses in. Refuge implies shelter, safety, and intentional proximity.

Times of trouble often reveal where trust truly rests. When pressure increases, it becomes tempting to rely on self-protection, control, or withdrawal. God invites you instead to trust His care. Perseverance strengthens when you believe that God is not distant from your struggle. He is attentive to it.

This scripture also affirms God's goodness. Trouble does not negate His character. Waiting seasons do not cancel His care. Even when circumstances feel unstable, God remains a refuge. His care is not conditional or fleeting. It is consistent and personal.

Today, perseverance may look like returning to God as your refuge rather than attempting to endure alone. You are not meant to absorb difficulty without support. God sees those who trust Him, and His care surrounds them fully.

Reflection

Where have you been carrying pressure without seeking refuge?
How does trusting God's care reshape how you endure this season?

Life Application

When stress or uncertainty rises today, intentionally turn to God as your refuge rather than relying on your own strength or control.

Prayer

Lord, thank You for being my refuge in times of trouble. Help me trust Your care and goodness when the season feels heavy. Strengthen my heart to persevere while resting in the safety of Your presence. Amen.

September 24

Strength for Today

Deuteronomy 33:25 (ESV)
"Your bars shall be iron and bronze, and as your days, so shall your strength be."

Devotional

Perseverance is sustained one day at a time. This verse offers reassurance for seasons when the road ahead feels long and demanding. God does not promise strength for every future challenge all at once. He promises strength that matches each day as it comes.

The image of iron and bronze speaks to durability and protection. God equips you to withstand what you are facing now, not by overwhelming you with future concerns, but by reinforcing you for the present moment. Endurance grows when you focus on today's faithfulness rather than tomorrow's unknowns.

This scripture also addresses fear of insufficiency. You do not need to borrow strength from tomorrow or replay yesterday's fatigue. God supplies what you need for each day you walk through. Perseverance becomes manageable when you trust God to meet you daily with what is required.

Today, endurance may look like releasing anxiety about what lies ahead and trusting God for the strength He is providing right now. You are equipped for this day, and tomorrow's strength will come when tomorrow arrives.

Reflection

Where have you been worrying about future demands rather than focusing on today?
How does this verse reshape your understanding of daily strength?

Life Application

When you feel overwhelmed today, pause and remind yourself that God is giving you the strength you need for this day alone.

Prayer

God, thank You for meeting me with strength that matches each day. Help me trust You for today and release my concerns about tomorrow. Strengthen my heart to persevere with confidence in Your daily provision. Amen.

September 25

Anchored in Hope

Romans 15:4 (NIV)

"For everything that was written in the past was written to teach us, so that through the endurance taught in the Scriptures and the encouragement they provide we might have hope."

Devotional

Perseverance is strengthened when hope is anchored in truth. This verse reminds you that Scripture is not only informative but sustaining. The stories, promises, and instructions written before you were born were preserved to strengthen your endurance today.

Endurance grows through encouragement. When the journey feels long, God uses His Word to remind you that others have walked difficult paths and remained faithful. Their stories are not distant history. They are evidence that perseverance is possible and that hope can endure through uncertainty.

This scripture also reframes how you engage with the Word. Reading Scripture is not simply a discipline. It is a source of encouragement designed to keep hope alive. Perseverance weakens when hope fades, but hope is renewed when truth is revisited consistently.

Today, perseverance may look like returning to God's Word not for answers alone, but for encouragement. As you remain anchored in what God has spoken, hope strengthens your endurance and steadies your faith.

Reflection

Where have you been struggling to maintain hope?
How might engaging Scripture differently strengthen your perseverance?

Life Application

Spend time today reading a portion of Scripture with the intention of receiving encouragement rather than instruction alone.

Prayer

God, thank You for Your Word that strengthens my endurance and renews my hope. Help me stay anchored in truth when the journey feels long. Encourage my heart and sustain my faith as I continue to persevere. Amen.

September 26

Stronger as You Go

Job 17:9 (ESV)
"Yet the righteous holds to his way, and he who has clean hands grows stronger and stronger."

Devotional

Perseverance does not always feel like progress, but it often produces it quietly. This verse speaks to strength that develops over time, not overnight. Even in the midst of suffering and unanswered questions, Job acknowledges a truth that endurance reveals. The righteous continue forward, and strength increases along the way.

Holding to your way requires resolve. It means remaining committed to integrity, obedience, and faith even when circumstances are discouraging. Perseverance is not proven by ease. It is refined through pressure. As you continue walking faithfully, God uses the journey itself to strengthen you.

This scripture also offers reassurance. You may not feel stronger yet, but growth is happening. Endurance compounds. Each faithful step builds upon the last, forming strength that is steady and lasting. Perseverance is not wasted effort. It is shaping who you are becoming.

Today, perseverance may look like continuing without visible affirmation. Trust that God is strengthening you as you go. What feels demanding now is producing resilience that will serve you well in the seasons ahead.

Reflection

Where have you noticed quiet growth even in difficult seasons?
What does it look like for you to hold firmly to your way right now?

Life Application

Choose today to remain faithful in one area where perseverance feels challenging, trusting that strength is developing even if you cannot yet see it.

Prayer

God, help me hold firmly to the path You have set before me. Strengthen me as I continue forward, even when the journey feels heavy. Thank You for growing strength within me as I persevere with faith and integrity. Amen.

September 27

Patient and Steady

James 5:7 (ESV)
"Be patient, therefore, brothers, until the coming of the Lord. See how the farmer waits for the precious fruit of the earth, being patient about it, until it receives the early and the late rains."

Devotional

Perseverance is closely tied to patience. This verse offers a grounded picture of endurance through the image of a farmer who understands timing. Growth cannot be rushed. Fruit develops through seasons of waiting, tending, and trust.

The farmer does not abandon the field because harvest is not immediate. He continues to prepare, care, and wait, trusting that what has been planted will grow in its proper time. Perseverance works the same way. Faithfulness continues even when results are not yet visible.

This scripture reminds you that waiting is not inactivity. It is participation in a process you cannot control but must trust. Perseverance strengthens when you accept that some outcomes require time and cannot be forced. God works through seasons, and each one plays a role in what is being produced.

Today, endurance may look like remaining patient without questioning the value of your effort. What you have planted is not forgotten. God is tending what you cannot see, and fruit will come in its appointed time.

Reflection

Where have you been tempted to rush a process God is still developing?
How does the image of the farmer reshape your understanding of patience?

Life Application

Practice patience today by resisting the urge to force an outcome and instead trusting God's timing for what you are cultivating.

Prayer

God, help me remain patient as I wait for what You are growing. Teach me to trust the process and persevere with faith, knowing You are working through every season. Amen.

September 28

Waiting With Confidence

Psalm 33:20 (NIV)

"We wait in hope for the Lord; he is our help and our shield."

Devotional

Perseverance is strengthened when waiting is paired with confidence rather than fear. This verse is short but grounded, reminding you that waiting does not leave you exposed. God is both your help and your protection as you endure.

Waiting in hope requires trust. It means believing that God is actively involved even when answers are delayed. Perseverance weakens when waiting feels unsupported, but Scripture reassures you that God stands as a shield around you. You are not vulnerable while you wait. You are covered.

This verse also clarifies where help comes from. When endurance is tested, it can be tempting to look for quick relief or external reassurance. God invites you instead to wait in hope, anchored in His presence. Perseverance grows when you trust that God Himself is sustaining you.

Today, endurance may look like choosing hope again, even if the waiting continues. God remains your help. He remains your shield. As you wait, you are not standing alone.

Reflection

Where has waiting begun to feel discouraging rather than hopeful? How does knowing God is your help and shield change how you endure?

Life Application

When waiting feels heavy today, intentionally remind yourself that God is actively helping and protecting you, even if outcomes are still unfolding.

Prayer

Lord, help me wait in hope rather than frustration. Thank You for being my help and my shield as I persevere. Strengthen my trust and sustain my faith as I continue to wait on You. Amen.

September 29

Hope That Holds

Hebrews 6:19 (CSB)

"We have this hope as an anchor for the soul, firm and secure."

Devotional

Perseverance is sustained by what keeps your soul anchored. This verse offers a steady image for seasons when emotions fluctuate and circumstances feel uncertain. An anchor does not eliminate movement around it, but it prevents drifting. Hope in God serves that same purpose for your soul.

When life feels unpredictable, endurance weakens if hope is not secured. This scripture reminds you that biblical hope is not wishful thinking. It is firm and secure. It holds you steady when waves of doubt, delay, or fatigue attempt to pull you off course.

Anchored hope allows you to remain grounded without needing constant reassurance. Perseverance becomes possible when your confidence is rooted in God's faithfulness rather than immediate outcomes. Even when progress feels slow, hope keeps you from being swept away by discouragement.

Today, perseverance may look like tightening your grip on hope rather than searching for certainty elsewhere. God has given you an anchor that holds. As you remain secured in Him, your endurance will remain steady.

Reflection

What has been testing the stability of your hope?
Where might your soul need stronger anchoring right now?

Life Application

Identify one area where discouragement has caused drifting and intentionally reaffirm your hope in God today.

Prayer

God, thank You for being the anchor for my soul. When uncertainty surrounds me, help me remain firm and secure in hope. Strengthen my endurance and keep me grounded as I continue to persevere. Amen.

September 30

Steady to the End

Psalm 130:5 (NIV)
"I wait for the Lord, my whole being waits, and in his word I put my hope."

Devotional

Perseverance is most clearly revealed at the end of a season. This verse reflects a deep, settled posture of trust. Waiting here is not partial or hesitant. It involves the whole being. It is a decision to remain anchored in God even when answers are still unfolding.

This kind of waiting is not passive resignation. It is intentional hope rooted in God's Word. When circumstances fluctuate and emotions rise and fall, Scripture becomes the place where hope is renewed. Perseverance strengthens when trust is anchored in what God has spoken rather than what is currently seen.

As September closes, this verse serves as a quiet summary of endurance. You have waited. You have continued. You have remained faithful through uncertainty, delay, and growth. Perseverance has not required perfection. It has required presence, trust, and consistency.

Today marks the close of a month focused on pressing forward. Carry this posture with you. Waiting with your whole being and placing hope in God's Word is not limited to a season. It is a way of walking forward with strength, patience, and faith.

Reflection

How has your understanding of perseverance shifted this month? Where has God strengthened your ability to wait with trust?

Life Application

Take time today to reflect on how you have endured this month and intentionally reaffirm your hope in God's Word as you prepare to move forward.

Prayer

God, thank You for carrying me through this season. As I wait, I place my hope fully in You and in Your Word. Strengthen my heart to continue forward with patience, trust, and perseverance in the days ahead. Amen

October

Abiding in Peace & Rest

September required strength. It asked you to keep going, to remain steady, and to press on even when the journey felt long. October invites something different. This month is not about pushing through or proving endurance. It is about learning how to remain. Peace and rest are not rewards you earn after surviving difficulty. They are gifts God offers in the midst of it.

Abiding means staying connected, rooted, and present with God rather than striving for control or clarity. Peace is not the absence of noise, pressure, or responsibility. It is the presence of trust. Rest is not inactivity or withdrawal. It is alignment. When your soul is aligned with God, you can move, decide, and lead without carrying unnecessary weight. October calls you to release urgency and rediscover stillness that restores rather than stalls.

This month will guide you into a slower, steadier posture. You will be invited to quiet your inner world, trust God more deeply, and allow peace to guard your heart and mind. As you abide in Him, you will find that rest does not weaken you. It strengthens you. Peace does not delay purpose. It sustains it. Let this month be a sacred pause where your soul exhales and your faith settles securely in God's presence.

October 1

Come Back to Rest

Psalm 116:7 (NIV)

"Return to your rest, my soul, for the Lord has been good to you."

Devotional

This verse reads like an invitation and a reminder. It assumes that the soul has wandered from rest and gently calls it back. Rest is not something you stumble into by accident. It is something you return to intentionally. God speaks directly to the inner life and invites it to settle again in what is safe and sustaining.

The phrase "return to your rest" suggests that rest is familiar. It is not foreign or unreachable. It belongs to you. Yet seasons of pressure, responsibility, and perseverance can quietly pull the soul away from it. October begins by calling you back, not because you failed to endure, but because God's goodness has already been proven.

Rest here is anchored in remembrance. The Lord has been good to you. Peace deepens when you stop striving and start recalling God's faithfulness. Abiding begins when you allow that truth to calm what has been overextended. This is not a command to stop living. It is an invitation to live from a rested place.

Today, let your soul return. You do not have to carry what God never asked you to hold. Peace starts by remembering who God is and allowing that truth to quiet you from the inside out.

Reflection

Where has your soul drifted from rest?
What reminds you most clearly of God's goodness in your life?

Life Application

Pause today and intentionally choose one moment of stillness where you remind your soul that it is safe to rest in God.

Prayer

God, help my soul return to rest. Thank You for Your goodness that surrounds me and sustains me. Teach me to abide in peace and trust You deeply as I begin this new season. Amen.

October 2

A Quieted Soul

Psalm 131:2 (NIV)
"But I have calmed and quieted myself, I am like a weaned child with its mother; like a weaned child I am content."

Devotional

Peace is not always something that happens to you. Sometimes it is something you choose. This verse reveals a deliberate posture. The psalmist does not wait for life to settle before finding rest. He actively calms and quiets his soul.

The image of a weaned child is powerful. A weaned child no longer cries for what once brought comfort. Instead, it rests securely, content simply to be close. This kind of peace is not dependent on getting answers, relief, or reassurance. It comes from trust and maturity. It reflects a soul that has learned how to rest in God's presence without striving.

Abiding in peace often means releasing the need to control outcomes or demand clarity. Contentment grows when your soul learns that God's nearness is enough. This does not minimize your desires or prayers. It simply places them in a posture of trust rather than urgency.

Today, peace may look like choosing calm instead of reaction. Quieting your soul does not mean disengaging from life. It means anchoring yourself in God so deeply that contentment is no longer tied to what is happening around you.

Reflection

What has been stirring restlessness in your soul?
What would it look like to quiet yourself before God today?

Life Application

When you notice restlessness today, pause and intentionally calm your thoughts, reminding yourself that God's presence is enough.

Prayer

God, help me quiet my soul before You. Teach me to rest in Your presence with contentment and trust. Release me from striving and help me abide in the peace You freely give. Amen.

October 3

Rest for the Weary

Matthew 11:28 (CSB)
"Come to me, all of you who are weary and burdened, and I will give you rest."

Devotional

Rest begins with invitation, not effort. Jesus does not ask the weary to fix themselves before coming to Him. He simply says, come. Weariness is not a disqualifier. It is the reason for the invitation.

This verse reframes rest as something received rather than achieved. Many burdens are carried quietly, especially by those who are faithful, responsible, and dependable. Over time, even good responsibilities can weigh heavily on the soul. Jesus acknowledges that weight and offers rest that does not require explanation or justification.

Abiding in peace starts when you stop trying to carry what was never meant to be borne alone. Coming to Jesus is an act of trust. It is a choice to lay down self-reliance and allow Him to provide relief that reaches deeper than physical rest. His rest restores the inner life, not just the outward pace.

Today, peace may begin with a simple decision to come. You do not need a plan or perfect words. You only need willingness. Rest is not something you postpone. It is something Jesus offers now.

Reflection

Where have you been carrying weariness silently?
What makes it difficult for you to come to Jesus for rest?

Life Application

When you feel burdened today, intentionally pause and bring that weight to Jesus rather than pushing through it on your own.

Prayer

Jesus, I come to You with my weariness and burdens. Thank You for offering rest without condition. Teach me to abide in Your peace and receive the rest You freely give. Amen.

October 4

Peace That Guards

Philippians 4:7 (NIV)
"And the peace of God, which transcends all understanding, will guard your hearts and your minds in Christ Jesus."

Devotional

Peace from God does not require full understanding to be effective. This verse reminds you that peace is not something you figure out. It is something you receive. God's peace operates beyond logic and explanation, meeting you at the level of the heart and mind.

Guarding implies protection. God's peace does not merely calm you momentarily. It stands watch over your inner life. When anxiety presses in or thoughts begin to spiral, peace acts as a boundary that keeps unrest from taking over. Abiding in peace means allowing God to protect what you cannot always control.

This peace is rooted in Christ. It is sustained through connection, not circumstance. When you remain close to Him, peace becomes a steady presence rather than a fleeting feeling. Rest deepens when you trust God to guard your thoughts and emotions without needing constant reassurance.

Today, peace may look like releasing the need to understand everything that is happening. God's peace does not require clarity to function. It simply requires trust and connection.

Reflection

Where have anxious thoughts been competing for your attention? How does knowing God's peace guards your heart and mind change your response?

Life Application

When anxious thoughts arise today, pause and intentionally invite God's peace to guard your heart and mind.

Prayer

God, thank You for Your peace that goes beyond understanding. Guard my heart and mind as I abide in You. Help me trust You deeply and rest securely in Your presence. Amen.

October 5

Resting in God's Nearness

Zephaniah 3:17 (NIV)
"The Lord your God is with you, the Mighty Warrior who saves. He will take great delight in you; in his love he will no longer rebuke you, but will rejoice over you with singing."

Devotional

Peace deepens when you remember where God is. This verse centers rest not on stillness alone, but on nearness. God is with you. Not watching from a distance. Not waiting for you to get it right. He is present, active, and attentive.

Rest becomes possible when you no longer feel the need to perform for God. This scripture paints a picture of delight, not demand. God rejoices over you. His love quiets accusation and replaces it with assurance. Abiding in peace begins when you allow yourself to believe that God's posture toward you is joyful, not critical.

Knowing God is near changes how you carry responsibility. You are not managing life alone. His presence steadies you, and His delight invites you to rest without fear of falling short. Peace grows when you trust that you are held, not evaluated.

Today, rest may look like releasing self-judgment and allowing God's nearness to quiet your soul. You do not need to strive for approval. You are already surrounded by His love.

Reflection

Where have you been striving instead of resting in God's nearness? What would change if you believed God delights in you?

Life Application

Throughout the day, remind yourself that God is with you and delights in you, especially in moments when pressure or self-criticism rises.

Prayer

God, thank You for being near to me. Help me rest in Your presence and receive Your love without striving. Quiet my heart with the assurance that I am held and delighted in by You. Amen.

October 6

Settled by Peace

Isaiah 32:17 (NIV)
"The fruit of that righteousness will be peace; its effect will be quietness and confidence forever."

Devotional

Peace is not something you force. It is something that grows. This verse reveals peace as fruit, not a performance. It develops naturally when your life is aligned with God's ways. Quietness and confidence are not manufactured. They are produced through trust and right alignment.

Notice the effect of peace. Quietness does not mean silence around you. It means calm within you. Confidence here is not loud or self-driven. It is steady and enduring. Abiding in peace creates an inner stability that remains even when circumstances fluctuate.

This scripture also reframes righteousness. It is not about perfection or pressure. It is about living in step with God. When your heart is aligned with Him, peace becomes the byproduct. Rest deepens not because everything is resolved, but because your soul is settled.

Today, peace may look like allowing your inner world to slow down. You do not need to rush clarity or outcomes. As you remain aligned with God, quiet confidence will continue to grow.

Reflection

Where have you been seeking peace through effort rather than alignment?
What would quiet confidence look like for you in this season?

Life Application

Pay attention today to moments when your spirit feels unsettled and gently realign your thoughts toward trust and confidence in God.

Prayer

God, thank You for the peace that grows from living aligned with You. Settle my heart with quiet confidence and help me abide in rest rather than striving. Let Your peace take root deeply within me. Amen.

October 7

Rest Without Fear

Psalm 4:8 (NIV)
"In peace I will lie down and sleep, for you alone, Lord, make me dwell in safety."

Devotional

True rest requires trust. This verse reflects a decision to rest rooted not in perfect circumstances, but in confidence in God's protection. Peace here is not conditional on everything being resolved. It is grounded in knowing who watches over you.

Sleep represents vulnerability. When you rest, you release control. You stop monitoring, planning, and guarding outcomes. This scripture acknowledges that kind of surrender and declares why it is possible. God alone makes you dwell in safety. Peace grows when you trust God to do what you cannot do while you rest.

Abiding in peace means allowing yourself to be human. You were not designed to stay alert, guarded, or anxious at all times. God invites you to lay down both your body and your concerns, trusting that His care continues even when you are still.

Today, peace may look like allowing yourself to rest without fear. God does not require constant vigilance from you. As you dwell in His safety, rest becomes an act of faith rather than a sign of weakness.

Reflection

What worries make it difficult for you to fully rest?
How does trusting God's protection change how you view rest?

Life Application

As you prepare to rest today, intentionally release your concerns to God and remind yourself that He is watching over you.

Prayer

God, thank You for the peace that allows me to rest safely in You. Help me release fear and trust Your protection fully. Teach me to abide in peace and receive the rest You provide. Amen.

October 8

Strengthened by Peace

Psalm 29:11 (NIV)

"The Lord gives strength to his people; the Lord blesses his people with peace."

Devotional

Peace is not passive. It carries strength within it. This verse reminds you that God does not offer peace as a soft escape from life, but as a sustaining blessing that fortifies you from the inside out. Strength and peace are not separate gifts here. They are connected.

Many people associate strength with effort and peace with rest, as if they must choose one or the other. God offers both together. When peace is present, strength becomes sustainable. When strength is rooted in peace, it does not exhaust you. Abiding in God allows both to coexist without tension.

This scripture also reframes how peace functions in your life. Peace is not simply a feeling that comes and goes. It is a blessing God actively gives. As you remain connected to Him, peace settles into your spirit and strengthens your capacity to move forward without strain.

Today, peace may look like receiving strength without pushing. You do not have to brace yourself for every challenge. God blesses His people with peace that steadies and sustains them.

Reflection

Where have you been relying on effort rather than peace for strength? How does knowing peace strengthens you change how you approach today?

Life Application

When you feel drained today, pause and ask God to strengthen you through His peace rather than through effort alone.

Prayer

God, thank You for the strength that comes through Your peace. Help me receive both without striving. Teach me to abide in You so that my strength is steady and my heart remains at rest. Amen.

October 9

Peace God Establishes

Isaiah 26:12 (NIV)
"Lord, you establish peace for us; all that we have accomplished you have done for us."

Devotional

Peace is not something you build through effort or control. This verse makes it clear that peace is established by God. It is set in place by His hand, not sustained by your ability to keep everything aligned. Rest deepens when you stop trying to create peace and allow God to establish it within you.

This scripture also reframes accomplishment. Even what you have worked hard for has been supported, guided, and enabled by God. Recognizing this truth releases pressure. You no longer carry the weight of proving, maintaining, or holding everything together on your own.

Abiding in peace means trusting God with both outcomes and process. When you acknowledge that God is the source of what has been accomplished, your soul is freed from striving. Peace settles when responsibility is placed back where it belongs.

Today, peace may look like letting go of self-reliance and acknowledging God's steady work in your life. You are not required to secure peace. God has already established it for you.

Reflection

Where have you been trying to maintain peace through control?
How does recognizing God's role in your accomplishments bring rest?

Life Application

Release one area today where you have been carrying unnecessary pressure and intentionally trust God to establish peace there.

Prayer

God, thank You for establishing peace in my life. Help me release the pressure to create or maintain it on my own. Teach me to abide in the peace You provide and rest in Your faithful work. Amen.

October 10

Dwelling in Peace

Psalm 23:2 (CSB)
"He lets me lie down in green pastures; he leads me beside quiet waters."

Devotional

Peace is often received through permission. This verse reminds you that rest is not something you must force yourself into. God leads you there. He creates the conditions for rest and invites you to dwell within them.

Green pastures and quiet waters speak to provision and calm. They are not places of hurry or pressure. God does not rush you into rest. He gently leads, knowing exactly what your soul needs. Abiding in peace means trusting His guidance rather than pushing yourself beyond what is sustainable.

This scripture also reveals God's attentiveness. He notices when rest is needed and provides space for renewal. Peace deepens when you allow yourself to be led rather than insisting on constant movement. Rest does not mean abandoning responsibility. It means receiving care along the way.

Today, peace may look like allowing God to guide your pace. You do not have to prove strength by staying busy. God offers quiet spaces where your soul can breathe and be restored.

Reflection

Where have you been resisting rest?
What would it look like to allow God to lead you into peace today?

Life Application

Pay attention today to moments when God is inviting you to slow down and intentionally follow His lead into rest.

Prayer

God, thank You for leading me into places of peace and restoration. Help me trust Your guidance and receive the rest You provide. Teach me to abide with You in quiet confidence and renewed strength. Amen.

October 11

Kept in Peace

John 14:27 (NKJV)

"Peace I leave with you, My peace I give to you; not as the world gives do I give to you. Let not your heart be troubled, neither let it be afraid."

Devotional

Peace from God is distinct. It is not fragile, temporary, or dependent on conditions. Jesus makes a clear distinction here between the peace the world offers and the peace He gives. Worldly peace depends on stability, control, or resolution. God's peace remains even when those things are absent.

This verse also speaks directly to the heart. Trouble and fear are acknowledged, not dismissed. Jesus does not deny that circumstances can be unsettling. Instead, He offers peace that steadies the heart in the midst of uncertainty. Abiding in peace means receiving what Jesus has already given rather than striving to create calm on your own.

Notice that peace is described as a gift. It is left with you. It is given to you. You are not asked to earn it or prove you deserve it. Rest deepens when you allow yourself to receive God's peace without resistance or skepticism.

Today, peace may look like choosing to trust what Jesus has already provided. You do not have to let fear dictate your posture. God's peace is present, available, and strong enough to quiet a troubled heart.

Reflection

What has been troubling your heart recently?
How does knowing God's peace is already given change your response?

Life Application

When fear or anxiety surfaces today, pause and remind yourself that God's peace has already been given to you and choose to receive it fully.

Prayer

Jesus, thank You for the peace You have given me. Help me receive it without fear or striving. Quiet my heart and strengthen my trust as I abide in Your peace and rest in Your presence. Amen.

October 12

Secure in His Presence

Psalm 16:8 (NLT)
"I know the Lord is always with me. I will not be shaken, for he is right beside me."

Devotional

Peace deepens when you are aware of God's nearness. This verse is not rooted in circumstance but in confidence. The psalmist does not say life is stable. He says God is present. That awareness becomes the source of security.

Being unshaken does not mean untouched by difficulty. It means not displaced by it. When God is set before you and recognized as near, peace steadies your inner world. Abiding in rest means you stop scanning for threats and start resting in presence. God beside you changes how you interpret everything else.

This scripture also emphasizes intentional awareness. "I know the Lord is always with me" is a practiced truth. Peace grows when you consistently remind yourself where God is. His nearness anchors you, allowing rest to take root even when circumstances feel uncertain.

Today, peace may look like acknowledging God's presence throughout your day. You do not need to brace yourself against what might happen. God is beside you, and that nearness keeps you steady.

Reflection

Where have you been feeling unsettled or shaken?
How does remembering God's nearness bring calm to your spirit?

Life Application

Throughout today, pause and remind yourself that God is with you and beside you, especially in moments that feel uncertain or demanding.

Prayer

God, thank You for being near to me. Help me remain aware of Your presence and rest in the security it brings. Steady my heart and keep me grounded as I abide in Your peace. Amen.

October 13

Unafraid at Rest

John 15:4 (NKJV)
"Abide in Me, and I in you. As the branch cannot bear fruit of itself, unless it abides in the vine, neither can you, unless you abide in Me."

Devotional

Peace is sustained through connection, not effort. This verse shifts the focus away from self-management and back to relationship. Jesus does not ask you to produce peace on your own. He invites you to remain connected to Him, where peace naturally flows.

Abiding is a posture of dependence. A branch does not strain to bear fruit. It remains attached and receives what it needs to grow. In the same way, rest deepens when you stop trying to generate calm and instead stay rooted in Christ. Peace is not forced. It is supplied.

This verse also removes fear from the equation. When you are abiding, you are not disconnected or unsupported. You are held. Fruitfulness, stability, and peace are outcomes of remaining in Christ, not outcomes of striving harder or controlling outcomes.

Today, rest may look like returning to connection. You do not need to solve everything to experience peace. You only need to remain close. Abiding is where fear loosens its grip and peace quietly settles in.

Reflection

Where have you been trying to produce peace instead of abiding? What helps you remain connected to Christ throughout your day?

Life Application

Pause today and intentionally reconnect with Christ through prayer or stillness, reminding yourself that peace flows from abiding, not effort.

Prayer

Jesus, help me abide in You. Teach me to remain connected rather than striving for peace on my own. As I stay rooted in You, let Your peace settle my heart and guide my steps. Amen.

October 14

Rest Is an Invitation

Mark 6:31 (NLT)
"Then Jesus said, 'Let's go off by ourselves to a quiet place and rest awhile.' He said this because there were so many people coming and going that Jesus and his apostles didn't even have time to eat."

Devotional

Rest is not something you take only after everything is finished. Sometimes it is something Jesus invites you into right in the middle of responsibility. This verse shows that even good work can become draining when there is no pause. Jesus notices the pace and responds with invitation, not correction.

What stands out is that the work was still ongoing. Needs were still present. People were still coming. Yet Jesus prioritized rest anyway. Abiding in peace means recognizing that rest is not a sign of neglect. It is a form of wisdom. God does not require you to exhaust yourself to prove faithfulness.

This invitation to a quiet place reflects care for the whole person. Rest restores clarity, strength, and perspective. When you step away briefly, you return renewed rather than depleted. Peace grows when you allow yourself to receive rest without guilt.

Today, rest may look like honoring Jesus' invitation rather than pushing through fatigue. You do not have to wait until everything is complete to pause. God meets you in quiet places and restores what constant motion drains.

Reflection

Where have you been pushing without pause?
What would it look like to accept Jesus' invitation to rest today?

Life Application

Create a small moment today to step away from noise or demands and intentionally rest, even briefly, without guilt.

Prayer

Jesus, thank You for inviting me to rest. Help me recognize when I need to pause and receive restoration from You. Teach me to abide in peace and trust that rest strengthens, not hinders, my walk with You. Amen.

October 15

Ruled by Peace

Colossians 3:15 (NLT)
"And let the peace that comes from Christ rule in your hearts. For as members of one body you are called to live in peace. And always be thankful."

Devotional

Peace is meant to guide, not just visit. This verse describes peace as something that takes the lead. When the peace of Christ governs your heart, it becomes the reference point for how you respond, choose, and rest. Abiding in peace means allowing Christ's peace to direct your inner life instead of urgency, fear, or pressure.

The idea of peace ruling suggests alignment. It means allowing your thoughts, emotions, and decisions to come into agreement with what Christ provides. This kind of peace is active, not passive. It brings order to internal conflict, quiets unnecessary noise, and steadies your reactions.

This scripture also connects peace to calling. You are called to live in peace, not pursue it endlessly. Gratitude reinforces this posture. A thankful heart stays open to rest because it recognizes God's presence even when circumstances feel unresolved.

Today, peace may look like choosing alignment over control. You do not need every answer in place to rest. You simply need to allow Christ's peace to guide where tension has been demanding attention.

Reflection

Where has tension been competing with peace in your heart?
What would it look like to let Christ's peace rule that area?

Life Application

When faced with a decision or emotional response today, pause and ask whether peace is ruling your heart before moving forward.

Prayer

Jesus, let Your peace rule in my heart. Quiet what has been restless and guide my thoughts and responses. Teach me to abide in peace and live from a place of gratitude and trust. Amen.

October 16

Rest Comes With His Presence

Exodus 33:14 (NLT)
"The Lord replied, 'I will personally go with you, Moses, and I will give you rest - everything will be fine for you.'"

Devotional

Rest is not found in perfect conditions. It is found in God's presence. This verse makes a powerful connection between the two. God does not promise Moses an easier assignment or fewer responsibilities. He promises Himself. And with His presence comes rest.

Notice that rest is not something Moses has to achieve. It is something God gives. Peace deepens when you stop trying to manage outcomes and instead trust that God is with you. His presence steadies what feels uncertain and calms what feels overwhelming.

Abiding in peace means believing that God's nearness is enough. You do not need every answer before you rest. You do not need every detail resolved. When God goes with you, rest is not dependent on circumstances. It flows from relationship.

Today, peace may look like releasing the need for reassurance beyond God's presence. He is with you. That alone is enough to quiet your heart and allow rest to settle deeply within you.

Reflection

Where have you been looking for rest outside of God's presence?
How does knowing God goes with you change how you carry today?

Life Application

Throughout today, remind yourself that God is with you in every moment and allow that awareness to guide your pace and posture.

Prayer

God, thank You for going with me. Help me rest in Your presence rather than striving for certainty. Let Your nearness quiet my heart and remind me that everything I truly need is found in You. Amen.

October 17

Peace in the Middle

Mark 4:39 (NLT)
"When Jesus woke up, he rebuked the wind and said to the waves, 'Silence! Be still!' Suddenly the wind stopped, and there was a great calm."

Devotional

This verse reminds you that peace is not dependent on the absence of storms. It is dependent on the presence of Jesus. The disciples were surrounded by chaos, yet peace arrived the moment Jesus spoke. Nothing about the setting was calm until His authority intervened.

What is striking is how Jesus responds. He does not match the storm's intensity. He speaks with clarity and command. Peace follows His voice. Abiding in peace means trusting that God can bring calm even when circumstances are loud, unpredictable, or overwhelming.

Often, rest is delayed because you assume peace must wait until conditions improve. This scripture reframes that belief. Peace can exist in the middle. Calm does not require escape. It requires trust in who is present with you.

Today, peace may look like inviting Jesus into the center of what feels unsettled. You do not need to quiet everything yourself. His presence and authority are enough to bring calm to what feels out of control.

Reflection

What situation in your life feels stormy right now?
How might trusting Jesus' authority change how you respond?

Life Application

When tension rises today, pause and invite Jesus into the situation, trusting Him to bring calm where you cannot.

Prayer

Jesus, thank You for speaking peace into chaos. Help me trust Your authority when life feels overwhelming. Teach me to abide in rest, knowing You are present and able to bring calm even in the middle of the storm. Amen.

October 18

Led Out in Peace

Isaiah 55:12 (NKJV)

"For you shall go out with joy and be led out with peace; the mountains and the hills shall break forth into singing before you, and all the trees of the field shall clap their hands."

Devotional

Peace is not always found by stopping. Sometimes it is found by being led. This verse presents peace as a guide, not a destination you must figure out on your own. God does not push you forward with pressure. He leads you out with peace.

Being led implies trust. It requires surrendering control over pace, direction, and outcome. Abiding in peace means allowing God to guide you rather than forcing clarity or certainty ahead of time. Peace accompanies obedience when it flows from trust instead of urgency.

This scripture also reminds you that peace is not narrow or fragile. It is expansive. Creation itself responds to God's leading with joy. When you move in step with Him, peace does not feel restrictive. It feels freeing. Rest deepens when you stop resisting God's lead and allow His peace to shape the journey.

Today, peace may look like releasing the need to rush or overthink your next step. Trust that God is leading you forward with peace and let that assurance steady your heart.

Reflection

Where have you been trying to force direction instead of being led? What would change if you trusted God to lead you out with peace?

Life Application

As you move through today, pay attention to where God is gently leading you and choose to follow without rushing or resisting.

Prayer

God, thank You for leading me with peace. Help me trust Your guidance and release the need to control my steps. Let Your peace accompany me as I move forward, resting in Your direction and care. Amen.

October 19

Peace Given by God

2 Thessalonians 3:16 (NKJV)
"Now may the Lord of peace Himself give you peace always in every way. The Lord be with you all."

Devotional

Peace is not something you manufacture. It is something God gives. This verse makes that unmistakably clear. The Lord of peace does not outsource calm to your circumstances or your coping skills. He gives peace Himself, personally and intentionally.

Notice the scope of this promise. Peace is given always and in every way. That includes busy seasons, uncertain moments, and situations that remain unresolved. Abiding in peace means trusting God's ability to supply rest even when life does not slow down.

This scripture also ties peace to presence. "The Lord be with you all" reminds you that peace flows from nearness. When God is present, peace is possible. Rest deepens when you stop waiting for conditions to change and instead receive what God is already offering.

Today, peace may look like letting God be the source rather than the solution you keep trying to find. You are not responsible for producing peace. You are invited to receive it from the One who is peace.

Reflection

Where have you been trying to create peace on your own?
What changes when you trust God to give peace in every way?

Life Application

When tension rises today, pause and intentionally receive peace from God rather than attempting to control the situation.

Prayer

God, You are the Lord of peace. I receive the peace You give, always and in every way. Help me rest in Your presence and trust You to supply what my heart needs. Teach me to abide in peace rather than striving for it. Amen.

October 20

Peace in the Gentle Whisper

1 Kings 19:12 (NIV)
"After the earthquake came a fire, but the Lord was not in the fire. And after the fire came a gentle whisper."

Devotional

Peace often arrives quietly. This verse reminds you that God is not always revealed through noise, force, or dramatic moments. Sometimes His presence is made known through nearness. Abiding in peace means learning to recognize God in subtle invitations rather than overwhelming displays.

Elijah experienced wind, earthquake, and fire, yet God chose the gentle whisper. This reveals how peace often works in your life. It does not compete with chaos or demand attention. It becomes noticeable when you slow your pace and allow space for stillness.

A gentle whisper requires presence, not urgency. It invites you to quiet internal distractions and remain attentive. When you create margin for silence, peace becomes easier to discern. God does not rush to overpower noise. He draws close and waits for you to listen.

Today, peace may look like choosing closeness over commotion. God is present, speaking softly, offering rest through awareness and intimacy rather than intensity.

Reflection

Where has noise or urgency been crowding out stillness?
How can you create space to listen for God's gentle whisper today?

Life Application

Intentionally create a quiet moment today without distractions and ask God to speak peace into your heart.

Prayer

God, help me recognize You in stillness. Quiet my heart and tune my spirit to Your gentle voice. Teach me to abide in peace and receive rest through Your presence. Amen.

October 21

Entering God's Rest

Hebrews 4:9 (NIV)

"There remains, then, a Sabbath-rest for the people of God."

Devotional

Rest is not an afterthought in God's design. This verse reminds you that rest is still available and still intended for you. It has not expired, and it has not been reserved for a later season. God's rest remains.

A Sabbath-rest speaks to more than physical pause. It reflects a posture of trust. It is the decision to stop striving, stop proving, and stop carrying what God never asked you to hold. Abiding in peace means recognizing that rest is part of obedience, not a reward for exhaustion.

This scripture also offers reassurance. Rest is not something you have missed or failed to reach. It remains. You are invited to enter it. Peace deepens when you stop postponing rest and start receiving it as a gift God has already made available.

Today, peace may look like allowing yourself to stop striving internally. You do not need to earn rest. God has already made space for it in your life.

Reflection

Where have you been delaying rest instead of receiving it?
What would it look like to enter God's rest without guilt?

Life Application

Identify one place today where you can stop striving and intentionally choose rest, trusting that God has made room for it.

Prayer

God, thank You that rest remains for me. Help me release striving and receive the peace You have already provided. Teach me to abide in Your rest and trust You fully with what I lay down. Amen.

October 22

Quietness Over Striving

Ecclesiastes 4:6 (NIV)
"Better one handful with tranquility than two handfuls with toil and chasing after the wind."

Devotional

Peace often requires a choice. This verse contrasts two ways of living. One values more, faster, and fuller hands. The other values tranquility. God does not glorify excess when it costs your peace. Rest is not found in accumulation. It is found in alignment.

Chasing after the wind describes effort without satisfaction. It is motion without rest and striving without fulfillment. Abiding in peace means recognizing when your pursuit is costing more than it is giving. Sometimes the most faithful decision is to hold less and rest more.

This scripture invites you to reassess what you are reaching for. Peace grows when you choose contentment over constant striving. Tranquility does not mean lack. It means knowing when enough is enough and trusting God within that boundary.

Today, peace may look like releasing unnecessary pressure. You do not need to carry everything to live well. God offers rest when you choose simplicity over strain.

Reflection

Where have you been striving instead of resting?
What might God be inviting you to release to regain peace?

Life Application

Identify one commitment, expectation, or pressure today that can be loosened so you can choose tranquility over striving.

Prayer

God, help me choose peace over striving. Show me where I am chasing more at the expense of rest. Teach me to live with contentment and abide in the tranquility You provide. Amen.

October 23

Released From Worry

Matthew 6:34 (NKJV)

"Therefore do not worry about tomorrow, for tomorrow will worry about its own things. Sufficient for the day is its own trouble."

Devotional

Peace is often restored when you stop living ahead of yourself. This verse brings your attention back to today. Worry pulls your mind into the future, asking you to carry what has not yet arrived. Jesus redirects that impulse and reminds you that today already has enough of its own concerns.

Abiding in peace means learning how to stay present. When you project yourself into tomorrow, rest is disrupted. Peace deepens when you release the need to anticipate every outcome and instead trust God with what you cannot yet see.

This scripture does not dismiss responsibility. It corrects burden. There is a difference between preparation and worry. Rest comes when you allow God to meet you one day at a time rather than demanding certainty far in advance.

Today, peace may look like returning your focus to what is directly in front of you. You are not required to solve tomorrow today. God's grace is sufficient for the moment you are in.

Reflection

Where has worry been pulling your attention into the future?
How might peace grow if you focused fully on today?

Life Application

When anxious thoughts about the future arise today, gently redirect your focus to the present moment and trust God with what is ahead.

Prayer

Jesus, help me release worry about tomorrow. Teach me to live present and trust You with what I cannot control. Let Your peace settle my heart as I abide fully in today. Amen.

October 24

Choosing the Better Part

Luke 10:41–42 (NIV)

"Martha, Martha," the Lord answered, "you are worried and upset about many things, but few things are needed – or indeed only one. Mary has chosen what is better, and it will not be taken away from her."

Devotional

Peace is often lost in the effort to manage too much at once. In this moment, Martha is not doing anything wrong. She is simply doing too much. Jesus does not criticize her work. He gently redirects her focus. Rest is found not in abandoning responsibility but in choosing priority.

This passage reveals how worry multiplies when attention is scattered. Mary's posture is not passive. It is intentional. She chooses presence over pressure. Abiding in peace means learning when to pause productivity in order to protect connection with God.

Jesus calls Mary's choice "the better part" because it nourishes the soul. Tasks will always return. Demands will always exist. What sustains peace is the decision to anchor yourself in what restores you before returning to what requires you.

Today, peace may look like choosing presence over performance. You do not need to carry everything at once. God invites you to slow down, refocus, and choose what brings rest to your spirit.

Reflection

Where have you been overwhelmed by many things?
What might it look like to choose the better part today?

Life Application

Intentionally pause today and give God your full attention, even briefly, before returning to your responsibilities.

Prayer

Jesus, help me recognize when I am carrying too much. Teach me to choose what truly matters and rest in Your presence. Quiet my worries and guide me into peace as I abide with You. Amen.

October 25

Quietness That Lasts

Isaiah 32:17 (NIV)

"The fruit of that righteousness will be peace; its effect will be quietness and confidence forever."

Devotional

Peace is not produced by effort or circumstance. It is the fruit of alignment. This verse reveals that peace flows naturally from righteousness, from living in right relationship with God. When your life is rooted in Him, peace becomes an outcome rather than a pursuit.

Quietness here does not mean silence. It speaks to an inner stillness, a settled soul that is no longer agitated by fear or urgency. Confidence grows alongside that quietness, not because everything is perfect, but because trust has replaced striving. Abiding in peace means allowing God's order to shape your inner world.

This scripture also points to longevity. The effect of righteousness is not temporary calm. It is lasting peace and steady confidence. Rest deepens when you stop chasing reassurance and begin living from alignment. Peace stays when it is rooted in God rather than circumstances.

Today, peace may look like returning to alignment. When your heart is anchored in God, quietness follows, and confidence settles in without effort.

Reflection

Where have you been striving instead of resting in alignment?
How does knowing peace is fruit, not force, change your perspective?

Life Application

Take time today to realign your thoughts and actions with God's truth, trusting that peace will follow naturally.

Prayer

God, thank You that peace flows from alignment with You. Quiet my soul and strengthen my confidence as I walk in righteousness. Help me abide in peace that lasts and rest in the assurance You provide. Amen.

October 26

Sweet Rest Without Fear

Proverbs 3:24 (NKJV)
"When you lie down, you will not be afraid; Yes, you will lie down and your sleep will be sweet."

Devotional

Rest is deeply connected to trust. This verse paints a picture of peace that follows you into stillness, even into sleep. Fear does not accompany you when you lie down because your confidence is anchored in God's care. Peace settles when vigilance is no longer required.

Sweet sleep reflects more than physical rest. It speaks to a mind that is not rehearsing worry and a heart that is not bracing for what might happen next. Abiding in peace means allowing yourself to release control at the end of the day, trusting that God remains watchful even when you rest.

This scripture reassures you that fear does not have to govern your quiet moments. God's presence provides safety that allows your body and soul to fully relax. Rest deepens when you trust that nothing is required of you in that moment except surrender.

Today, peace may look like intentionally letting go before you lie down. You do not need to stay alert to stay safe. God is faithful, present, and attentive. Sweet rest follows trust.

Reflection

What fears tend to surface when you try to rest?
How does trusting God's care change your ability to relax?

Life Application

Before resting today, pause and intentionally place your fears in God's hands, choosing trust over vigilance.

Prayer

God, thank You for the promise of rest without fear. Help me release control and trust You fully as I lie down. Quiet my thoughts and give me sweet rest as I abide in Your peace. Amen.

October 27

Strength in Quiet Trust

Isaiah 30:15 (NIV)
"In repentance and rest is your salvation, in quietness and trust is your strength."

Devotional

Peace is not found in constant movement. It is found in returning. This verse invites you back to a posture of rest and trust, reminding you that strength does not come from striving harder but from quiet dependence on God.

Quietness here is not passivity. It is restraint. It is the discipline of not reacting immediately, not rushing to fix or prove, and not allowing anxiety to lead. Abiding in peace means recognizing that your strength grows when you trust God enough to slow down and listen.

This scripture also reframes salvation as ongoing. Rest is not separate from spiritual health. It is part of it. When you choose quiet trust over urgency, you align yourself with how God sustains you. Peace deepens when you stop resisting rest and allow it to strengthen you from the inside out.

Today, peace may look like choosing stillness instead of speed. You do not lose momentum when you rest in God. You gain strength that lasts.

Reflection

Where have you been relying on effort instead of trust?
How might quietness strengthen you in this season?

Life Application

Intentionally slow your pace today in one area and choose trust over urgency, allowing rest to become a source of strength.

Prayer

God, help me return to You in rest and trust. Quiet my spirit and strengthen me as I lean on You. Teach me to abide in peace and receive the strength that comes from stillness in Your presence. Amen.

October 28

Lightening the Weight

Proverbs 12:25 (NLT)
"Worry weighs a person down; an encouraging word cheers a person up."

Devotional

Worry has weight. It presses on the mind and settles in the body, often without you realizing how heavy it has become. This verse names that reality plainly. Peace begins when that weight is acknowledged rather than ignored.

The contrast in this scripture is powerful. Worry weighs down, but encouragement lifts. Encouragement is not shallow positivity. It is truth that reminds you of what is solid and trustworthy. Abiding in peace means choosing voices, words, and thoughts that lighten rather than burden your spirit.

Sometimes peace comes through receiving encouragement. Other times it comes through offering it, even to yourself. God often uses words to bring relief, clarity, and calm. Rest deepens when you allow encouragement to interrupt worry's grip.

Today, peace may look like speaking life into a place where heaviness has been lingering. You are not meant to carry the full weight of worry. God provides encouragement that lifts and restores your heart.

Reflection

What worries have been weighing you down?
What encouraging word or truth does your heart need today?

Life Application

Intentionally replace a worried thought today with an encouraging truth from God's Word or a reminder of His faithfulness.

Prayer

God, thank You for lifting the weight of worry from my heart. Help me receive encouragement and speak it where heaviness remains. Teach me to abide in peace and walk lighter in Your care. Amen.

October 29

Peace That Flows

Isaiah 48:18 (NIV)
"If only you had paid attention to my commands, your peace would have been like a river, your righteousness like the waves of the sea."

Devotional

Peace is meant to move through your life, not appear in short bursts. This verse paints peace as a river, steady, continuous, and sustaining. God's design for peace is not fragile or seasonal. It is meant to flow, carrying you forward with consistency and grace.

Paying attention to God's commands is not about rigid rule-following. It is about alignment. When your life flows in rhythm with God's wisdom, peace becomes the natural result. Abiding in peace means allowing God's direction to shape your choices so that rest is not interrupted by constant resistance or correction.

The imagery of waves reinforces this idea. Righteousness moves with power and purpose, not chaos. Peace grows when you stop fighting the current of God's guidance and allow yourself to move with it. Rest deepens when you trust that God's way leads to stability rather than strain.

Today, peace may look like yielding to God's direction instead of pushing against it. When you align with Him, peace flows freely, steady and life-giving.

Reflection

Where have you been resisting God's direction?
How might peace flow more freely if you aligned with His guidance?

Life Application

Identify one area today where you can intentionally align your actions or mindset with God's truth and allow peace to flow from that decision.

Prayer

God, help me align my life with Your wisdom. Teach me to move with Your direction rather than against it. Let Your peace flow through my heart like a steady river as I abide in rest and trust You fully. Amen.

October 30

Secure in His Care

Proverbs 14:26 (NLT)
"Those who fear the Lord are secure; he will be a refuge for their children."

Devotional

Peace grows when you know where your security comes from. This verse points directly to the source of rest that does not waver. Reverence for God produces a deep sense of safety, not anxiety. When your trust is anchored in Him, peace becomes a steady foundation rather than a fleeting feeling.

Security here is not about control or certainty. It is about refuge. A refuge is a place you return to when life feels unpredictable. Abiding in peace means knowing you have a place of safety in God, regardless of what surrounds you. That awareness allows your heart to rest instead of staying on alert.

This scripture also widens the view of peace. God's care extends beyond you. It reaches into legacy, responsibility, and those you love. Rest deepens when you trust that God is not only holding you but also watching over what matters to you most.

Today, peace may look like releasing the need to guard everything yourself. You are secure in God's care. He is your refuge, and that truth allows your heart to rest.

Reflection

Where have you been seeking security outside of God?
How does knowing God is your refuge bring peace to your heart?

Life Application

When anxiety tries to rise today, remind yourself that your security is found in God and intentionally rest in His care.

Prayer

God, thank You for being my refuge and my security. Help me rest in You and trust that You are watching over me and those I love. Teach me to abide in peace, confident in Your care. Amen.

October 31

The God of Peace With You

Romans 15:33 (NIV)
"The God of peace be with you all. Amen."

Devotional

Peace does not end with striving resolved or questions answered. Sometimes peace is simply the awareness of God's presence with you. This verse offers no instruction, no correction, and no condition. It is a declaration. God, who is peace Himself, is with you.

As October closes, this scripture serves as a reminder that peace is not something you leave behind when a season ends. It is something you carry forward because God goes with you. Abiding in peace means trusting that His presence remains steady, even as circumstances shift and chapters turn.

There is rest in simplicity. This verse does not ask you to do more or become more. It affirms what already is. God is with you. That truth settles the soul. Peace deepens when you stop reaching and allow presence to be enough.

Today, peace may look like resting in the assurance that God is near. As this month closes, you are not walking forward alone. The God of peace goes with you into what comes next.

Reflection

How does knowing God is with you bring a sense of peace?
What would it look like to carry this assurance into the next season?

Life Application

As you close out this month, take a moment to acknowledge God's presence and intentionally step forward in peace, trusting that He goes with you.

Prayer

God, thank You for being the God of peace. As this month comes to a close, I rest in the truth that You are with me. Help me carry Your peace forward and abide in Your presence in every season. Amen.

November

Living in Gratitude & Abundance

November invites you to slow down long enough to recognize what God has already done. Gratitude is not a seasonal response or a polite habit. It is a posture of awareness. When you live gratefully, you begin to see God's hand not only in what you have received, but also in what He has sustained, protected, and carried you through. This month is an invitation to notice His faithfulness with fresh eyes.

Living in abundance does not mean having everything you want. It means recognizing the fullness of what God has provided. Abundance is rooted in perspective, not possession. It is the ability to see sufficiency where you once focused on lack. As gratitude grows, contentment follows, and peace settles deeper into the soul. You begin to understand that God's provision shows up in many forms, strength, wisdom, timing, grace, and daily sustenance.

Throughout this month, you will be encouraged to live from a place of fullness rather than striving. Gratitude will shape how you see your life, your relationships, and your journey with God. As you reflect, give thanks, and acknowledge His goodness, you will discover that abundance is not something you chase. It is something you recognize when your heart is aligned with Him.

November 1

Remembering the Benefits

Psalm 103:2 (NIV)
"Praise the Lord, my soul, and forget not all his benefits."

Devotional

Gratitude begins with remembrance. This verse calls your soul to pay attention, to pause long enough to recall what God has already done. It is possible to move forward so focused on what is next that you overlook what has sustained you. Living in gratitude requires intentional remembering.

Forgetting does not always mean denying God's goodness. Sometimes it simply means becoming distracted by what feels unfinished or unmet. This scripture invites you to bring your soul back into alignment. When you remember God's benefits, your perspective shifts. Gratitude grows not because life is perfect, but because God has been faithful.

Abundance often reveals itself through reflection. When you take inventory of God's provision, mercy, protection, and grace, you begin to see how full your life truly is. Abiding in gratitude means training your heart to notice what has already been given instead of focusing only on what you are still waiting for.

Today, peace and abundance may begin with a simple act of remembrance. When you recall God's benefits, gratitude rises naturally and steadies your heart.

Reflection

What benefits of God have you been overlooking?
How does remembering His faithfulness change how you view your life?

Life Application

Take time today to intentionally list specific ways God has shown His goodness and faithfulness in your life.

Prayer

God, thank You for Your many benefits in my life. Help me remember Your faithfulness and live with a grateful heart. Open my eyes to the abundance You have already provided and teach me to praise You with awareness and trust. Amen.

November 2

Gratitude in Every Season

1 Thessalonians 5:18 (NKJV)
"In everything give thanks; for this is the will of God in Christ Jesus for you."

Devotional

Gratitude is not dependent on circumstances. This verse does not say to give thanks for everything, but in everything. That distinction matters. It acknowledges that life includes difficulty, uncertainty, and loss, yet still calls you to a posture of gratitude within it.

Living in gratitude and abundance means recognizing that God's presence does not leave when conditions are less than ideal. His will is not that you deny pain or pretend hardship does not exist. His will is that gratitude anchors you, reminding you that He is still at work even when the outcome is not yet clear.

Abundance begins to shift when gratitude becomes a steady practice rather than a situational response. When you learn to give thanks in every season, your heart is no longer ruled by what is lacking. You begin to see provision, strength, and grace woven through every experience.

Today, gratitude may look like acknowledging God's faithfulness even in the middle of unresolved situations. This posture does not minimize difficulty. It magnifies trust.

Reflection

Where do you find it hardest to give thanks?
How might gratitude change your perspective in that area?

Life Application

Choose one situation today where gratitude feels challenging and intentionally thank God for His presence and faithfulness within it.

Prayer

God, help me learn to give thanks in every season. Teach me to trust Your will and recognize Your presence no matter what I am facing. Shape my heart to live in gratitude and abundance, anchored in You. Amen.

November 3

Satisfied by His Provision

Psalm 107:8–9 (NIV)
"Let them give thanks to the Lord for his unfailing love and his wonderful deeds for mankind, for he satisfies the thirsty and fills the hungry with good things."

Devotional

Gratitude deepens when you recognize who truly satisfies. This verse connects thanksgiving directly to God's provision, not only for survival, but for fullness. God does not merely meet needs. He fills. He satisfies. Living in gratitude means acknowledging that what sustains you comes from His unfailing love.

Thirst and hunger represent more than physical need. They reflect longing, emptiness, and desire. God responds to those places with goodness. When you begin to see how He has filled the hungry places in your life, gratitude rises naturally. Abundance becomes visible when you stop measuring what you lack and start recognizing how God has provided.

This scripture invites you to give thanks intentionally. Thanksgiving is a response to awareness. When you notice God's deeds and reflect on His care, your heart shifts from striving to appreciation. Gratitude keeps you grounded in what is already present rather than consumed by what feels missing.

Today, abundance may look like recognizing where God has already satisfied you. When you see His goodness clearly, gratitude becomes a natural response.

Reflection

Where has God satisfied a need or longing in your life?
How does recognizing His provision increase your gratitude?

Life Application

Take time today to thank God for specific ways He has met your needs and filled empty places in your life.

Prayer

God, thank You for Your unfailing love and provision. You have satisfied my needs and filled my life with good things. Help me live with a grateful heart and recognize the abundance You have already provided. Amen.

November 4

Remembering the Source

Deuteronomy 8:18 (NLT)
"Remember the Lord your God. He is the one who gives you power to be successful, in order to fulfill the covenant he confirmed to your ancestors with an oath."

Devotional

Gratitude grows when you remember where your strength truly comes from. This verse gently redirects your attention away from self-reliance and back to God as the source of ability, provision, and opportunity. Success is not something you generate on your own. It is something God empowers.

Living in gratitude and abundance means recognizing that every ability you possess has been entrusted to you. Skills, wisdom, endurance, and opportunity are not accidents. They are part of God's provision working through your life. When you remember this, pride gives way to humility and anxiety gives way to trust.

This scripture also ties provision to purpose. God's empowerment is not random. It is connected to His promises and His plan. Abundance is not just about what you receive. It is about how God equips you to walk in alignment with what He has already spoken over your life.

Today, gratitude may look like acknowledging God as the source of your progress and provision. When you remember Him, abundance becomes clearer and confidence becomes grounded rather than pressured.

Reflection

Where have you been tempted to credit yourself instead of God? How does remembering God as your source change your view of success?

Life Application

Take a moment today to thank God for the abilities, opportunities, and strength He has given you, recognizing Him as the source of all you have.

Prayer

God, thank You for being the source of my strength and provision. Help me remember You in every season and acknowledge that what I have comes from You. Teach me to live with gratitude and walk confidently in the abundance You provide. Amen.

November 5

Experiencing His Goodness

Psalm 34:8 (NIV)

"Taste and see that the Lord is good; blessed is the one who takes refuge in him."

Devotional

Gratitude deepens when it moves from belief to experience. This verse invites you to do more than acknowledge God's goodness. It invites you to encounter it. "Taste and see" suggests personal participation. God's goodness is not distant or theoretical. It is meant to be experienced in real and tangible ways.

Taking refuge in God speaks to trust. Refuge is chosen when you need protection, rest, or reassurance. When you turn to God in those moments, you begin to see His goodness more clearly. Abundance becomes visible when you recognize how often God has been your shelter, your help, and your source of peace.

This scripture reminds you that blessing flows from proximity. The closer you draw to God, the more aware you become of His care. Gratitude grows when you reflect on moments where God met you personally, guided you gently, or sustained you quietly through uncertainty.

Today, abundance may look like recognizing how God has shown His goodness through experience, not just provision. When you taste and see, gratitude becomes heartfelt and lasting.

Reflection

Where have you personally experienced God's goodness?
How does trusting God as your refuge increase your gratitude?

Life Application

Reflect today on a moment when God met you in a meaningful way and intentionally thank Him for that experience.

Prayer

God, thank You for allowing me to experience Your goodness personally. Help me trust You as my refuge and recognize the many ways You have shown Your care in my life. Teach me to live with gratitude and awareness of Your presence. Amen.

November 6

Gratitude Rooted in Mercy

Psalm 136:1 (NKJV)
"Oh, give thanks to the Lord, for He is good! For His mercy endures forever."

Devotional

Gratitude becomes steady when it is anchored in who God is. This verse calls you to give thanks not because everything is perfect, but because God's goodness and mercy are constant. His mercy does not fluctuate with seasons, outcomes, or emotions. It endures.

Living in gratitude and abundance means recognizing that mercy itself is provision. God's mercy covers what you cannot fix, redeems what you regret, and sustains you when strength runs low. When you remember how often His mercy has met you, gratitude rises naturally.

This scripture also reminds you that abundance is not only about what you receive. It is about what God continues to extend. Mercy is renewed again and again. When you live aware of that truth, your heart rests in sufficiency rather than striving.

Today, abundance may look like acknowledging how God's mercy has carried you through moments you could not have handled on your own. Gratitude deepens when you recognize that His mercy has never failed you.

Reflection

Where have you experienced God's mercy in your life?
How does remembering His enduring mercy shape your gratitude?

Life Application

Take time today to reflect on specific moments where God's mercy sustained or protected you and thank Him intentionally.

Prayer

God, thank You for Your goodness and enduring mercy. Help me recognize how often Your mercy has carried me and shaped my life. Teach me to live with a grateful heart, grounded in the abundance of who You are. Amen.

November 7

Responding to His Goodness

Psalm 116:12 (NIV)

"What shall I return to the Lord for all his goodness to me?"

Devotional

Gratitude eventually asks a question. When you become aware of God's goodness, provision, and mercy, your heart naturally responds. This verse reflects that moment of pause where recognition turns into reflection. God's goodness invites a response, not out of obligation, but out of love.

Living in gratitude and abundance means understanding that thanksgiving is more than words. It shapes how you live, give, and serve. When you acknowledge how God has been good to you, your life becomes a response to that goodness. Abundance shows itself when gratitude moves beyond acknowledgment into action.

This scripture does not demand repayment. It invites devotion. God's goodness cannot be earned or returned in equal measure. What He desires is a heart that recognizes Him and lives accordingly. Gratitude deepens when you allow it to influence your choices, priorities, and posture toward others.

Today, abundance may look like responding to God's goodness with obedience, generosity, or worship. When your life reflects gratitude, it becomes a testimony of God's faithfulness.

Reflection

How has God been good to you recently?
What response might gratitude be inviting from you?

Life Application

Choose one intentional way today to respond to God's goodness, whether through prayer, generosity, obedience, or encouragement toward someone else.

Prayer

God, thank You for Your goodness in my life. Help me respond with a heart that honors You. Show me how to live out my gratitude through my actions, choices, and love for others. Teach me to walk in abundance shaped by thankfulness. Amen.

November 8

Trust That Leads to Joy

Proverbs 16:20 (NKJV)
"He who heeds the word wisely will find good,
And whoever trusts in the Lord, happy is he."

Devotional

Gratitude and joy often grow from the same root: trust. This verse connects wisdom, trust, and happiness in a way that feels both simple and profound. When you pay attention to God's word and trust Him with your life, goodness follows. Joy becomes a byproduct of alignment rather than something you chase.

Living in gratitude and abundance means learning to trust God not only when things are clear, but also when outcomes are uncertain. Trust steadies the heart. It quiets the need to control and opens space for peace. When trust deepens, contentment follows, and gratitude becomes more consistent.

This scripture reminds you that happiness is not dependent on circumstance. It is tied to confidence in God's care. When you trust Him, you begin to recognize good even in ordinary moments. Abundance shows up as a settled assurance that God is present and faithful.

Today, abundance may look like choosing trust over worry. As you lean into God's word and rely on Him, joy rises naturally and gratitude finds a steady place in your heart.

Reflection

Where is God inviting you to trust Him more fully?
How does trust influence your sense of joy and contentment?

Life Application

Identify one area today where you can intentionally choose trust over anxiety and remind yourself of God's faithfulness in that space.

Prayer

God, thank You for inviting me to trust You. Help me heed Your word with wisdom and rest in the goodness You provide. Teach me to live with gratitude and joy that flow from trusting You completely. Amen.

November 9

Abundance That Outlives You

Proverbs 13:22 (NLT)
"Good people leave an inheritance to their grandchildren, but the sinner's wealth passes to the godly."

Devotional

Abundance is not measured only by what you hold. It is revealed in what you pass on. This verse shifts the lens of gratitude from immediate gain to lasting impact. A life lived with wisdom and integrity produces fruit that extends beyond one generation.

Living in gratitude and abundance means recognizing that God's provision is not just for personal comfort. It is meant to shape lives, influence families, and leave something meaningful behind. Inheritance here speaks to more than finances. It includes values, faith, wisdom, character, and examples worth following.

When you view abundance through the lens of legacy, gratitude deepens. You begin to see how God has been faithful not only to meet your needs, but to position you as a steward of what He has entrusted to you. Abundance grows when you live with awareness that your life has ripple effects.

Today, abundance may look like honoring what God has given you by how you live and what you model. Gratitude is expressed when you recognize that your faithfulness today shapes the future in ways you may never fully see.

Reflection

What kind of legacy are you building with your life?
How does gratitude influence the way you steward what God has given you?

Life Application

Consider one intentional way today to invest in someone else, through encouragement, wisdom, generosity, or example, recognizing that abundance is meant to be shared.

Prayer

God, thank You for the abundance You have entrusted to me. Help me live with gratitude and wisdom so that what You place in my hands blesses others beyond me. Teach me to steward Your provision well and build a legacy that honors You. Amen.

November 10

Lacking Nothing

Psalm 23:1 (NIV)
"The Lord is my shepherd, I lack nothing."

Devotional

Abundance begins with knowing who leads you. This verse does not deny challenges or needs. It declares trust. When the Lord is your shepherd, provision is not accidental. It is intentional, guided, and consistent. Gratitude grows when you recognize that God's care is active, not distant.

Lacking nothing does not mean having everything you desire. It means trusting that what you truly need is supplied. A shepherd watches, guides, protects, and provides. Living in gratitude and abundance means resting in the assurance that God sees ahead and leads you wisely through every season.

This scripture invites you to shift your focus. Instead of measuring life by what feels absent, you begin to recognize what has been faithfully provided. Abundance becomes a posture of confidence rather than accumulation. Peace settles when you trust that God's leadership is enough.

Today, abundance may look like releasing comparison and embracing contentment. When you trust the Shepherd, gratitude flows naturally, and your heart rests in sufficiency.

Reflection

Where have you been focusing on what you lack?
How does trusting God as your shepherd reshape your view of abundance?

Life Application

Take a moment today to thank God for specific ways He has guided and provided for you, choosing to rest in His care rather than compare your life to others.

Prayer

God, thank You for being my shepherd. Help me trust Your guidance and rest in the truth that I lack nothing under Your care. Teach me to live with gratitude and contentment, confident in Your faithful provision. Amen.

November 11

Receiving Today With Gratitude

Psalm 118:24 (NKJV)
"This is the day the Lord has made; We will rejoice and be glad in it."

Devotional

Gratitude is often lost when your focus stays fixed on yesterday or reaches too far into tomorrow. This verse gently brings you back to today. Not a perfect day. Not a completed day. Simply this day. A day God intentionally made and entrusted to you.

Rejoicing here is a choice, not a reaction. It does not depend on circumstances aligning or plans unfolding exactly as hoped. Living in gratitude and abundance means recognizing that today itself is a gift. Breath, opportunity, presence, and grace are already here, waiting to be acknowledged.

Abundance grows when you stop postponing joy. When you learn to receive the day as it is, gratitude takes root in the ordinary. You begin to notice God's faithfulness woven into simple moments. Peace settles when you stop resisting the present and start honoring it.

Today, abundance may look like welcoming this day without comparison or complaint. When you choose to rejoice, you are not ignoring reality. You are affirming that God is still at work within it.

Reflection

What has kept you from fully receiving today?
How might gratitude change the way you experience this moment?

Life Application

Intentionally pause today and thank God for the gift of this day, choosing to be present and grateful in whatever it holds.

Prayer

God, thank You for this day You have made. Help me receive it with gratitude and choose joy without condition. Teach me to live aware of Your presence and recognize the abundance found in each moment You give. Amen.

November 12

Delight Before Desire

Psalm 37:4 (NIV)
"Take delight in the Lord, and he will give you the desires of your heart."

Devotional

Gratitude and abundance begin with where your heart rests. This verse invites you to delight in God first, not as a strategy to receive more, but as a posture of relationship. Delight shifts your focus from what you want to who God is. When your joy is rooted in Him, your perspective begins to change.

Delighting in the Lord aligns your desires with His will. Over time, what you long for becomes shaped by His wisdom and goodness. Abundance is not just about receiving what you ask for. It is about discovering that your deepest desires are refined and fulfilled as you walk closely with God.

Living in gratitude and abundance means trusting that God knows what satisfies your heart better than you do. As you delight in Him, you begin to recognize how He meets your needs in ways that are deeper and more lasting than you imagined. Contentment grows when your joy is anchored in God rather than outcomes.

Today, abundance may look like choosing delight over demand. When your heart is aligned with God, gratitude flows naturally, and desire finds its proper place.

Reflection

What does it look like for you to delight in the Lord?
How might delighting in God reshape your desires?

Life Application

Intentionally spend time today enjoying God's presence through prayer, worship, or reflection, focusing on delight rather than requests.

Prayer

God, help me delight in You above all else. Align my heart with Your will and shape my desires according to Your wisdom. Teach me to live with gratitude and recognize the abundance that flows from walking closely with You. Amen.

November 13

Naming What God Has Done

Psalm 126:3 (NIV)
"The Lord has done great things for us, and we are filled with joy."

Devotional

Gratitude often grows strongest when you pause long enough to look back. This verse is not rooted in hope alone. It is rooted in memory. The people speaking here are not imagining what God might do. They are acknowledging what He has already done.

Joy follows recognition. When you take time to name God's faithfulness, gratitude becomes grounded rather than vague. Living in gratitude and abundance means learning to reflect honestly on your journey and see God's hand woven through it. Even seasons that felt uncertain or painful often reveal His care in hindsight.

This scripture reminds you that joy does not have to be forced. It rises naturally when gratitude is sincere. When you acknowledge the great things God has done, your heart fills with appreciation rather than striving. Abundance becomes visible when you stop minimizing your story and start honoring God's work within it.

Today, abundance may look like taking inventory of God's faithfulness. When you recognize how far He has brought you, joy finds room to grow.

Reflection

What great things has God done in your life?
How does reflecting on His faithfulness affect your sense of joy?

Life Application

Take time today to write down specific moments where you can clearly see God's hand at work in your life and thank Him intentionally.

Prayer

God, thank You for the great things You have done in my life. Help me remember Your faithfulness and allow joy to rise from gratitude. Teach me to live aware of Your goodness and recognize the abundance You have already provided. Amen.

November 14

Gratitude That Is Intentional

Psalm 92:1 (NIV)
"It is good to praise the Lord and make music to your name, O Most High,"

Devotional

Gratitude is not only something you feel. It is something you choose. This verse reminds you that praise is intentional. It is an act of the will, not merely a reaction to circumstances. Giving thanks is described as good because it aligns your heart with truth, not because life is always easy.

Praising God brings awareness. When you stop and acknowledge Him, you begin to see how present He has been all along. Living in gratitude and abundance means creating space to notice God's goodness rather than rushing past it. Praise slows you down long enough to recognize what is already in your life.

Music and praise also invite expression. Gratitude does not have to look the same every day. Sometimes it is quiet reflection. Other times it is spoken acknowledgment or joyful worship. Abundance grows when gratitude is allowed to flow naturally instead of being confined to one form.

Today, abundance may look like intentionally praising God without waiting for a specific outcome. When gratitude becomes a daily choice, your heart remains open to joy, peace, and awareness of God's presence.

Reflection

How intentional is your gratitude toward God?
What helps you express thankfulness most naturally?

Life Application

Choose one intentional way today to express gratitude to God, through prayer, music, journaling, or spoken praise.

Prayer

God, thank You for the goodness of praising You. Help me choose gratitude intentionally and recognize Your presence throughout my day. Teach me to live with a thankful heart that remains open to the abundance You provide. Amen.

November 15

Seeing the Abundance Around You

Psalm 104:24 (NIV)
"How many are your works, Lord! In wisdom you made them all; the earth is full of your creatures."

Devotional

Gratitude often begins with noticing. This verse draws your attention outward, inviting you to see the abundance already surrounding you. God's wisdom is evident not only in grand moments but in the details of creation, provision, and order woven into everyday life.

Living in gratitude and abundance means learning to observe rather than rush past. When you slow down enough to recognize God's work, your perspective shifts. You begin to see fullness where you once overlooked it. Abundance is not always about increase. Sometimes it is about awareness.

This scripture reminds you that God's wisdom fills the earth. Nothing He creates is careless or lacking purpose. When you recognize that same intentionality at work in your own life, gratitude deepens. You begin to trust that God has been present and active even in places you did not immediately understand.

Today, abundance may look like opening your eyes to what is already good. When you notice God's handiwork, gratitude becomes a natural response rather than a forced discipline.

Reflection

Where have you seen evidence of God's wisdom in your life?
What blessings might you be overlooking simply because you are moving too fast?

Life Application

Pause today and intentionally notice something around you that reflects God's care or creativity and thank Him for it.

Prayer

God, thank You for the wisdom and care You have poured into creation and into my life. Help me slow down and recognize Your work around me. Teach me to live with gratitude that flows from awareness of Your abundance. Amen.

November 16

Valued and Provided For

Luke 12:24 (NIV)
"Consider the ravens: They do not sow or reap, they have no storeroom or barn; yet God feeds them. And how much more valuable you are than birds!"

Devotional

Gratitude grows when you understand your value. Jesus invites you to observe something simple, birds being fed, to reveal something profound. God's care reaches even the smallest parts of creation. If He attends to them, how much more attentive is He to you.

This verse shifts abundance away from storage and control. The ravens do not stockpile or strategize, yet they are sustained. Jesus is not discouraging responsibility. He is addressing worry. Living in gratitude and abundance means trusting that God's provision is active and ongoing, not something you must anxiously secure on your own.

Abundance also shows up in how God sees you. You are not overlooked. You are not forgotten. Your life carries value in God's eyes, and that truth becomes the foundation for gratitude. When you trust His care, fear loosens its grip and peace settles in.

Today, abundance may look like releasing worry and resting in God's provision. When you recognize your value to Him, gratitude becomes a natural response rather than a forced one.

Reflection

Where have you been worrying about provision or the future?
How does knowing your value to God shift your perspective?

Life Application

When worry arises today, pause and remind yourself that God is attentive to your needs and values you deeply. Choose trust over anxiety.

Prayer

Jesus, thank You for reminding me of my worth and Your faithful care. Help me trust Your provision, release worry, and live each day with gratitude, confident that You see and sustain me. Amen.

November 17

Gratitude Born From Grace

Luke 7:47 (NIV)

"Therefore, I tell you, her many sins have been forgiven—as her great love has shown. But whoever has been forgiven little loves little."

Devotional

Gratitude deepens when you remember what you have been forgiven from. In this moment, Jesus connects love directly to awareness of grace. The woman's response is not exaggerated or emotional excess. It is proportionate to her understanding of mercy received.

Living in gratitude and abundance means recognizing that forgiveness itself is a form of provision. Grace covers what you could not undo and restores what shame tried to steal. When you understand how much has been forgiven, gratitude grows naturally. Love becomes the overflow of grace, not obligation.

This verse invites honest reflection. When gratitude feels thin, it is often because grace has been minimized. Abundance becomes clearer when you acknowledge how much God has extended to you freely. Forgiveness is not small. Mercy is not limited. Awareness of grace reshapes how you love, worship, and live.

Today, abundance may look like remembering the depth of grace God has shown you. When you recognize what has been forgiven, gratitude moves from words to posture and love flows without restraint.

Reflection

What has God forgiven you from that you may have minimized? How does remembering His grace deepen your gratitude?

Life Application

Take time today to reflect on God's forgiveness in your life and intentionally thank Him for the grace that has restored and freed you.

Prayer

Jesus, thank You for the grace and forgiveness You have given me so freely. Help me live with a heart shaped by gratitude, aware of Your mercy, and reflecting the love I have received. Amen.

November 18

Following After Receiving

Matthew 20:34 (NIV)

"Jesus had compassion on them and touched their eyes. Immediately they received their sight and followed him."

Devotional

Gratitude often reveals itself through what you choose next. In this moment, Jesus heals the blind men, but the story does not end with their sight restored. Their response matters. They follow Him. Gratitude here is not spoken. It is demonstrated through direction.

Living in gratitude and abundance means allowing what God has done for you to shape how you move forward. When healing, provision, or clarity comes, the natural response is alignment. Abundance is not just receiving. It is responding with a life that reflects thankfulness.

This verse reminds you that gratitude does not require elaborate expression. Sometimes it is simply choosing to follow Jesus more closely than before. When you allow God's compassion to change your path, gratitude becomes embodied. Your steps begin to reflect your awareness of His goodness.

Today, abundance may look like aligning your choices with the grace you have received. When gratitude guides your direction, your life becomes a living response to God's compassion.

Reflection

How has God's compassion changed your life?
What does following Him look like for you right now?

Life Application

Identify one area today where you can align your actions more closely with what God has already done for you.

Prayer

Jesus, thank You for Your compassion and restoring grace. Lead me to follow You with a grateful heart, allowing my life to reflect the goodness I have received through faithful obedience and trust. Amen.

November 19

Satisfied in Him

John 6:35 (NIV)
"Then Jesus declared, 'I am the bread of life. Whoever comes to me will never go hungry, and whoever believes in me will never be thirsty.'"

Devotional

Gratitude deepens when you understand what truly satisfies you. Jesus does not describe Himself as an addition to life, but as sustenance. Bread was essential, daily, and necessary. By calling Himself the bread of life, Jesus points to a deeper abundance that goes beyond temporary provision.

Living in gratitude and abundance means recognizing that fulfillment is found in Christ, not in constant pursuit. Hunger and thirst often show up as restlessness, comparison, or striving. Jesus offers a different way. When you come to Him, the deeper needs of your heart are met.

This verse invites you to examine where you seek satisfaction. Gratitude grows when you stop expecting people, achievements, or possessions to fill what only Christ can. Abundance becomes steady rather than fleeting when your source is secure.

Today, abundance may look like returning to Christ as your source. When you trust Him to satisfy you, gratitude replaces striving and peace takes root.

Reflection

Where have you been looking for satisfaction outside of Christ?
How does trusting Jesus as your source change your perspective?

Life Application

Pause today and intentionally bring your needs, longings, and concerns to Jesus, trusting Him to satisfy what truly matters.

Prayer

Jesus, thank You for being my true source of life and satisfaction. Draw me to come to You first, trusting You to meet my deepest needs, and help me rest in the abundance found in You. Amen.

November 20

Seeking First What Matters Most

Matthew 6:33 (NLT)
"Seek the Kingdom of God above all else, and live righteously, and he will give you everything you need."

Devotional

Gratitude grows when your priorities are clear. Jesus speaks directly to the tension between worry and trust, reminding you that abundance flows from alignment. Seeking God's Kingdom first is not about striving harder. It is about ordering your life around what truly matters.

This verse reframes abundance. Provision is not something you chase. It follows. When your heart is focused on God's ways, His presence, and His purposes, your needs are not ignored. They are addressed in the right order. Living in gratitude and abundance means trusting that God sees what you need before you ask.

Often, anxiety rises when priorities are misplaced. Jesus offers peace by redirecting your focus. When God comes first, gratitude replaces fear because you are no longer carrying the weight of provision alone. Abundance becomes a byproduct of trust rather than constant effort.

Today, abundance may look like releasing control and choosing trust. When you seek God first, gratitude grows because you recognize that He is faithful to supply what is needed, exactly when it is needed.

Reflection

What tends to compete for first place in your life?
How does trusting God with your needs change your sense of peace?

Life Application

Identify one area today where you can intentionally put God first, trusting Him to handle the rest.

Prayer

God, help me seek Your Kingdom above all else. Teach me to trust You with my needs and align my heart with Your priorities. Thank You for being faithful to provide and for inviting me to live with gratitude and peace. Amen.

November 21

Rest Is Part of the Gift

Matthew 11:29 (NIV)
"Take my yoke upon you and learn from me, for I am gentle and humble in heart, and you will find rest for your souls."

Devotional

Abundance is often misunderstood as constant movement or visible gain. Jesus offers a different picture. He invites you into rest. Not escape. Not avoidance. Rest for your soul. This kind of rest comes from walking closely with Him rather than carrying everything on your own.

A yoke connects two who move together. Jesus does not remove responsibility, but He shares it. Living in gratitude and abundance means recognizing that you were never meant to carry life alone. When you learn from Christ, you discover a rhythm marked by grace rather than pressure.

This verse reminds you that rest is not weakness. It is wisdom. When you accept Jesus' invitation, gratitude grows because striving loosens its grip. Abundance becomes evident not in how much you do, but in how deeply you trust.

Today, abundance may look like allowing yourself to rest without guilt. When you receive rest as a gift, your soul regains clarity, strength, and peace.

Reflection

Where have you been carrying more than you were meant to?
How does Jesus' invitation to rest challenge your current pace?

Life Application

Choose one intentional way today to slow down and invite Jesus into the weight you have been carrying.

Prayer

Jesus, thank You for inviting me into rest. Help me learn from You and walk at Your pace. Teach me to release what I was never meant to carry and receive the abundance of peace You offer. Amen.

November 22

Gratitude That Overflows

Luke 18:43 (NIV)
"Immediately he received his sight and followed Jesus, praising God. When all the people saw it, they also praised God."

Devotional

Gratitude has a way of spreading. In this moment, healing does not remain private. The man receives his sight, follows Jesus, and praises God openly. His response becomes an invitation. Others see what God has done and join in praise.

Living in gratitude and abundance means allowing God's work in your life to be visible. Not for attention, but for testimony. When gratitude is expressed freely, it reminds others of God's power and presence. Abundance multiplies when praise moves beyond silence.

This verse shows that gratitude is not only personal. It can be communal. When you acknowledge what God has done, it creates space for others to reflect on His goodness as well. Gratitude becomes a shared experience that draws hearts toward worship.

Today, abundance may look like giving God credit openly. When you choose to praise Him without restraint, gratitude overflows and encourages others to recognize His faithfulness too.

Reflection

How openly do you express gratitude for what God has done?
Who might be encouraged by hearing your testimony?

Life Application

Share one specific way God has shown His faithfulness in your life with someone today, giving Him praise openly.

Prayer

God, thank You for the ways You work in my life. Help me express my gratitude freely and openly. May my praise point others toward You and reflect the abundance of Your goodness. Amen.

November 23

Gratitude That Acts

John 13:17 (NLT)

"Now that you know these things, God will bless you for doing them."

Devotional

Gratitude is not meant to stop at understanding. Jesus speaks these words after modeling humility and service. The blessing does not come from knowledge alone. It comes from action. Living in gratitude and abundance means allowing what you know to shape how you live.

This verse reminds you that obedience is an expression of thankfulness. When you choose to live out what God has shown you, gratitude moves from words to behavior. Abundance follows when your life reflects what you believe.

Often, gratitude grows as you act. When you serve, forgive, or love intentionally, you begin to see how God meets you in obedience. Blessings are not always immediate or visible, but they are real. It flows from aligning your actions with God's truth.

Today, abundance may look like taking one step of obedience. When you act on what you know, gratitude deepens, and God's blessing becomes part of your lived experience.

Reflection

What has God shown you that requires action?
How might obedience deepen your gratitude?

Life Application

Identify one simple way today to live out something God has already placed on your heart.

Prayer

Jesus, thank You for showing me how to live. Help me move beyond knowledge into obedience. Teach me to express my gratitude through action and trust You to bless my steps as I follow You. Amen.

November 24

Do You See What Has Been Given

Luke 7:44–45 (NIV)

"Do you see this woman? I came into your house… she has not stopped kissing my feet."

Devotional

You can be in the presence of something sacred and still miss it. Familiarity has a way of dulling awareness. What was once extraordinary can quietly become expected. In this moment, Jesus pauses the room and asks a simple question that carries weight. Do you see?

The difference between the host and the woman is not access. It is recognition. One treats Jesus as routine. The other responds as if she understands the magnitude of what she has received. Her gratitude is not measured. It is expressed freely because her heart sees clearly.

Living in gratitude and abundance means learning to recognize what is already present. Sometimes abundance is overlooked not because it is absent, but because it has become ordinary. When awareness fades, gratitude follows. When awareness returns, gratitude flows naturally.

Jesus' question still matters today. It invites reflection rather than correction. When you truly see God's presence in your life, gratitude moves beyond habit and becomes heartfelt. Abundance is revealed not in more, but in seeing rightly.

Today, abundance may look like paying attention again. When you slow down long enough to see God's grace, gratitude deepens and your response becomes sincere.

Reflection

What might you be overlooking out of familiarity?
How does awareness change the way you express gratitude?

Life Application

Pause today and intentionally acknowledge something you have taken for granted, thanking God for it with fresh awareness.

Prayer

Jesus, help me see clearly what You have given and who You are in my life. Remove complacency from my heart and renew my awareness of Your grace. Teach me to live with gratitude that flows from truly seeing You. Amen.

November 25

Thankful Before the Answer

John 11:41 (NLT)
"So they rolled the stone aside. Then Jesus looked up to heaven and said, 'Father, thank you for hearing me.'"

Devotional

Gratitude does not always wait for visible results. In this moment, Jesus gives thanks before anything changes. The stone is moved, but the miracle has not yet occurred. His gratitude is rooted in relationship, not outcome. He trusts the Father before the answer is revealed.

Living in gratitude and abundance means learning to thank God in advance. Thanksgiving becomes an expression of trust rather than proof that everything has worked out. When gratitude comes first, it shifts your focus from fear to faith.

This verse invites you to consider how often you delay thanksgiving until circumstances improve. Jesus models a different posture. He acknowledges God's faithfulness before the breakthrough, demonstrating confidence in who God is rather than what He will do.

Today, abundance may look like choosing gratitude even when you are still waiting. When you thank God before the answer, your heart remains anchored in trust, and peace takes root.

Reflection

Where are you waiting for an answer from God?
What would it look like to thank Him before the outcome?

Life Application

Offer a prayer of thanksgiving today for something you are still believing God for, trusting His faithfulness ahead of the result.

Prayer

Father, thank You for hearing me. Help me trust You fully and choose gratitude even while I wait. Teach me to live with a thankful heart that rests in who You are, not just what You do. Amen.

November 26

Gratitude as a Way of Life

Ephesians 5:20 (NIV)
"Always giving thanks to God the Father for everything, in the name of our Lord Jesus Christ."

Devotional

Gratitude is not meant to be occasional. This verse calls you into a way of living. Giving thanks always and for everything does not mean denying difficulty. It means recognizing that God remains present and faithful in every circumstance.

Living in gratitude and abundance means allowing thankfulness to shape how you move through life. When gratitude becomes a habit, it transforms your perspective. You begin to notice God's hand in moments you once overlooked. Abundance is revealed not by perfection, but by awareness.

This scripture invites consistency. Gratitude does not fluctuate based on mood or outcome. It flows from trust in who God is. When thankfulness becomes your posture, peace follows, and contentment settles in.

Today, abundance may look like choosing gratitude intentionally, even in small or ordinary moments. When you live thankful, your heart stays open to God's ongoing work in your life.

Reflection

How consistent is gratitude in your daily life?
What shifts when you choose thankfulness regardless of circumstances?

Life Application

Practice intentional gratitude today by thanking God for both the big and small things you experience.

Prayer

God, help me live with a grateful heart in all things. Teach me to recognize Your presence and trust You fully. May gratitude become my posture and abundance my perspective as I walk with You each day. Amen.

November 27

Gratitude That Trusts the Bigger Picture

Romans 8:28 (NKJV)
"And we know that all things work together for good to those who love God, to those who are the called according to His purpose."

Devotional

Thanksgiving is not only about celebrating what feels good. It is about trusting God with what has not yet made sense. This verse anchors gratitude in confidence rather than circumstance. It does not say all things are good. It says God works all things together for good.

Living in gratitude and abundance means choosing trust when clarity is incomplete. Some seasons are joyful. Others are stretching. Yet God remains intentional in every part of your story. Gratitude grows when you believe that nothing is wasted, even the parts you would not have chosen.

This scripture invites you to zoom out. When you step back, you begin to see how God weaves purpose through both blessings and burdens. Abundance is not found only in outcomes you celebrate. It is found in knowing that God is at work, shaping something meaningful through it all.

Today, abundance may look like giving thanks for God's faithfulness even when the full picture is still unfolding. When gratitude is rooted in trust, peace replaces pressure and hope steadies your heart.

Reflection

Where have you struggled to see God at work?
How does trusting His purpose change the way you view your journey?

Life Application

Take a moment today to thank God not only for what you understand, but also for what you are still trusting Him to work out.

Prayer

God, thank You for working all things together for good. Help me trust You fully and live with gratitude even when I do not see the full picture. Strengthen my faith and remind me that You are always at work in my life. Amen.

November 28

Abundance Redefined

2 Corinthians 8:9 (NIV)

"For you know the grace of our Lord Jesus Christ, that though he was rich, yet for your sake he became poor, so that you through his poverty might become rich."

Devotional

Gratitude matures when you understand what abundance truly costs. This verse reframes everything. Jesus did not give from excess. He gave through sacrifice. His richness was not material, yet His willingness to lay it down became the source of your abundance.

Living in gratitude and abundance means recognizing that what you have is rooted in grace, not entitlement. Christ's sacrifice was intentional and personal. Through His humility, you gained access to life, freedom, and hope that cannot be measured by earthly standards.

This scripture challenges shallow definitions of abundance. True richness is found in what Christ secured for you through love. When you grasp the depth of His sacrifice, gratitude deepens beyond words. It becomes reverence, humility, and commitment to live differently.

Today, abundance may look like honoring what Christ has done by living with generosity and gratitude. When you remember the cost of grace, your heart remains grounded and thankful.

Reflection

How does this verse reshape your understanding of abundance?
What does Christ's sacrifice stir in your heart today?

Life Application

Pause today and thank Jesus specifically for what His sacrifice has made possible in your life, choosing to live with humility and gratitude.

Prayer

Jesus, thank You for Your sacrifice and grace. Help me never take lightly what You have done for me. Teach me to live with gratitude that honors You and reflects the abundance You secured through love. Amen.

November 29

Abundance Through Connection

John 15:5 (NIV)
"I am the vine; you are the branches. If you remain in me and I in you, you will bear much fruit; apart from me you can do nothing."

Devotional

Abundance is not something you produce on your own. Jesus makes this clear by using the image of a vine and branches. Fruit does not come from striving. It comes from staying connected. Gratitude deepens when you recognize that everything flowing through your life begins with Him.

Living in gratitude and abundance means learning to remain rather than rush. When you stay connected to Christ, growth happens naturally. Fruit is not forced. It is the result of relationship. When you abide in Him, your life reflects nourishment, stability, and purpose.

This verse also invites honesty. Apart from Christ, effort becomes exhausting and outcomes feel empty. Gratitude grows when you acknowledge your dependence and choose connection over control. Abundance is revealed not in independence, but in intimacy with God.

Today, abundance may look like slowing down and remaining present with Christ. When you stay connected to Him, your life bears fruit that lasts and gratitude becomes your steady posture.

Reflection

Where have you been relying on your own effort instead of abiding in Christ?
What helps you stay connected to Him consistently?

Life Application

Set aside intentional time today to remain with Christ through prayer or quiet reflection, focusing on connection rather than productivity.

Prayer

Jesus, thank You for being my source. Help me remain connected to You and trust You for growth and fruit in my life. Teach me to live with gratitude that flows from abiding in You each day. Amen.

November 30

Recognizing the Source

James 1:17 (NIV)
"Every good and perfect gift is from above, coming down from the Father of the heavenly lights, who does not change like shifting shadows."

Devotional

Gratitude becomes steady when you recognize where everything truly comes from. This verse draws your attention upward, reminding you that every good and perfect gift has a source. Nothing meaningful in your life arrived by accident. It was given with intention by a faithful God.

Living in gratitude and abundance means learning to trace blessings back to their origin. When you know the source, gratitude deepens and entitlement fades. God's generosity is consistent, not seasonal. He does not change with circumstances or moods. His goodness remains constant, even when life feels uncertain.

As this month closes, this scripture anchors your heart in truth. Abundance is not defined by what you accumulated or achieved. It is defined by recognizing God's hand at work throughout your life. Gratitude grows when you acknowledge that what you have reflects who God is.

Today, abundance may look like quiet recognition. When you honor God as the giver of every good gift, gratitude settles into your spirit and prepares you to move forward with trust and humility.

Reflection

What good gifts have you received that you may have overlooked? How does recognizing God as the source change your gratitude?

Life Application

Take time today to intentionally thank God for specific gifts in your life, acknowledging Him as their source.

Prayer

Father, thank You for every good and perfect gift You have given me. Help me recognize Your hand in my life and live with gratitude rooted in truth. As I move forward, keep my heart anchored in Your unchanging goodness. Amen.

December

Hope That Sustains & Redeems

Hope is not wishful thinking. It is the quiet strength that holds you when answers are incomplete and the future feels uncertain. As this year comes to a close, hope becomes less about what you expect to happen and more about who you trust to carry you through. This month invites you to anchor your heart in a hope that does not fluctuate with circumstances but remains steady through every season.

Hope that sustains is not loud or hurried. It settles your spirit when weariness sets in and reminds you that God has been present in every moment of the journey. It assures you that even when progress felt slow or setbacks felt heavy, nothing was wasted. God has been working beneath the surface, strengthening your faith and shaping your character in ways you may only now begin to recognize.

Hope that redeems looks back without regret and forward without fear. It acknowledges what has been lost, delayed, or broken, while trusting God's power to restore meaning and purpose. As you move through December, this devotional will guide you toward a hope rooted in God's promises, sustained by His presence, and redeemed by His grace. This is not the end of the story. It is preparation for what comes next.

December 1

Hope That Cannot Be Extinguished

John 1:5 (NLT)
"The light shines in the darkness, and the darkness can never extinguish it."

Devotional

Hope does not wait for darkness to pass before it appears. It shines in the middle of it. This verse reminds you that light is not fragile. Darkness does not overpower it, diminish it, or cancel it out. No matter how heavy the season has felt, hope remains present and active.

As this final month begins, you are invited to remember that God's light has been shining even when the path felt unclear. Hope that sustains does not depend on ideal conditions. It holds steady when answers are delayed and when strength feels low. The darkness you have faced has not won. It has not erased what God is doing in you.

Hope that redeems allows you to look back without shame and forward without fear. It declares that even the hardest moments could not extinguish God's presence in your life. His light has been constant, guiding, and faithful through every season.

Today marks more than the start of a new month. It is a reminder that hope remains alive. God's light continues to shine, and it will carry you forward into what comes next.

Reflection

Where have you seen God's light even in difficult moments?
What does this verse remind you about the nature of hope?

Life Application

Take a moment today to acknowledge one area where God's light has sustained you, even when circumstances felt dark.

Prayer

God, thank You for being my light. Thank You that hope does not fade when life feels heavy. Help me trust that Your light continues to shine and guide me forward. As this month begins, anchor my heart in hope that sustains and redeems. Amen.

December 2

Anchored in Hope

Hebrews 6:19 (NIV)
"We have this hope as an anchor for the soul, firm and secure."

Devotional

Hope is not meant to drift. This verse reminds you that true hope has weight and purpose. An anchor does not remove the storm, but it keeps you from being carried away by it. In the same way, hope steadies your soul when life feels uncertain or overwhelming.

As this month unfolds, you are invited to consider where your soul is anchored. Hope that sustains does not depend on everything being calm or resolved. It holds firm in the middle of movement, tension, and waiting. When your hope is anchored in God, you remain secure even when circumstances shift.

This scripture also speaks to endurance. Anchors are built to last. They are not temporary solutions. Hope rooted in God is not fragile or fleeting. It is dependable, firm, and secure, holding you steady through every season.

Today, abundance may look like stability rather than change. When your hope is anchored in God, peace becomes possible even before answers arrive. You are not adrift. You are held.

Reflection

What is your soul currently anchored to?
How does this verse reshape your understanding of hope?

Life Application

Take time today to identify any areas where your hope has been drifting and intentionally re-anchor them in God through prayer and trust.

Prayer

God, thank You for being my anchor. When life feels uncertain, help me remain grounded in hope that is firm and secure. Teach me to trust You fully and rest in the stability You provide. Amen.

December 3

Hope While You Wait

Romans 8:24–25 (NIV)
"For in this hope we were saved. But hope that is seen is no hope at all. Who hopes for what they already have? But if we hope for what we do not yet have, we wait for it patiently."

Devotional

Hope does not eliminate waiting. It gives waiting purpose. This verse reminds you that hope often lives in what you cannot yet see. If everything were already clear or resolved, hope would not be necessary. Hope sustains you in the space between promise and fulfillment.

Living in hope that sustains and redeems means learning to wait without despair. Waiting does not mean God is inactive. It means He is working beyond what you can presently see. Patience becomes an act of trust, not passivity. Hope holds steady while the story continues to unfold.

This scripture also reframes expectations. Salvation itself is rooted in hope, not instant clarity. As you wait, hope reminds you that what is unseen is still real. God's promises remain trustworthy, even when progress feels slow.

Today, abundance may look like endurance. When you wait with hope, your heart remains open to what God is shaping in you. Hope sustains you now and prepares you for what is ahead.

Reflection

What are you currently waiting on God for?
How does this verse encourage you to wait with hope?

Life Application

Choose one area where waiting feels difficult and intentionally entrust it to God today, practicing patience anchored in hope.

Prayer

God, help me wait with hope. When answers are delayed, remind me that You are still working. Strengthen my trust and teach me to be patient, confident that Your promises will be fulfilled in Your time. Amen.

December 4

Speaking Hope to Your Soul

Psalm 42:11 (NIV)
"Why, my soul, are you downcast? Why so disturbed within me? Put your hope in God, for I will yet praise him, my Savior and my God."

Devotional

Hope sometimes begins as a conversation within. This verse captures a moment of honesty rather than denial. The psalmist does not ignore the heaviness of the soul. He acknowledges it, names it, and then redirects it. Hope that sustains does not pretend everything is fine. It chooses where to place trust even when emotions feel unsettled.

Living in hope that sustains and redeems means learning to speak truth to your inner life. Feelings are real, but they are not always reliable guides. This verse reminds you that you can acknowledge discouragement without surrendering to it. Hope becomes an intentional choice rooted in who God is.

The phrase "I will yet praise him" points forward. It is a declaration that current feelings do not have the final word. Redemption often begins when you decide that hope and praise will remain present, even when clarity has not arrived.

Today, abundance may look like emotional honesty paired with spiritual resolve. When you speak hope to your soul, you make room for God to steady your heart and renew your strength.

Reflection

What emotions have been weighing on your soul?
How can you intentionally redirect your hope toward God today?

Life Application

When discouragement surfaces today, pause and intentionally speak this verse over yourself, choosing hope instead of despair.

Prayer

God, when my soul feels heavy or unsettled, help me place my hope in You. Teach me to speak truth over my emotions and trust You as my Savior and my God. Renew my strength and anchor my heart in hope that endures. Amen.

December 5

Hope That Walks With You

Isaiah 43:2 (NIV)
"When you pass through the waters, I will be with you… When you walk through the fire, you will not be burned; the flames will not set you ablaze."

Devotional

Hope does not promise an easy path. It promises presence. This verse does not say you will avoid the waters or the fire. It says you will not face them alone. Hope that sustains understands that hardship is part of the journey, but it is never the whole story.

Living in hope that sustains and redeems means trusting God's nearness when circumstances feel overwhelming. The waters may feel deep and the fire intense, yet God remains with you in every step. His presence does not eliminate the challenge, but it ensures you are not consumed by it.

This scripture reminds you that survival is not the goal. Transformation is. Walking through difficulty with God refines faith, strengthens trust, and reveals His faithfulness in ways comfort never could. Hope grows stronger when you realize you are held, protected, and guided through it all.

Today, abundance may look like reassurance rather than relief. When you trust that God walks with you through every season, hope steadies your heart and gives you courage to keep moving forward.

Reflection

Where do you need to be reminded of God's presence today?
How does this verse change the way you view your current challenges?

Life Application

When facing a difficult moment today, pause and remind yourself that God is with you, choosing trust over fear.

Prayer

God, thank You for walking with me through every season. When the path feels hard, remind me that I am not alone. Strengthen my faith and anchor my hope in Your constant presence. Amen.

December 6

Hope Proven Over Time

Psalm 71:5 (NIV)
"For you have been my hope, Sovereign Lord, my confidence since my youth."

Devotional

Hope deepens when you look back and recognize consistency. This verse is not spoken from a place of new belief, but from lived experience. The psalmist acknowledges that hope has been present across seasons, not just in moments of need. Confidence grows when you realize God has been faithful longer than you realized.

Living in hope that sustains and redeems means remembering your history with God. Even when faith felt small or circumstances were uncertain, He remained steady. Hope becomes stronger when it is rooted in memory as much as promise. What God has done before builds trust for what lies ahead.

This verse invites reflection on the longevity of God's presence in your life. Hope does not emerge overnight. It is formed through years of walking, learning, failing, and being restored. Redemption often becomes clearer when you recognize how God has carried you from the beginning.

Today, abundance may look like perspective. When you acknowledge God's long-standing faithfulness, hope feels less fragile and more secure. Your confidence is not misplaced. It has been shaped by time and sustained by God.

Reflection

Where have you seen God's faithfulness over time?
How does remembering your history with Him strengthen your hope?

Life Application

Take time today to reflect on a season where God carried you through and thank Him for His ongoing faithfulness.

Prayer

Sovereign Lord, thank You for being my hope through every season of my life. Help me remember Your faithfulness and trust You with what lies ahead. Strengthen my confidence in You and anchor my hope in Your unchanging presence. Amen.

December 7

Pressed But Still Standing

2 Corinthians 4:8–9 (NIV)
"We are hard pressed on every side, but not crushed; perplexed, but not in despair; persecuted, but not abandoned; struck down, but not destroyed."

Devotional

Hope that sustains does not deny pressure. It survives it. This verse names the reality of hardship without surrendering to it. Life can press in from every direction, creating moments of confusion and weariness. Yet hope remains present, steadying you when circumstances feel overwhelming.

Living in hope that sustains and redeems means understanding that struggle does not equal defeat. Being pressed does not mean you are crushed. Feeling uncertain does not mean you are without hope. God's presence ensures that even when life hits hard, you are not abandoned or undone.

This scripture reminds you that resilience is not about avoiding difficulty. It is about enduring it with God's strength. Redemption often shows up in your ability to remain standing when you thought you would fall. Hope reveals itself not by the absence of trouble, but by your ability to keep going through it.

Today, abundance may look like perseverance. When you realize that you are still here, still held, and still moving forward, hope proves itself faithful once again.

Reflection

Where do you feel pressed or challenged right now?
How does this verse redefine what it means to endure?

Life Application

When pressure rises today, remind yourself that difficulty does not define the outcome. Choose to stand firm in hope.

Prayer

God, when life feels heavy and pressing, remind me that I am not crushed or abandoned. Strengthen my endurance and anchor my hope in You. Help me trust that You are sustaining me through every challenge. Amen.

December 8

Hope That Calms the Mind

Psalm 94:19 (NLT)
"When doubts filled my mind, your comfort gave me renewed hope and cheer."

Devotional

Hope does not always arrive as strength. Sometimes it comes as comfort. This verse acknowledges an internal battle that many experience quietly. Doubts crowd the mind, questions linger, and clarity feels distant. Yet God meets the mind as surely as He meets the heart.

Living in hope that sustains and redeems means allowing God to tend to your inner life. When thoughts spiral or uncertainty weighs heavy, His comfort brings renewal. Hope does not always silence doubt immediately, but it steadies you in the midst of it.

This scripture reminds you that God is attentive to what you carry mentally and emotionally. His comfort does not dismiss your concerns. It restores your ability to keep going. Renewed hope often comes not through answers, but through reassurance that you are not alone in your questioning.

Today, abundance may look like peace of mind. When God's comfort settles your thoughts, hope becomes lighter and your spirit steadied. Even in uncertainty, His presence brings renewal.

Reflection

What doubts or worries have been filling your mind?
How has God comforted you in moments of uncertainty before?

Life Application

When anxious thoughts arise today, pause and invite God's comfort, trusting Him to renew your hope and calm your mind.

Prayer

God, when my mind feels overwhelmed or uncertain, thank You for meeting me with Your comfort. Renew my hope and steady my thoughts. Help me trust You even when answers are not yet clear. Amen.

December 9

Hope Anchored in the Word

Psalm 119:114 (NIV)
"You are my refuge and my shield; I have put my hope in your word."

Devotional

Hope becomes steady when it has a place to rest. This verse reminds you that God's Word is not only something to read, but somewhere to dwell. In moments of uncertainty, it offers shelter. When fear presses in, it becomes protection. Hope finds strength when it is anchored in truth that does not change.

Living in hope that sustains and redeems means choosing where you place your trust. The psalmist names God as both refuge and shield, emphasizing safety and defense. Hope rooted in God's Word guards your heart and mind when circumstances feel unstable or overwhelming.

This scripture also speaks to intention. Hope does not drift aimlessly. It is placed deliberately. When you choose to put your hope in God's Word, you align yourself with promises that endure beyond emotion or circumstance. Redemption often begins when truth replaces fear.

Today, abundance may look like security. When your hope is anchored in God's Word, you are not easily shaken. His truth becomes a steady place for your soul to rest.

Reflection

Where do you turn for refuge when uncertainty arises?
How can you more intentionally place your hope in God's Word?

Life Application

Spend time today reading or reflecting on a passage of Scripture that reminds you of God's faithfulness, allowing it to steady your heart.

Prayer

God, thank You for being my refuge and shield. Help me place my hope firmly in Your Word and trust Your truth when life feels uncertain. Anchor my heart in hope that sustains and redeems. Amen.

December 10

Strength for the Weary

Isaiah 40:29 (NIV)
"He gives strength to the weary and increases the power of the weak."

Devotional

Hope sustains when strength runs low. This verse speaks directly to moments when energy is depleted and perseverance feels costly. God does not wait for you to feel strong before He meets you. He responds to weariness with provision and to weakness with renewed power.

Living in hope that sustains and redeems means releasing the pressure to hold everything together on your own. Weariness is not a failure of faith. It is an invitation to receive what God freely gives. When you acknowledge your limits, hope opens the door for God's strength to take root.

This scripture reframes weakness as a place of encounter rather than inadequacy. God's strength is not reserved for the capable. It is poured out on those who are honest about their need. Redemption often begins when you stop striving and allow God to carry what feels heavy.

Today, abundance may look like renewed energy or quiet endurance. When God strengthens you, hope becomes practical. It shows up as the ability to keep going, one faithful step at a time.

Reflection

Where are you feeling weary or stretched thin?
How might God be inviting you to receive His strength today?

Life Application

Pause today and acknowledge an area of weariness, asking God to meet you there with renewed strength.

Prayer

God, thank You for meeting me in my weakness. When I feel weary, remind me that Your strength is available and sufficient. Help me receive what You freely give and walk forward in hope that sustains and redeems. Amen.

December 11

Hope That Is Taught Over Time

Romans 15:4 (NIV)
"For everything that was written in the past was written to teach us, so that through the endurance taught in the Scriptures and the encouragement they provide we might have hope."

Devotional

Hope is not only something you feel. It is something you learn. This verse reminds you that Scripture carries a long memory. The stories, promises, and truths written long ago were preserved to strengthen you now. They teach endurance and offer encouragement for every season of waiting and growth.

Living in hope that sustains and redeems means allowing God's Word to shape your perspective over time. Scripture does not rush you. It walks with you. Through it, you learn how others endured hardship, trusted God through uncertainty, and found hope that carried them forward. Their stories become reminders that you are not alone in your journey.

This verse also speaks to continuity. God's faithfulness did not begin with you, and it will not end with you. The same encouragement that sustained believers before you is available today. Hope grows as you return to Scripture, allowing it to teach, steady, and reassure your heart.

Today, abundance may look like reassurance drawn from God's Word. When you allow Scripture to teach and encourage you, hope becomes rooted, resilient, and enduring.

Reflection

How has Scripture encouraged you during difficult seasons?
What story or promise from God's Word has sustained your hope before?

Life Application

Spend time today revisiting a passage of Scripture that has encouraged you in the past, allowing it to renew your hope once again.

Prayer

God, thank You for Your Word that teaches and encourages me. Help me draw hope from the truths You have preserved for my growth and endurance. Strengthen my faith and anchor my hope in the wisdom of Scripture. Amen.

December 12

Hope That Restores

Isaiah 61:3 (NIV)

"…to bestow on them a crown of beauty instead of ashes, the oil of joy instead of mourning, and a garment of praise instead of a spirit of despair."

Devotional

Hope that redeems does not erase the past. It transforms it. This verse speaks to exchange. What once symbolized loss, grief, or despair is not discarded. It is replaced. God's redemptive hope does not deny pain. It meets it with restoration.

Living in hope that sustains and redeems means trusting God with what feels ruined or unfinished. Ashes represent what has burned down or fallen apart. Yet God promises beauty in its place. Mourning gives way to joy. Despair is met with praise. Redemption is not about pretending the ashes never existed. It is about believing God can create something meaningful from them.

This scripture reminds you that hope carries creative power. God does not simply comfort you where you are. He reshapes your story. What once weighed heavy on your heart can become a testimony of His faithfulness and care.

Today, abundance may look like healing that unfolds gradually. When you trust God with what feels broken, hope begins to restore your spirit and renew your outlook. Redemption is already at work, even when you cannot yet see the full picture.

Reflection

What ashes are you still carrying from past seasons?
How does this verse reshape your understanding of redemption?

Life Application

Offer God one area of loss or disappointment today, trusting Him to bring restoration and renewed hope.

Prayer

God, thank You for being a restorer. Take what feels broken or heavy in my life and replace it with Your beauty, joy, and praise. Help me trust You with my story and anchor my hope in Your redemptive power. Amen.

December 13

Rooted in Trust

Jeremiah 17:7–8 (NIV)
"But blessed is the one who trusts in the Lord, whose confidence is in him."

Devotional

Hope becomes steady when trust takes root. This verse does not describe a momentary decision, but a settled posture. Trust placed in the Lord shapes how you stand, how you wait, and how you move forward. Confidence anchored in God does not sway with every circumstance.

Living in hope that sustains and redeems means choosing where to place your weight. Trust grows when you rely on God consistently, not only in moments of need. Over time, that trust produces stability. It allows hope to remain firm even when seasons change or uncertainty arises.

This scripture reminds you that blessing is connected to confidence. When your trust is rooted in the Lord, your hope becomes resilient. Redemption often unfolds quietly as trust deepens, allowing growth that is not dependent on outward conditions.

Today, abundance may look like steadiness. When your confidence rests in God, hope does not rush or falter. It remains grounded, nourished, and prepared to endure whatever lies ahead.

Reflection

Where is your confidence currently placed?
How does trusting God reshape your experience of hope?

Life Application

Identify one area today where you can intentionally place your trust in God, choosing confidence over uncertainty.

Prayer

Lord, help me place my trust fully in You. Anchor my confidence in Your faithfulness and guide me as I move forward in hope. Teach me to remain rooted in You through every season. Amen.

December 14

A Refuge for Your Heart

Psalm 62:8 (NIV)
"Trust in him at all times, you people; pour out your hearts to him, for God is our refuge."

Devotional

Hope becomes sustaining when you stop holding everything inside. This verse offers a clear invitation. Trust God at all times and bring your whole heart with you. Hope that redeems does not require polished prayers or perfect faith. It welcomes honesty and openness.

Living in hope that sustains and redeems means learning where to place what weighs on you. When you pour out your heart to God, you are not burdening Him. You are responding to His invitation. Refuge is not found in self-control or silence. It is found in bringing everything to the One who can hold it.

This scripture reminds you that trust and vulnerability belong together. God does not ask you to trust Him while hiding your fears or disappointments. He asks you to bring them openly. In that exchange, hope settles in. Redemption begins when you stop carrying alone what God has already offered to shelter.

Today, abundance may look like relief. When you pour out your heart to God, hope finds space to breathe. His refuge becomes a place of rest, reassurance, and renewal.

Reflection

What have you been holding back from God?
How might pouring out your heart deepen your trust and hope?

Life Application

Take a few moments today to speak honestly with God about what you are carrying, trusting Him as your refuge.

Prayer

God, thank You for being my refuge. Help me trust You fully and bring my whole heart before You. Teach me to pour out my fears, hopes, and burdens, knowing that You receive them with care. Anchor my hope in Your steady presence. Amen.

December 15

Hope That Welcomes You In

John 6:37 (NLT)
"Whoever comes to me I will never drive away."

Devotional

Hope becomes deeply personal when you realize it is rooted in welcome, not performance. This verse offers assurance without conditions. Jesus does not qualify who may come or how they must arrive. He simply promises that anyone who comes will not be turned away.

Living in hope that sustains and redeems means trusting that you are received just as you are. There is no requirement to be stronger, more faithful, or more put together. Hope rests in the certainty that Christ's invitation is open and His response is consistent. He does not withdraw His welcome when you struggle or question.

This scripture speaks gently to moments of self-doubt or hesitation. Redemption begins when you stop holding back and choose to come forward. Hope grows as you realize that God's grace is not fragile. It is steady, patient, and secure.

Today, abundance may look like belonging. When you come to Christ honestly, you are met with acceptance that sustains you. Hope is not something you earn. It is something you receive.

Reflection

What has made you hesitate to come fully to Christ?
How does this promise reshape your understanding of hope?

Life Application

Take a moment today to come to Christ honestly, without pretense, trusting His promise to receive you fully.

Prayer

Jesus, thank You for welcoming me without conditions. Help me come to You freely and trust Your promise to receive me with grace. Anchor my hope in Your faithfulness and remind me that I am never turned away. Amen.

December 16

Hope That Holds Steady

Isaiah 26:4 (NIV)
"Trust in the Lord forever, for the Lord, the Lord himself, is the Rock eternal."

Devotional

Hope that sustains is built on something that does not shift. This verse points you toward permanence in a world that often feels unstable. God is not described as temporary support or occasional help. He is named as the Rock eternal. That truth invites confidence that goes beyond the moment you are in.

Living in hope that sustains and redeems means learning where to place lasting trust. Circumstances change. Emotions fluctuate. Seasons come and go. Yet God remains steady. When your hope is anchored in Him, it is not easily shaken by uncertainty or delay.

This scripture also speaks to longevity. Trusting God forever is not about perfection. It is about persistence. Hope grows stronger when you choose to return to God again and again, trusting His faithfulness across every stage of life. Redemption often unfolds when you stop looking for stability elsewhere and rest in who God has always been.

Today, abundance may look like reassurance. When you remember that God is eternal and unmovable, hope settles your heart. You are not standing on fragile ground. You are held by a Rock that will not give way.

Reflection

What has been challenging your sense of stability?
How does seeing God as eternal change the way you trust Him?

Life Application

When uncertainty arises today, pause and remind yourself that God is unchanging and trustworthy, choosing to rest your hope in Him.

Prayer

Lord, thank You for being my Rock and my steady foundation. Help me trust You fully and anchor my hope in Your unchanging nature. When life feels uncertain, remind me that You remain faithful and eternal. Amen.

December 17

Hope That Watches Over You

Psalm 121:7–8 (NIV)

"The Lord will keep you from all harm - he will watch over your life; the Lord will watch over your coming and going both now and forevermore."

Devotional

Hope is strengthened when you know you are being watched over. This verse offers reassurance that God's care is not distant or occasional. It is constant and personal. He watches over your life in its entirety, attending to both the visible moments and the quiet transitions in between.

Living in hope that sustains and redeems means trusting God's protection beyond what you can see. His watchfulness does not depend on your awareness or effort. Whether you are moving forward confidently or feeling uncertain, God remains attentive to every step you take.

This scripture reminds you that hope does not require constant vigilance on your part. You are not responsible for holding everything together. God's care extends to your coming and going, now and always. Redemption often unfolds when you release the need to control and rest in His oversight.

Today, abundance may look like peace of mind. When you trust that God is watching over your life, hope settles into your spirit. You are not navigating this season alone. You are being kept, guided, and sustained.

Reflection

Where do you need reassurance of God's care today?
How does knowing God watches over your life affect your sense of hope?

Life Application

As you move through your day, remind yourself that God is watching over every step, choosing trust over worry.

Prayer

God, thank You for watching over my life. Help me rest in the assurance that You are keeping me and guiding my steps. Anchor my hope in Your faithful care, now and forever. Amen.

December 18

Called by Name

Isaiah 43:1 (NIV)
"Do not fear, for I have redeemed you; I have summoned you by name; you are mine."

Devotional

Hope deepens when it becomes personal. This verse does not speak in generalities. God declares redemption with intention and care. You are not overlooked or forgotten. You are known, named, and claimed. Hope that redeems reminds you that fear loses its grip when identity is secure.

Living in hope that sustains and redeems means understanding who you belong to. Redemption is not only about what God has done. It is about who He has called you to be. When God names you as His own, your past no longer defines you. Your failures do not have the final word. Hope rises from knowing you are held by a faithful God.

This scripture also addresses fear directly. Fear often grows when identity feels uncertain. God counters that uncertainty with ownership and love. Redemption restores confidence, reminding you that you are not navigating life alone or unprotected.

Today, abundance may look like assurance. When you remember that God has redeemed you and called you by name, hope becomes steady. You are His, and that truth sustains you through every season.

Reflection

Where have you struggled with fear or uncertainty?
How does knowing you are redeemed and known by God strengthen your hope?

Life Application

Speak this verse over yourself today, reminding your heart that you are redeemed, known, and securely held by God.

Prayer

God, thank You for redeeming me and calling me by name. Help me release fear and rest in the truth that I belong to You. Anchor my hope in Your love and remind me daily that I am Yours. Amen.

December 19

Held Steady

Psalm 66:9 (NIV)

"He has preserved our lives and kept our feet from slipping."

Devotional

Hope often reveals itself in what did not happen. This verse draws attention to God's quiet, faithful preservation. There were moments when you could have fallen, faltered, or lost your footing, yet you remained standing. Not because of your own strength, but because God was holding you steady.

Living in hope that sustains and redeems means recognizing the ways God has protected you along the way. Preservation is not always dramatic. Sometimes it shows up as restraint, redirection, or unseen support. Hope grows when you realize that even in uncertain seasons, God has been keeping you.

This scripture invites gratitude for God's steady hand. He does not only rescue after a fall. He prevents many falls you never notice. Redemption often unfolds through His ability to guard your steps and preserve your life, even when the path feels uneven.

Today, abundance may look like stability. When you reflect on how God has kept you from slipping, hope becomes grounded in gratitude. You are still here, still moving forward, and still being sustained.

Reflection

Where have you seen God preserve you without realizing it at the time? How does acknowledging His protection strengthen your hope?

Life Application

Take time today to thank God for the ways He has kept you steady, especially in moments you once overlooked.

Prayer

God, thank You for preserving my life and keeping me steady. Help me recognize Your protection and trust You to continue guiding my steps. Anchor my hope in Your faithful care and sustaining presence. Amen.

December 20

Hope Has a Name

John 11:25 (NIV)
"I am the resurrection and the life. The one who believes in me will live, even though they die."

Devotional

Hope that sustains and redeems is not an idea or a feeling. It is a person. Jesus does not point to hope as something external. He declares that hope is found in who He is. Resurrection and life are not distant promises. They are present realities rooted in Christ.

This verse speaks directly to moments when hope feels fragile. When loss, disappointment, or exhaustion weighs heavy, Jesus reminds you that life is not defined by what ends. Redemption flows from His ability to bring life where it once seemed impossible. Hope remains alive because He is alive.

Living in hope that sustains and redeems means trusting beyond what you can see. Even when circumstances suggest finality, Jesus offers continuity. He reassures you that belief in Him leads to life that is not limited by time, seasons, or outcomes.

Today, abundance may look like assurance. Hope rests securely when it is anchored in Christ, not circumstances. Because He lives, hope does not fade. It endures, redeems, and carries you forward.

Reflection

Where have you been tempted to believe something was over?
How does knowing Jesus is resurrection and life reshape your hope?

Life Application

Declare today that your hope is anchored in Christ, choosing to trust Him even in areas that feel unresolved.

Prayer

Jesus, thank You for being my resurrection and my life. Help me anchor my hope in You, especially when I feel weary or uncertain. Remind me that nothing is beyond Your power to redeem and restore. Amen.

December 21

When Light Breaks Through

Luke 1:78–79 (NLT)

"Because of God's tender mercy, the morning light from heaven is about to break upon us, to give light to those who sit in darkness and in the shadow of death, and to guide us to the path of peace."

Devotional

Hope often arrives quietly, like light breaking at dawn. This verse reminds you that hope is born from God's tender mercy, not human effort. Even in darkness, God is already at work, preparing light that will guide, restore, and bring peace.

Living in hope that sustains and redeems means trusting that darkness does not have the final word. Light does not rush, but it is certain. God's mercy ensures that hope will rise, even when you feel surrounded by uncertainty or waiting for clarity.

This scripture speaks to the promise of guidance. Hope does not simply illuminate your surroundings. It directs your steps. When God's light breaks through, it leads you toward peace, offering assurance that redemption is unfolding, even if you cannot yet see the full picture.

Today, abundance may look like anticipation. When you trust God's mercy, hope steadies your heart. Light is coming. Peace is ahead. And you are being gently guided forward.

Reflection

Where have you been waiting for light or clarity?
How does trusting God's mercy reshape your hope?

Life Application

Pause today and acknowledge one area where you are trusting God to bring light, choosing patience and hope over discouragement.

Prayer

God, thank You for Your tender mercy and the promise of light. Help me trust You in moments of darkness and wait with hope for the peace You are bringing. Guide my steps and anchor my heart in Your faithfulness. Amen.

December 22

The God Who Waits to Show Compassion

Isaiah 30:18 (NIV)
"Yet the Lord longs to be gracious to you; therefore he will rise up to show you compassion. For the Lord is a God of justice. Blessed are all who wait for him."

Devotional

Hope becomes steady when you realize God is not reluctant with grace. This verse reveals a powerful truth. God longs to show compassion. He is not distant or withholding. His patience is purposeful, and His grace is intentional.

Living in hope that sustains and redeems means trusting God's timing without questioning His heart. Waiting can feel heavy when answers are delayed, but this scripture reminds you that delay does not mean denial. God's compassion is active even when you cannot see immediate movement.

This verse also connects waiting with blessing. Hope grows when you trust that God is working for justice and good, even in seasons that require patience. Redemption often unfolds quietly, shaped by grace that arrives at the right moment.

Today, abundance may look like reassurance. When you understand that God desires to be gracious to you, hope shifts from frustration to trust. Waiting becomes an act of faith, grounded in confidence that God's compassion is certain.

Reflection

Where are you being asked to wait?
How does knowing God longs to show you compassion change your perspective?

Life Application

Choose patience today by trusting God's heart, reminding yourself that His grace and compassion are at work even in the waiting.

Prayer

God, thank You for Your grace and compassion. Help me trust You as I wait and believe that Your timing is shaped by love and justice. Anchor my hope in Your faithfulness and teach me to wait with confidence. Amen.

December 23

Hope Came Near

John 1:14 (NLT)
"So the Word became human and made his home among us. He was full of unfailing love and faithfulness."

Devotional

Hope became tangible when God chose nearness. This verse reminds you that redemption was not distant or abstract. God entered fully into humanity. He did not speak hope from afar. He came close and made His home among us.

Living in hope that sustains and redeems means trusting that God understands every part of the human experience. Jesus lived among people, sharing their joys, burdens, questions, and pain. Hope is strengthened when you remember that God did not remain removed from your reality. He stepped into it with love and faithfulness.

This scripture also speaks to permanence. God did not visit briefly. He made His home among us. Redemption is rooted in presence. Hope grows when you realize that God desires relationship, closeness, and connection. He does not remain distant or formal.

Today, abundance may look like comfort. When you remember that God came near, hope feels personal and accessible. You are not reaching for something far away. Hope is present, dwelling with you.

Reflection

Where have you felt distant from hope or connection?
How does knowing God chose nearness change your understanding of redemption?

Life Application

Pause today and acknowledge God's presence with you, reminding yourself that hope is not distant but dwelling near.

Prayer

God, thank You for choosing nearness. Help me remember that You are present in every moment and season of my life. Anchor my hope in Your unfailing love and faithfulness as I continue forward. Amen.

December 24

Hope Is Announced

Luke 2:11 (NIV)

"Today in the town of David a Savior has been born to you; he is the Messiah, the Lord."

Devotional

Hope is announced before it is fully understood. This verse captures the moment when heaven speaks into the world and declares that everything has changed. A Savior has been born. Not quietly in theory, but openly in history. The news is released. The promise is made known.

Living in hope that sustains and redeems means recognizing the power of God's declaration. Before people fully grasped the meaning of Jesus' birth, they first had to hear that it had happened. Hope enters the world through proclamation. God does not wait for readiness. He announces redemption.

This scripture reminds you that hope often arrives as an interruption. It breaks into ordinary life with divine clarity. The announcement itself carries weight. It signals that waiting has ended and fulfillment has begun, even if understanding unfolds later.

Today, abundance may look like awareness. Hope has been spoken into the world and into your life. The Savior has been announced. Redemption is no longer approaching. It has begun.

Reflection

What has God already declared over your life?
How does recognizing hope as an announcement shift your perspective?

Life Application

Pause today and acknowledge what God has already spoken, choosing to trust His declaration even as understanding continues to grow.

Prayer

God, thank You for announcing hope to the world and to my life. Help me trust what You have already declared and rest in the truth that redemption has begun. Prepare my heart to receive all that this hope means. Amen.

December 25

When the Time Was Right

Galatians 4:4–5 (NKJV)
"But when the fullness of the time had come, God sent forth His Son, born of a woman, born under the law, to redeem those who were under the law, that we might receive the adoption as sons."

Devotional

Christmas reminds us that hope arrived exactly on time. Not early. Not late. When the fullness of time had come, God acted. Redemption was not rushed, and it was not delayed. It unfolded with divine intention, rooted in God's perfect understanding of what humanity needed most.

Living in hope that sustains and redeems means trusting God's timing, even when waiting feels long. The birth of Jesus confirms that God sees the whole picture. Hope entered the world at the precise moment it was meant to, wrapped in humility, purpose, and love.

This verse also reveals the depth of redemption. Jesus was sent not only to rescue, but to restore relationship. Adoption is at the heart of Christmas. Through Christ, you are brought into belonging, identity, and inheritance. Hope is not just about salvation from something but being welcomed into something new.

Today, abundance looks like belonging. Christmas celebrates a Savior who came to redeem and to draw you close. Hope sustains because it is rooted in God's perfect timing and His desire for relationship with you.

Reflection

Where have you struggled to trust God's timing?
How does the truth of redemption and adoption reshape your hope?

Life Application

Pause today to reflect on God's perfect timing in your life, choosing trust over impatience and gratitude over striving.

Prayer

God, thank You for sending Your Son at just the right time. Help me trust Your timing in my own life and rest in the gift of redemption and belonging. Anchor my hope in Your faithfulness and remind me that You are always at work, even when I am waiting. Amen.

December 26

Holding Hope Close

Luke 2:19 (NIV)
"But Mary treasured up all these things and pondered them in her heart."

Devotional

After the announcement and the celebration, there is a quieter work that begins. This verse invites you into that sacred space. Mary did not rush past what had happened. She held it. She reflected. She allowed the moment to sink deep into her heart.

Living in hope that sustains and redeems means learning how to treasure what God has done. Not every movement of God calls for immediate action. Some moments are meant to be carried inward, reflected on, and revisited over time. Hope matures when it is pondered, not hurried.

This scripture reminds you that reflection is not passive. It is intentional. Mary's posture teaches you that holding hope close allows it to shape you from the inside out. Redemption continues not only through what God does, but through how you receive and remember it.

Today, abundance may look like stillness. As the celebration fades, hope remains. When you treasure what God has done and take time to reflect, hope becomes something you carry forward, steady and enduring.

Reflection

What has God done recently that you need to pause and reflect on? How can holding hope close strengthen you moving forward?

Life Application

Set aside a quiet moment today to reflect on what God has revealed to you this season, choosing to treasure it rather than rush ahead.

Prayer

God, help me treasure what You have done and take time to reflect on Your work in my life. Teach me to hold hope close and allow it to shape me as I move forward. Anchor my heart in remembrance and trust. Amen.

December 27

Returning Changed

Luke 2:20 (NLT)
"The shepherds went back to their flocks, glorifying and praising God for all they had heard and seen. It was just as the angel had told them."

Devotional

Hope does not end when the moment passes. The shepherds did not stay in the fields marveling forever. They returned to their responsibilities, but they returned changed. What they had seen and heard reshaped how they lived and worshiped.

Living in hope that sustains and redeems means learning how to carry what God has revealed back into ordinary life. The shepherds did not receive new assignments or dramatic titles. They went back to their flocks, but they carried praise with them. Hope had altered their perspective.

This scripture reminds you that transformation does not always look like relocation or reinvention. Sometimes redemption shows up in how you return. You resume familiar routines with renewed faith, deeper gratitude, and steady trust. Hope becomes real when it follows you into daily life.

Today, abundance may look like continuity with purpose. As the celebrations fade, hope remains active. You are invited to live changed, even in familiar places, allowing what God has shown you to continue shaping how you move forward.

Reflection

What has God shown you this season that you are meant to carry forward?
How can praise remain part of your daily life?

Life Application

As you return to routine today, intentionally bring gratitude and worship with you, choosing to live changed rather than unchanged.

Prayer

God, help me carry what You have revealed into my everyday life. Teach me to return with gratitude, praise, and trust. May hope continue to shape how I live, even in ordinary moments. Amen.

December 28

Hope That Learned to Wait

Psalm 40:1 (NLT)
"I waited patiently for the Lord to help me, and he turned to me and heard my cry."

Devotional

Hope that sustains is often shaped in waiting. This verse reflects a posture that is neither rushed nor resigned. Waiting patiently does not mean being passive. It means choosing trust while time unfolds. The psalmist waited, and in that waiting, God responded.

Living in hope that sustains and redeems means recognizing that waiting is not wasted time. God hears before He moves. He sees before He answers. Hope grows stronger when you learn that God's response is rooted in care, not urgency.

This scripture also reminds you that God turns toward you. Waiting does not push Him away. It draws His attention. Redemption often begins quietly as God listens, attends, and prepares to act. Hope is sustained not by speed, but by assurance that God is present in the waiting.

Today, abundance may look like trust refined. As the year comes to a close, you can look back and see places where waiting shaped your faith. Hope remains steady when you believe that God hears every cry and responds in His perfect time.

Reflection

Where have you been waiting for God's help?
How has waiting strengthened or challenged your hope?

Life Application

Choose patience today by trusting that God hears you and is responding, even if the answer is still unfolding.

Prayer

God, thank You for hearing my cries and meeting me in seasons of waiting. Help me trust You fully and remain patient as You work. Anchor my hope in Your faithfulness and remind me that You always turn toward me. Amen.

December 29

Hope That Endures to the End

Hebrews 6:11–12 (NIV)
"We want each of you to show this same diligence to the very end, so that what you hope for may be fully realized."

Devotional

As the year comes to a close, hope invites perseverance. This verse acknowledges that hope is not only something you feel. It is something you sustain through diligence and faith. What God has promised is meant to be fully realized, but it requires endurance along the way.

Living in hope that sustains and redeems means continuing even when momentum slows. Faithfulness near the end matters just as much as enthusiasm at the beginning. This scripture reminds you that hope matures through consistency, not urgency. It is shaped by choosing to remain steady when distractions, fatigue, or doubt arise.

This verse also speaks to realization. Hope is not meant to remain abstract. God desires fulfillment. Redemption unfolds as you continue trusting, believing, and walking forward with patience. Endurance positions you to receive what hope has been pointing toward all along.

Today, abundance may look like resolve. As the year winds down, you are invited to finish with intention. Hope is strengthened when you commit to seeing God's work through, trusting that what He has promised will come to pass.

Reflection

Where have you felt tempted to slow down or disengage?
What does diligence look like for you in this season?

Life Application

Choose one way today to remain diligent in faith, trusting God to bring His promises to completion in His time.

Prayer

God, help me remain faithful and diligent as I move toward the end of this season. Strengthen my hope and remind me that You are at work bringing Your promises to fulfillment. Teach me to endure with trust and confidence in You. Amen.

December 30

Hope You Are Convinced Of

2 Timothy 1:12 (NKJV)

"For I know whom I have believed and am persuaded that He is able to keep what I have committed to Him until that Day."

Devotional

As the year draws to a close, hope becomes less about anticipation and more about conviction. This verse speaks from a place of certainty. It does not say, "I hope God is able." It declares, "I know whom I have believed." Hope that sustains and redeems is anchored in relationship, not outcomes.

Living in this kind of hope means resting in who God is, even when answers are incomplete. Paul's confidence was not rooted in circumstances or timing. It was grounded in trust. He was persuaded. He had settled the question of God's faithfulness in his heart.

This scripture invites you to reflect on what you have entrusted to God. Your prayers. Your future. Your unanswered questions. Redemption does not require you to resolve everything before the year ends. Hope rests in the assurance that God is able to keep what you have placed in His hands.

Today, abundance may look like peace. As the year closes, you are not required to carry everything forward alone. You can end this season confident, persuaded, and secure, trusting that God is faithful to guard every commitment made to Him.

Reflection

What have you committed to God this year?
Where do you need to move from uncertainty to conviction?

Life Application

Take a moment today to name what you are entrusting to God, choosing confidence in His ability rather than anxiety about outcomes.

Prayer

God, thank You for being faithful and trustworthy. Help me end this year confident in who You are and persuaded of Your ability to keep all that I have committed to You. Anchor my hope in You as I prepare to step forward. Amen.

December 31

The Year Is Crowned

Psalm 65:11 (NLT)
"You crown the year with a bountiful harvest; even the hard pathways overflow with abundance."

Devotional

This year does not end unfinished. It is crowned.

God does not measure your year only by ease or outcome. He sees the full landscape. The prayers whispered. The strength it took to keep going. The growth that happened quietly beneath the surface. Scripture declares that God crowns the year, not with perfection, but with harvest.

Even the hard pathways overflow. That means the difficult moments were not wasted. The long seasons were not empty. The places where you questioned, waited, or endured were still producing something meaningful. Hope sustained you there. Redemption was working even when it was not obvious.

Living in hope that sustains and redeems means trusting God's perspective over your own. What you may have labeled as delay, God calls development. What felt heavy, He names fruitful. This verse affirms that abundance does not cancel hardship. It emerges from it.

As this year closes, you are not closing a chapter marked by lack. You are closing a year crowned by God Himself. Hope has carried you through. Redemption has been at work. And what God has done will continue to unfold beyond this moment.

Today, abundance looks like completion. The year is finished, and it is crowned.

Reflection

Where have you seen growth you did not expect?
How does viewing the year as crowned by God change how you remember it?

Life Application

Take time today to thank God for the entire year, including the hard pathways, trusting that He has brought abundance from every step.

Prayer

God, thank You for crowning this year with Your faithfulness. I trust that even the hard pathways were filled with purpose and growth. As I close this year, I rest in Your work and step forward with hope, gratitude, and peace. Amen.

Continue the Journey

If you are here, you have walked through an entire year with intention. Day by day, you made space for God. Some days may have felt powerful and affirming. Other days may have felt heavy, quiet, or uncertain. Still, you showed up. That matters.

My prayer is that these pages reminded you that you are never walking alone. God is present in the ordinary moments, the unanswered questions, the waiting seasons, and the victories you did not even realize were forming as you kept going.

This devotional may be ending, but your journey is not. There is still growth ahead, still purpose unfolding, still grace meeting you exactly where you are. I would love to stay connected and continue walking alongside you as God leads us forward.

You can find encouragement, teaching, and ongoing reflections at:

Website: www.winningwithjustlatoya.com
YouTube: @WinningwithJustLaToya

Thank you for trusting me with your time, your heart, and your faith throughout this year.

With gratitude,

LaToya Banks

About the Author

LaToya Banks is a faith-centered writer and leader committed to helping others cultivate a steady, daily walk with God. Her writing emphasizes consistency over perfection, surrender over performance, and faith that is formed in the ordinary moments of life.

She is the author of *I Surrender All* and *I'm Every Woman: Designed for Purpose*, devotionals created to guide readers into deeper spiritual alignment and personal growth.

Through her books, teaching, and digital platforms, LaToya encourages believers to slow down, remain rooted in God's presence, and walk faithfully through every season.

www.ingramcontent.com/pod-product-compliance
Lightning Source LLC
LaVergne TN
LVHW100502110826
845146LV00002B/486